NOW HEAR THIS

Other books by Edwin P. Hoyt

KAMIKAZES

GUADALCANAL

THE MILITARISTS

JAPAN'S WAR

U-BOATS: A PICTORIAL HISTORY

AMERICA'S WARS AND MILITARY EXCURSIONS

DEATH OF THE U-BOATS

HITLER'S WAR

THE GI'S WAR

THE AIRMEN

THE RISE OF THE CHINESE REPUBLIC

CARRIER WARS

YAMAMOTO

THE DAY THE CHINESE ATTACKED

NOW HEAR THIS

The Story of American Sailors in World War II

Edwin P. Hoyt

Paragon House
New York

First edition, 1993

Published in the United States by
Paragon House
90 Fifth Avenue
New York, New York 10011

Library of Congress Cataloging-in-Publication Data

Hoyt, Edwin Palmer.
    Now hear this : the story of American sailors in World War II / by
Edwin P. Hoyt.—1st ed.
      p.   cm.
    Includes bibliographical references and index.
    ISBN 1-55778-483-3
    1. World War, 1939–1945—Naval operations, American. 2. World
War, 1939–1945—Personal narratives, American. 3. United States.
Navy—History—World War, 1939–1945. I. Title.
D773.H7   1993
940.54′5973′092—dc20   92-33502
                                        CIP

Manufactured in the United States of America

This book is for the officers and men and women of the United States Navy, who have served their country well since before the American Revolution and who continue to serve today.

Contents

Preface

Now Hear This is the third of a group of books intended to show how the Second World War appeared to the people who served in it. As with *The GI's War* and *The Airmen*, the purpose is not to trace or assess the strategy of the struggle but to give the personal experiences of the people involved, to show "the way it was," at least as the participants saw it. I am grateful to all those who saw fit to participate in this project, and only wish that more stories could have been included.

In World War II, the navy included many unsung activities. For example, John S. Murphy served as a reserve officer in the navy hydrographic office in Suitland, Maryland, from 1943 until 1946. One did not win medals in the hydrographic office, but the men who sailed the seas would have been hard put without its services in charting the seas. So it was too with training centers like the Great Lakes Naval Training Station at Chicago.

World War II brought the creation of a new navy. Before 1940 the men who went to sea were professionals. The officers were for the most part the product of the United States Naval Academy or of the air training programs that produced pilots for the planes. The enlisted men and petty officers came out of the service schools; most of them were in the navy as a career.

The men of the sea commands were competent and brave—as will be seen in the story of the Battle of the Java Sea, where a small force of American, Australian, British, and Dutch ships faced an overwhelming Japanese invasion force. The Japanese had better ships, better planes, and better weapons at this point in the war. The performance of the Americans in a battle they knew they could not win was exemplary in every way.

The expansion program begun in 1940 to meet the threat of Hitler's aggression caused an explosion in the navy community, and when war actually began another sort of explosion occurred. It was quickly discovered at the highest levels that the men who made fine officers in peacetime did not necessarily serve with distinction under war conditions. What was needed was daring and the willingness to risk a ship, an aircraft, or a fleet to achieve victory. For the navy, the epitome of this sort of man was William F. Halsey. He was not always right. As a result of errors by his meteorologists, he took his ships into two furious typhoons at considerable loss of ships, men, and materiel. But Halsey had the great quality of a fighter, and he was able to communicate this spirit to the fleet. Small wonder that he was the most popular admiral in the United States Navy and his reputation has stood the test of time, although his two typhoons and the decision to forsake San Bernardino Strait in the battles of Leyte Gulf are still controversial in naval circles. The fact remains that Halsey was the most inspirational sea commander of the navy in World War II, and for that reason his reputation will always survive. Typical of the man was his decision, when aircraft carriers became an important part of the navy and he was assigned to command one, that he must learn to fly. He was over fifty at the time, and there was no navy requirement that the commander of a carrier be a pilot; practically none of the officers senior enough to have such a command had any flight training. But Halsey said he must learn to fly if he was to command fliers—and he did, although his instructors never said he was the best of their pilots. "The worse the weather, the better he flew," said one of them. In a way, that too summed up Halsey. He always rose to adversity and always performed best under pressure. Since that is what war is about, it was small wonder that he was the best of the American naval commanders.

This opinion of Halsey spread like scuttlebutt through the fleet. Most of the men who loved him had never seen him or spoken to him, but still they revered him as a leader.

That is one of the aspects of World War II I have tried to probe

in these books. It is impossible to overestimate the degree of igno-
rance of facts and strategy on the part of enlisted men and junior
officers of the services in this war. It was said of the Chinese Com-
munists that the common soldiers were informed as to the plans of
their leaders, but this was certainly not true of the Western armies,
and it was not true of the American armed forces. That fact emerges
in these pages as in the pages of the other two books. The average
sailor, like Bill LeBaron, served through the war without knowing
until he read about it what had actually happened. Seaman
LeBaron served on the cruiser *Wichita*, which saw almost continuous
action in many areas, but what he knew was that he was on a ship
and sometimes it was in action. That was about the size of it.

The reader will notice that there are no stories about blacks or
women here. I solicited both from various sources but was unable to
arouse any interest. (This was also the case with *The GI's War* and *The
Airmen*.) One reason for the failure of women in the navy to come
forward may be that until relatively later in the war, WAVEs were not
sent overseas, even to Hawaii. Their duties in World War II were
almost entirely administrative and clerical, and they may believe
that no one wants to read about that. Sexual harassment was surely
as prevalent in the wartime navy as it has been later, but most women
in those days did not make an issue of it. Half a century later, no
navy women responded to my requests. What was well known during the war was that army and navy nurses and Red Cross girls were
courted by the "lucky guys" who, in the navy, included a number of
high-ranking officers—pilots in particular. Even now this is an
aspect of the war no one seems to want to talk about.

As for blacks, I have never been able to secure cooperation. With
the navy, the reason may be that blacks still feel a discrimination that
existed in the World War II services: Blacks were largely employed
as cooks and messmen. But on the warships every man had a combat
station and some of the black sailors served valiantly at the guns. I
am only sorry to have been unable to reach any of them who wanted
to have their stories told.

The stories that do appear have the ring of truth. They were
constructed from diaries, interviews, narratives, and letters from
the people involved. Some of them were written long after the fact,

but most of them came from closer to hand, and the sense of immediacy is always present in the diaries.

Altogether, I believe these stories provide a new look at the war and for that reason have some lasting value as well as for their entertaining reading.

Edwin P. Hoyt
Tokyo, 1992

tention. In September 1940 President Roosevelt made a deal with Britain in which Britain received fifty World War I American destroyers that were lying idle in various American backwaters. In return the Americans got naval and air bases in the West Indies and Bermuda. It was not long before Seaman Orbeck was transferred to U.S. Mobile Hospital No. 1 on Bermuda. There he helped take care of the survivors of ocean sinkings who made it to Bermuda.

In October 1940 Selective Service came into being in America, and with it the registration of young men for the draft. After his election to a third term, Roosevelt felt more secure in his leadership and began to move the United States closer to participation in the European war, still trying to avoid involvement in Asia.

But not until President Roosevelt announced a national alert and military expansion program in 1941 did the wheel of naval defense begin really turning. Even then, the shortage of money kept the scale of defense activity to a minimum—and by that time the American emphasis had shifted from Japan to Europe.

When the European war had begun in September 1939, the United States had announced a policy of neutrality. But as time went on it became apparent that American sympathies rested with England, and neutrality became less intense every season. By 1940 some Americans were enlisting in the British and Canadian forces to get into the war. Men of the merchant marine found themselves propelled into the war whether they wished to be or not, and many of them experienced the horrors of getting torpedoed and taking to open boats for salvation after a U-boat attack.

American involvement increased in December 1940 with the announcement of the Lend Lease plan, which allowed Britain to obtain American assistance on credit. President Roosevelt announced that he wanted the United States to become the "arsenal of democracy."

Lester A. Wood was a regular naval officer serving aboard the USS William B. Preston, a seaplane tender in 1940. The United States Navy was expecting war with Japan, although no one knew when it would come. But the Navy was doing its best to prepare for trouble, as Admiral Wood's narrative indicates.

It was December 1940, the Saturday of the Army/Navy game, the broadcast received spasmodically by radio early in the day. We were near the Island of Midway, scheduled to enter port the following morning. The message from our unit commander ordered "nominate one tender and one squadron of PBYs to proceed and report to C-in-C Asiatic Fleet and then to CDR Patrol Wings Asiatic."

Our ship, William B. Preston, was the only tender available, the USS Childs having received similar orders two months earlier. Returning to Pearl Harbor, we went about carrying out our orders, made ready and departed the following Friday, some six days after receiving our initial orders.

Our departure coincided with the decision by C-in-C Asiatic Fleet that war was sufficiently imminent to warrant sending all dependents home, meaning that we were leaving for a potential war zone with no fixed time of return.

As families, we faced the situation as best we could. We tried to explain to our daughter that I would be away for two years. Her reaction: "Goody Goody! I will be six when you come home!" It gave us strength, for in her childish way, she showed us there is some sunshine in every situation.

The Wright accompanied us to near Wake Island, where we fueled at sea in order to have sufficient fuel to get to Guam; not the smoothest operation because it was a first for both ships. Crossing the 180th meridian, we shifted reckoning of the Greenwich Hour Angle westward from the prime meridian to eastward from same, and were gratified when our navigational fix coincided with the dead reckoning from our morning star sights. Shortly thereafter, the PBYs flew over, fixed their positions and went on to Guam.

Apra Harbor in Guam was without most of its navigational aids, rendered inoperative by a severe typhoon a few days earlier. To enter, we made a 90 degree turn from south to east, and for the first time as navigator I experienced a tumbling gyro. It was to happen again and again until the Chief Electricians Mate found that it was a submarine gyro that had been cannibalized from an old "O" boat. When we arrived in Manila, EMs from the sub tender Canopus examined it, made the repairs and it caused us no further trouble.

The drift toward war with Germany became faster and faster. In January 1941, American and British representatives held secret meetings in which they agreed that in case of war with Japan and Germany, the United States would turn its attention first to Germany. By April 1941 the U.S. Navy had extended its defense zone into the Atlantic. By September President Roosevelt was talking about arming American merchant ships with deck guns and the next month he asked Congress for permission to do so. On September 4, the American destroyer *Greer* was attacked by a U-boat while convoying British ships. Later that month the destroyer *Kearny* was attacked. At the end of October the inevitable occurred and the destroyer *Reuben James* was sunk in a battle with German U-boats. A hundred American sailors were lost.

Meanwhile the imperial Japanese navy was expanding rapidly, building modern ships, including some of the largest war ships in the world. Two of them would become the battleships *Yamato* and *Musashi*, and the third would become the carrier *Shinano*. By 1941 the Japanese had ten major carriers, most of them more modern than the half-dozen effective American ones. They also had something even more valuable: combat experience gained at the expense of the Chinese (and of the Americans in the sinking of the U.S. gunboat *Panay* by Japanese carrier aircraft in 1937).

The Japanese navy in 1941 was on a war footing, while the American navy was still operating at its peacetime level, in which promotions and influence depended on spit and polish and cronyism. The worst thing that could be said about the American naval establishment in 1941 was that it was a hotbed of intrigue by groups of officers seeking to feather their own nests with promotions and power. One result of this deplorable situation was that the naval intelligence division in Washington guarded its secrets carefully and did not pass along vital information about Japanese activity to the Pacific fleet headquarters in Hawaii. Therefore the Hawaii command was never fully aware of the imminence of danger of attack in the first two weeks of December 1941. The Pacific fleet had been alerted to apparent Japanese intentions for many months and had been on alert basis all summer and fall. But such vigilance cannot be maintained at a high pitch constantly without refueling, and Washington's naval establishment was so jealous of its prerogatives that it refused one request after another from the Pacific fleet for information. That is how matters stood at Pearl Harbor on December 7, 1941.

Across the Pacific, the Japanese had meanwhile been gearing up to attack the British, Dutch, and Americans simultaneously in a bid to secure the natural resources they needed to pursue their China adventure. The decision to extend the war was made on the basis of America's sudden curtailment of oil and steel shipments to Japan after the Japanese invaded northern Indochina in 1940. Japan then began negotiations with America, looking to restore her most-favored-nation trade status. If she did not achieve it by negotiation, her military leaders were determined to achieve their aims by military action. The Americans by 1941 had adopted a firm and uncompromising policy toward Japan. As the price of peace she must abandon her efforts to conquer China. This ultimatum to Japan created a crisis. More than 100,000 Japanese soldiers had been killed in the China war by 1941, and the Japanese government would have been totally embarrassed and considered to have betrayed the memories of those brave soldiers if it now abandoned its conquest of China. There might have been room for a face-saving gesture. The Japanese never called their effort in China a war; it was always an incident. Had the Western powers been more imaginative they might have offered the Japanese a face-saving plan of withdrawal from China. There were many leaders in Japan who would have liked to be disengaged from that war, which was already seen as a mistake. But the American policy remained rocklike.

Aboard the flying boat tender *William B. Preston,* Lieutenant Wood and the others of the crew were on the watch in the Philippines.

> *Until December 1941, things were pretty much routine, war in Europe, storm clouds gathering in our area. We ran our advanced base exercises to various islands in the Philippines, tending the PBYs and training for what was eventually to happen.*
>
> *On 30 November, 1941, we left Manila for a routine cruise to the south coast of Mindanao and set up our base in Malalag Bay. The PBYs*

patrolled daily, scouting to the south and east to the Japanese-held Peleliu Islands.

Britain, engaged in a struggle for her existence with Germany and Italy, was in no position to exert leadership in the Far East. And so the world came to December 7 and the simultaneous attacks on Malaya, the Philippines, and Hawaii.

The attack on Pearl Harbor was not a part of the original Japanese war plan, which had been drawn at the insistence of the imperial army. Japan's primary goal was to capture the resources of the Dutch East Indies and of Malaya. The attack on the Philippines was conceived for two reasons: to eliminate a dangerous American base, and to prevent the Americans from granting independence to the Philippines and thus setting up a counterfoil to the Japanese plan for a Greater East Asia in which Japan would exert all the leadership.

Pearl Harbor was from the outset the brainchild of Admiral Isoroku Yamamoto, who feared the American Pacific fleet more than anything else. At the moment, Yamamoto knew, the Japanese fleet was the most powerful in the Pacific, but it would not always be so. In 1940 the Americans embarked on a major shipbuilding and aircraft-building program. Yamamoto, who had served as Japanese naval attaché in Washington and who had been involved in the two London naval-limitation conferences of the 1930s, knew very well the American war potential in its industrial plant, and he was certain that if Japan was to have any chance of carrying out the army's announced intentions the American fleet would have to be crippled in the beginning of the war so badly that it could not spring back for at least a year. In that time Japan would be able to capture and consolidate her victories and perhaps the Americans could be persuaded to accept them as the price for future peace in the Pacific. If it was going to be a long war, Yamamoto said, Japan would lose. The attack on Pearl Harbor was essential to any hope for victory, and Yamamoto staked his career on it, announcing to a recalcitrant naval establishment that if the Pearl Harbor plan were not included in the Japanese war plan, he would resign his commission.

For several years before the war broke out, U.S. naval officers who served in China, in particular, saw a world war coming in the Japanese belligerence and the arrogance of the Japanese army in China. Admiral Yardley had sounded warnings for several years and advocated a naval strengthening program that neither the American political leadership nor the American people were ready to undertake. Even after the expansion of the war in China, the decision of the army-dominated government to destroy Chiang Kai-shek's Kuomintang regime, and the establishment of the puppet Chinese government under Wang Ching-wei at Nanking, the Americans remained blind to the threat. Their major interest was on the other side of the world, where Hitler was running wild and taking over one country after another. Even in the face of this more obvious threat to American well-being, the United States government was slow to act. It was very hard to give up the peaceful life, and many Americans felt that they had been dragged into the First World War and that they were not going to pull anybody's chestnuts out of the fire once again.

President Roosevelt had moved cautiously, if steadily, toward entrance into the European conflict, and by 1941 the American naval structure was geared for that sort of involvement and was using bases in Canada, the West Indies, and Iceland.

But in the Pacific Roosevelt refused to act. Suggestions were made that the Aleutian Islands and Alaska be fortified, but they were not. The administration did not want to anger the Japanese. Various incidents along the Yangtze River were glossed over, exhibiting an American attitude that only increased the zest of the Japanese army for conquest and only furthered its contempt for the Westerners, whom it saw as weak and self-indulgent.

This attitude was encouraged by what the Japanese witnessed in China. The Americans and British lived like nobility, even the enlisted men of the military service. On the American gunboats of the Asiatic fleet, the seamen had their own Chinese cooks, laundrymen, and personal servants. They did not tote and carry; this was "coolie" work and would have caused them to lose face. Life in the Far East military was spongy and soft, and the foreign troops gave a very definite impression of self-indulgence and weakness.

The officers who advanced in the American army and navy played service politics to the hilt, and this usually meant seeking small advantages. In the Office of Naval Intelligence the top officers guarded their secrets almost as carefully from the fleet as they did from the enemy. Promotion depended on fitness reports, which depended on observation of regulations. It was almost suicidal for an officer to exhibit any resourcefulness or variation from the norm. An example was made of Admiral Richardson, commander of the Pacific fleet in 1940. President Roosevelt was persuaded that year to move the fleet's permanent base from San Diego to Pearl Harbor. Richardson objected. It would put the fleet out on a limb, he said. All fuel and food and everything else had to be brought in by sea, which made the supply line very vulnerable to possible submarine attack.

President Roosevelt was moving the fleet for political purposes, as part of his diplomacy to offer Japan a carrot and a stick. He was not pleased with Admiral Richardson's attitude, and so this energetic and forceful officer was removed from command of the fleet, and for all practical purposes his career ended. The command passed to Admiral Husband E. Kimmel, another forceful and active officer, who was exasperated by the Washington naval establishment's politicking from almost the first moment of his arrival as commander of the fleet.

That is how matters stood in the last few weeks of 1941, when the Japanese were poised for war, but the Western world was not quite sure when it would come or if it could be avoided and was waiting nervously for the Japanese to move.

TWO

Pearl Harbor Day

December 7, 1941.

Aviation Ordnance Mate Second Class Theodore LeBaron was stationed at Ford Island with a PBY squadron of the patrol wing. It was good duty:

> *I joined the squadron in 1940. It was a squadron which had been at Pearl Harbor for a few years and was living in a country-club style, particularly compared to some other duties with the fleet. We reported at the hangar for muster at 7 A.M. and our working day was over at 1 P.M., at which time we could take the liberty boat and bus to Honolulu. Except for every fourth weekend when we each had the duty, the weekend ran from 1 P.M. Friday until 7 A.M. on Monday. There was a small golf course on Ford Island, also movies, bowling alley, and beer parlor, handball and tennis courts, and a swimming pool. Laundry service came at very low fees, so your leisure time could all be leisure and not have to worry about dishwater (or washwater) hands. The barracks were very new and very clean. We slept in double bunks and mine was on a screened-in lanai. The chow was not submarine type but very good.*

In the fall of 1941 the squadron was put on alert and there was a good deal of talk about war with Japan. For several days every member of the squadron had to stay at the hangar or at least be callable. But no one knew what was really going on. One of the wise guys of the squadron said the only way to find out was to send someone over to one of the whorehouses in Honolulu to get the straight dope.

No one in the squadron knew that Admiral Husband E. Kimmel, commander of the Pacific Fleet, had been getting a series of confusing and incomplete reports that kept the fleet on edge, but without enough information to take action.

Kimmel did what he could. In the middle of October he sent the twelve-plane squadron of PBYs to Midway. The planes flew patrols out of Midway until the end of November without seeing any indications of Japanese naval activity in the central Pacific. Then they were ordered to Wake Island, where they arrived at the end of November. The men of the squadron knew it was serious business because they were ordered to load the PBYs with 500-pound bombs and patrol south, west, and north of Wake. Still no one saw any evidence of Japanese activity, although some of the patrols must have passed quite near the Japanese strike force in the north.

On December 5 the squadron was called back to Midway and then to Pearl Harbor. Because of the international dateline, they arrived at Pearl Harbor on December 5 too, coming in after dark and seeing the "whole fleet in all its incandescent glory" spread out below them.

AOM 2 c LeBaron went to bed early on the night of December 6. When he woke on Sunday morning the day was bright and clear. As he reached for his pants he noticed the time was 7:50. He was standing on the lanai when he heard an explosion. He looked up to see a cloud of black smoke hanging above what he knew was the squadron's hangar.

Then he heard men yelling on the other side of the lanai and ran over. There, not far above the ground, he saw a Japanese torpedo plane that had just finished its run on battleship row, specifically the battleship *California*, which was in drydock.

The pilot had his canopy open and was waving at the Americans on the ground.

Next thing LeBaron saw was the battleships lifting out of the water and then settling back again. It seemed odd, then it came to him that the movement was caused by torpedoes.

The men headed for the door, intent on getting to the hangar, but they were stopped by a chief petty officer who told them to stand fast. Nobody was to leave the barracks.

That order stood for only a few minutes and then the sailors were released. LeBaron headed for the hangar, running a few feet, then dropping at the sound of a bomb, getting up, and running again. He saw a plane bombing the battleship *Nevada*.

Seaman 2/c Charles T. Sehe was aboard the battleship *Nevada* on that morning of December 7. He had been serving on the *Nevada* since earlier in the year, after completing boot camp at the Great Lakes Naval Training Station. He had joined the navy because there wasn't anything else to do that he wanted to do. There were no jobs in these depression years.

"All I have to do is close my eyes and I can relive December 7, 1941," he wrote fifty years later.

The crew had just finished breakfast—about 7:55—and he was in the head when the explosion of bombs that hit the *Nevada* literally blew the men in the head off their seats. Moments later he was racing for his battle station, which was the No. 4 searchlight on a high platform on the mainmast. He got there before General Quarters sounded, but there was not much he could do but watch what was going on around him.

About fifteen minutes after the attack's start a low-flying Japanese plane was seen to release its torpedo, which slammed into the Nevada *on its port side, at about Frame 40, between the two forward gun turrets, causing a list which was corrected almost immediately. Of all the eight battleships stationed at Pearl Harbor the* Nevada *was the only one to get under way. As the slow-moving* Nevada *got under way, a sudden explosion on the USS* Arizona *showered the sky with a thick black smoke and flaming debris fell upon the decks of the starboard side of the* Nevada. *Then the topside crew of the* Nevada *saw the slow rolling over of the battleship* Oklahoma, *the sister ship of the* Nevada. *As our ship slowly passed into the channel, the* Nevada *became almost the sole target of attacking planes. It was bombed, strafed again and again, and set afire. Five more bombs exploded on the forecastle and the boat deck. The damage was so extensive that the burning and sinking ship was given orders to beach itself near shore at Waipio Peninsula to avoid blocking the channel. While beaching operations were under way, the destroyer*

Shaw, *moored near the* Pennsylvania, *blew up and showered the* Nevada's *decks again with flaming debris.*

Ted LeBaron watched from the shore as the Japanese zeroed in on the *Nevada*. He did not think they scored any hits. And although he was right in the middle of the action on Ford Island, he felt more or less safe. No bombs were aimed at the island after the initial bombing of the hangar. The danger was from shrapnel of the American antiaircraft fire. What impressed him most was the sight of the destroyer *Shaw* in drydock, which was hit by a bomb and blew up with a spectacular roar. The bomb must have hit the magazines; the *Shaw* just came completely apart.

LeBaron finally got to the hangar to see the squadron's planes going up in smoke. A plane from the carrier *Enterprise* was trying to land and was under fire by American gunners who seemed to be trigger-happy. One sailor was firing a .45-caliber automatic at the plane and other sailors were firing the machine guns on some of the PBYs parked at the adjacent hangar.

On that morning of December 7, the old four-stack destroyer *Ward* was duty destroyer for Pearl Harbor. Her job was to patrol a three-mile-by-three-mile square just off the entrance to the harbor. She had gone to sea on December 6 for a three-day duty tour with a new skipper aboard: Lieutenant William W. Outerbridge, a U.S. Naval Academy graduate. This was his first command. He had reported in on December 5 to the commander of the inshore patrol at Pearl Harbor and had been shown a new dispatch from the fleet that warned of the possibility of submarine attack on Pearl Harbor. Any submarine not escorted and not operating in the area assigned for submarine operations was to be attacked and sunk without warning. The order seemed a curious one, for none of the officers of the Pearl Harbor patrol had ever seen a submarine other than the U.S. Navy's, and they were sure that they would have plenty of warning before a submarine tried to attack. But the task of the *Ward* was to be alert and to patrol, and that is what the vessel did.

At two o'clock in the morning the minesweepers came into the channel and began their routine sweeps. Not quite two hours later the *Ward* received a message by signal lamp from the minesweeper *Condor*: "We have sighted a suspicious object which looks like a submarine. It appears to be standing to the westward from our present position."

The signalman acknowledged the message and called the officer of the deck, who woke the captain. He ordered General Quarters and the *Ward* increased speed to 20 knots and asked for additional information. The *Ward* then turned toward Barber's Point and began to search but did not find a submarine. After three-quarters of an hour the captain ordered the ship secured from General Quarters and went to bed in his sea cabin. Lieutenant O. W. Goepner took over the deck. He was a reserve officer, a graduate of the Northwestern University ROTC unit.

Lieutenant Goepner was not quite sure of the extent of his authority, so when the USS *Antares* approached the harbor with a lighter in tow, he awakened the captain to report. The captain acknowledged the fact, but said that was all right and turned over and went back to sleep.

At 6:30 Lieutenant Goepner awakened the captain again, this time abruptly.

"Captain, come on the bridge," he said. This was a command every captain must obey. But Outerbridge was not sure that the lieutenant knew what he was doing, and he was annoyed by being awakened so many times.

"Now look here, Goepner," he said, "that's stern talk for the officer of the deck. I've only been here one day but I want you to realize the seriousness of giving commands like that, that I fully expect to find something if you talk like that."

"Well, captain," said Lieutenant Goepner, "Come to the bridge."

Outerbridge hurried to the bridge.

"We have been watching that object that appears to be following the *Antares*. It looked like a buoy but it's moving and we believe it is a submarine." The skipper looked at the object.

"Goepner, I believe it is a submarine. Go to General Quarters."

So the lieutenant rang the gong for General Quarters and the crew responded. It was 6:35.

"If that's a submarine," the captain said, "we'll attack."

"I'll go to my battle station," said Lieutenant Goepner.

"Yes," said the captain. "The executive officer will take the deck."

Goepner was the gunnery officer, so he ordered all the guns loaded. The depth charges were on ready. The *Ward* moved on the object; the captain debated whether or not he should ram it and decided against it because he might damage or even sink the old four-stack destroyer. He decided to shoot and drop depth charges.

At seventy-five yards from the submarine they opened fire. A shell from Gun No. 3 struck the submarine at the water line, the base of the conning tower. The projectile went into the hull and then the submarine appeared to sink. The *Ward* resumed its patrol, notifying the fourteenth Naval District headquarters of the action. For a time the report was not believed, but when the bombing of Pearl Harbor began that morning the command quickly changed its attitude.

That day at least two other Japanese miniature submarines were sunk inside Pearl Harbor and one washed up on the beach of the north shore of Oahu.

Lieutenant Graham C. Bonnell of the Navy Supply Corps was aboard the cruiser *San Francisco* that day. The cruiser was being overhauled and was all torn up; she had no fuel or ammunition aboard, and the cradles in her turrets were out. At the moment she was only a hulk and there was no fighting to be done from her.

Lieutenant Bonnell saw the dive bomber that bombed LeBaron's hangar on Ford Island. He saw the plane come down, the red balls of the rising-sun flag clearly showing in the sunshine, and he saw the plane pull up and the bomb hit. But it did not even then register that this was an enemy plane and that the bombing was real. Not until the black smoke shot up and the hangar burned did Bonnell realize that Pearl Harbor was under enemy attack.

When the General Quarters call came on the *San Francisco* Bonnell went to his station—the communications room in the superstructure. The gun crews of the *San Francisco* were organized and sent to other ships to help fight off the Japanese. The boat crews were sent out to help the wounded and the men trapped on the battleships.

Lieutenant Bonnell had a ringside seat for the attack:

There was something going on at each different point in the harbor. It was like a circus of horrors. The Oklahoma *turned over, a 33,000-ton vessel capsizing!*

The first time I looked at my watch it was around four o'clock in the afternoon. We were waiting for the Japanese to invade. One rumor had it that they were already landing at various points on the island, so we were all on edge.

Three hours later, when the attack was all over, Seaman Sehe was part of a fire crew trying to stop the thirteen separate fires on the ship and remove the bodies of the dead. Nineteen of Sehe's shipmates died in that attack, about a hundred were wounded, and seventeen were never found. The fire crew was given shiny new galvanized buckets to pick up the fragmented body parts. He went into the secondary batteries of the five-inch, 51-caliber gun casements and there began picking up body segments strained through the cyclone wire security fences by the force of the explosions. He picked up several knee joints, shoulders, and parts of feet.

When the Japanese attack lessened and the planes disappeared, AOM 2/c LeBaron and the other men around the hangar headed for the barracks to get something to eat. The messhall was the first floor of their barracks. When they got there, they found that it had been turned into an emergency aid station for treatment of the victims of the bombing and torpedoing of the battleships. Many sailors had been blown into the water and others had jumped to swim to Ford Island. The harbor was so full of oil from the torpedoing of the ships that some men drowned just trying to swim. Some were burned or wounded. The messhall was the natural place to take them, and when LeBaron went in, he saw that every single table was covered by a body. Most of the men were black with oil.

Somehow LeBaron and his buddies got something to eat and then returned to the hangar area. Some of the men were put to work then servicing the *Enterprise* planes as they came in. Others were turning Ford Island into a little fortress, getting every available machine gun out of the wrecked aircraft and putting up machine-gun nests on the edge of the island. They expected a Japanese landing that night. A pair of SBD dive bombers was parked on the apron, and the men took turns sitting in the rear cockpits, waiting for Japanese planes, so they could fire the machine guns. But no Japanese planes came after the morning raids. During the evening all around Pearl Harbor itchy-fingered sailors were firing at this and that, but the firing was sporadic and did not ever last long.

Late that night word was received that six *Enterprise* fighter planes would be coming in to land. A blackout was being enforced but the ground crew turned on the light on the water tower and the pilots were told to come in with wingtip lights on but not their bright landing lights. The planes made their approach on the single runway. At the last moment the lead plane veered off and flew low over the fleet. The others followed him. Someone panicked and began firing at the planes. Every gun in the fleet seemed to be firing. LeBaron heard shrapnel dropping around him and he turned and ran, along with the others. He found cover under a roof of concrete over a loading platform at the rear of a hangar.

LeBaron thought all six of the fighters must have been shot down but in about ten minutes, after the firing had stopped, two of the fighters reappeared and landed. The pilots got out of their planes cursing the gunners of the fleet. But by the morning of December 8 everything had quieted down and the PBY squadron was back on patrol out of Pearl Harbor.

Like many thousands of the U.S. Navy's sailors and millions of American civilians, on Pearl Harbor Day Yeoman Van Watts was a long way from the action, although he was thoroughly familiar with the scene, having been detached from the carrier *Enterprise* a few weeks before and sent back to San Francisco for reassignment. He returned on the transport *Wharton*, which was full of evacuees from Shanghai and other Far Eastern ports, servicemen and their dependents who had gotten out in time.

Aboard the *Wharton* Watts had spent the week-long journey to

San Francisco ghostwriting tales of the adventures of the Shanghai Squadron in those last few months before the war broke.

When the Japanese struck Pearl Harbor at seven o'clock on the morning of Sunday, December 7, Watts was sitting in the Naval Receiving Station Library in San Diego, studying for the Supply Corps Warrant Officer's examinations. It was ten o'clock in the morning in San Diego. He was reading in a world history text about the Battle of Waterloo when suddenly the station loudspeakers piped up, "Now hear this. Now hear this. All hands to quarters. All hands to quarters."

That was the end of the Battle of Waterloo.

Yeoman Watts dropped the book, jumped up, and began to move.

In a few hours, after life had settled down a little, he was at an outdoor assembly, listening to the words of Captain McCandless, commanding officer of the station:

> *This Sunday morning, without warning, Japanese planes attacked Pearl Harbor. There have been heavy casualties. It is expected the President will momentarily ask Congress for a declaration of war. All liberty and leave are canceled until further notice. No one may leave the base without the Commanding Officer's permission. All hands will now fall out and stand by for orders.*

For several days Watts had been assigned to the disbursing office, to work on the growing naval reserve payroll with Chief Drake of San Diego and Disbursing Clerk Second Class Dick Edwards, both of them reserves who had been called to active duty in the "emergency" that had now become war. On December 8, Van Watts had new orders, and he was on the train heading for Puget Sound. On December 11, he boarded the seaplane tender USS *Mackinac*. He did not know it, but he would soon be headed once more for the South Pacific.

That December 7, aviationman LeBaron's younger brother Jack was serving as an ordinary seaman aboard the USS *Holly*, a net tender. The crew had already taken the ship down to Key West and back and just before war broke out they were trying to salvage an underwater cable that had been lying forgotten on the bottom of the Atlantic off Gloucester, Massachusetts.

On December 7 Jack LeBaron was visiting friends in the Boston suburbs when he heard on the radio that all sailors were to return to their ships. A few hours later they were on antisubmarine patrol in Massachusetts Bay. The fact that the *Holly* got such an assignment was a good indication of the state of American offshore defenses on December 7. The vessel's top speed was ten knots, about half that of a submarine on the surface. The ship had one gun with a range of 700 yards. Their underwater detection gear to fight submarines consisted of a set of earphones and a small underwater microphone. They were told to "listen" with it—but not what to listen for or how to manage the equipment. Every night the ship took a position and stayed there, and in the morning headed in to shore.

On December 8, the third LeBaron brother, eighteen-year-old Bill, showed up early at the navy recruiting station in Burlington, Vermont, and signed up to go into the navy. "I didn't think my brothers should fight the war alone," he said.

On the other side of the world it was December 8. The seaplane tender *William B. Preston* was on duty in the Philippines, its PBYs flying regular patrols and anticipating Japanese action at any time.

Early on Monday, December 8, the message came: "Japanese attack Pearl Harbor, a state of war now exists between the U.S. and Japan and her two axis partners Germany and Italy" What to do? We decided to move a little more to seaward to seek some visual protection from a headland that marked the eastern land mass. Ammunition was loaded in the canisters of the .50 caliber machine guns and distributed to our AA battery—four .50 calibers. When we anchored, we had the foresight to unshackle the anchor chain and hang it from a stopper. We kept steam to the main engine throttles. We didn't have to wait long. First came a section of Japanese fighters, attacking our two remaining PBYs (two had left earlier on a routine patrol) promptly setting them on fire. They were manned by skeleton crews in order to anchor them farther apart. One crew had already secured to the buoy and they hit the water, suffering no casualties. The other crew, not yet completing the maneuver, stayed with their plane. The pilot, Ens. Reuben Tills was killed and one crew member severely injured, the first casualties west of the date line.

> *Our turn followed shortly thereafter, first a formation of six horizontal bombers made a practice run on us. By the time they were ready to make a bombing run, we had knocked the anchor chain off the stopper and were underway with all the power we could squeeze out. They dropped their bombs, we maneuvered and fought them off with our four .50 calibers. They made no hits, although we had some sizeable bomb fragments on board. One half hour later they returned, this time with thirteen planes in two formations. Same results: a non-damaging stand-off. Our captain, Naval Aviator Cdr. E. Grant, estimated that they were making their runs at an altitude of about four thousand feet. We knew early on that we were in a war.*

Ensign Thomas A. Evins was based at the Alameda naval base on December 5, and late in the afternoon he went into San Francisco to meet his friend Randolph Hearst, who was working on the San Francisco *Examiner*, one of the chain of newspapers owned by the family. The pair went bar-hopping that evening, much to the disgust of Randolph's wife, Catherine. When they wandered into the Hearst mansion after hours, she was not impressed with their tales of having a drink with band leader Paul Whiteman and other adventures.

But the next day, Catherine Hearst had recovered and was very polite. In these days of the national emergency, the well-to-do were making it a habit to invite officers in uniform for weekends and show them off to their friends. William Randolph Hearst, Jr., came by for a drink. And everyone was well-behaved, at least until all the guests had left and Catherine had gone to bed. Then Ensign Evins and his host improved the evening with more drinks and several hours of nonsensical talk. They were planning a trip down to San Simeon, William Randolph Hearst's castle, for the next weekend.

"I was sleeping in the guest house a few yards away," wrote Ensign Evins, "when I heard Randy coming along from the main house with a portable radio on full blast. It was about eleven in the morning of December 7 and the radio said that the Japanese had attacked Pearl Harbor."

Ensign Evins' reaction at the moment was that the Japanese had just decided to commit suicide. "We could lick 'em blindfolded."

Since all naval personnel in the Bay area were being ordered back to their posts, Randolph Hearst took Ensign Evins on the long drive across the San Mateo Bridge to Alameda. As they went, they could see that the whole area was in a state of panic. Guards had been posted at every bridge and every conceivable public service installation. If Evins had not been in uniform, they would never have made it past the guards.

THREE

Getting Organized

The day after the Pearl Harbor attack, the naval supply depot at Pearl Harbor sent emissaries into Honolulu to commandeer supplies to take care of the men who had been made homeless because their ships were sunk or damaged. In the days that followed the antiaircraft guns were put back aboard the cruiser *San Francisco*, and she got ready to leave for war. The repair depot stepped up the tempo of the refit and Lieutenant Graham Bonnell was pleased and surprised to learn that they would be out of drydock on December 16 instead of January 20.

And so they were, joining the task force of Admiral Wilson Brown that was going to Wake Island to land reinforcements to send in a new marine fighter squadron. But the relief of Wake never happened, because the brass at Pearl Harbor got cold feet after Admiral Kimmel was abruptly relieved of command, charged with dereliction of duty. Those who were holding the fortress, waiting for Admiral Chester Nimitz to take over, were not about to stick out their necks. As they could see so easily, any sort of error could cost them their careers—or, as it had been in the case of Admiral Kimmel, perception of error—no matter how mistaken.

So the *San Francisco* returned to Pearl Harbor and then went out again, this time with Admiral Halsey.

AOM 2 c LeBaron's squadron spent the first few days after the Japanese attack trying to patch up the salvageable aircraft and go on patrol. They slept at the hangar because takeoff could be at a few moments' notice. The command was very jumpy after the attack, and some of the officials still expected a Japanese landing.

LeBaron flew on some of these patrols as bombardier, since he had been trained in Hawaii in that specialty. One patrol took off one December day at about 4:00 P.M. It was known by this time that the Japanese attack force had left the area, so they really did not expect to find anything unusual. They flew around Oahu and up the north shore of the island to the northwest, toward Midway. At the appointed time they turned around and headed back toward Oahu, but somehow they got lost. LeBaron did not know why and the pilots never enlightened him. They were flying at 2,000 feet, and the night was pitch-black. Oahu was under a strict blackout, and there was nothing to be seen. The big problem was that several mountains on Oahu are higher than 2,000 feet, so they had to climb to 3,000 feet to be sure they were safe.

The problem then became that at 3,000 feet a solid layer of cloud hid what was below; so they were at safe altitude but they could not see land if it was down there, and they did not know where they were. Finally at midnight the pilot broke radio silence to tell Honolulu their story. The solution offered was that the whole battery of searchlights at Pearl Harbor would focus toward the sky and turn on. Perhaps they could spot the lights. It was done, not once but twice, but the men in the PBY did not see any lights.

The pilot then did some navigational exercises and concluded that they had reached a point 200 miles south of Honolulu. Now their fuel supply became critical; they were running out of gas. The pilots figured that they might possibly make it back but would not have enough reserve left for a safe landing. They were carrying 2,000 pounds of 500-pound bombs, and it was AOM 2 c LeBaron's job to disarm them and jettison them. So he did. (These turned out to be the only bombs he dropped during the war.)

After the bombs, they dumped out everything else that could be spared. Still the future did not look bright. The pilot told everyone on the aircraft except those in the cockpit to get into the bunks, since that would be the safest position in case of a hard landing.

LeBaron got into a top bunk because he was the smallest member of the crew.

The pilot then prepared for an emergency landing at sea. He stalled the plane until it was a few feet above the water, while the co-pilot watched and directed him. They did a fine job but when the plane pancaked onto the water, it hit hard and the strap that held up the top bunk broke and LeBaron pancaked down on top of the man in the bunk below. After they got disentangled the crew sat in the airplane for twelve hours as it rode like a cork on the sea. LeBaron was seasick.

They had hit the water at 2:00 A.M. Six hours later another patrol PBY spotted them and at about noon a four-stack destroyer came up. They removed the guns and bombsight from the PBY and the destroyer sank the aircraft with machine-gun fire.

The old destroyer brought the crew of the PBY to Pearl Harbor the next morning in the middle of a submarine alert. Torpedo boats were racing all over the harbor, dropping depth charges on what was supposed to be another miniature submarine. Finally the excitement ended and the destroyer was allowed to enter the harbor and the crew of the PBY got back to their squadron.

A few days after Pearl Harbor, on the other side of America, Seaman Jack LeBaron's net tender *Holly* was on antisubmarine patrol again inside Cape Cod. The December night was black and oily. A lookout reported seeing a wake off the port beam. The signalmen sent the daily signal code request for identification and there was no answer. The process was repeated. No answer. The men of the *Holly* stripped for action, a process that meant taking the canvas cover off their single gun and unlocking the ammunition locker. They then began firing, and fired all around the ship, with no effect.

Next morning they arrived in port, prepared to file a report of the incident, when they encountered one of the other skippers, who was furious because "some damn fool started firing at me last night." The moment of heroism went unnoticed and unreported.

*   *   *

During that first week of war the destroyer *Ward* made many "contacts" at Pearl Harbor and the crew showed great enthusiasm for reporting submarines. Most of the Japanese submarine fleet that had surrounded the island had moved off, so they did not make any more attacks until January 2, when they attacked again and this time were given credit for sinking a full-sized submarine, but Lieutenant Outerbridge was convinced that the *Ward* and the other old four-stack destroyers of the Eightieth Division sank many more submarines and saved Pearl Harbor from more tragedies. Lieutenant Outerbridge got the Navy Cross for sinking the first submarine of America's war.

That was many weeks before the *Ward*'s counterparts on the Atlantic Coast of the United States sank their first submarine. The agent was the USS *Roper*, and the sinking came in April 1942. Meanwhile, in spite of the efforts of the net tender *Holly* and the other ragtag components of what was an almost laughable Eastern Sea Frontier Defense system, the German U-boats were having a field day off the East Coast of the United States. After all, the biggest craft in the antisubmarine fleet at the beginning was a 90-foot Coast Guard cutter. The destroyers of the fleet that were not essential for fleet work were almost all in use in convoys of war materials to Britain.

Ensign Frank Cummings was a ninety-day-wonder, a graduate of Northeastern University's U.S. Navy midshipman course. He had been assigned as communications officer to the old flush-deck four-stack destroyer USS *Sturtevant* at the end of 1941. The *Sturtevant*, DD 240, was one of the group of destroyers assigned by the U.S. Navy that year in the period of "un-neutral neutrality," when American warships had begun actively escorting British convoys on the high seas, actions that had led to the U-boat tracking of the battleship *Texas*, the torpedo damage to the USS *Kearney*, and the sinking of the *Reuben James*. But now that Hitler had declared war on the United States there was no further question, and no quarter was given.

One day in January 1942 a group of these 1,200-ton American destroyers bound for the British western approaches lay in the icy harbor of Argentia, Newfoundland. They were waiting for a convoy bound from Halifax, their boilers up, propellers turning slowly to keep them steaming to their anchors.

The escorts got under way in the forenoon watch and moved out of the anchorage. It was a cold, grim day, with gray skies overhead that meant snow, and ahead were the fog banks of the Newfoundland waters. Three old destroyers formed a scouting line and headed for the rendezvous with the convoy.

Tired old ships, relics of a different war, they were doing their duty, moving fast enough to have a bone in the teeth. As they approached the designated point at sea, a dot of longitude and latitude on the charts, the visibility decreased steadily. The new destroyers had radar, but not these old tubs; they would get it later if they lasted that long.

By this time visibility was down to 800 yards, but they could not use their foghorns because of the danger of alerting U-boats to their position. The destroyer division commander, riding in the *Roper*, led the destroyers steadily onward to the rendezvous point, slowing in the fog, but keeping on until they found the three-dozen-ship convoy they were to take across the Atlantic. They broke formation and headed to the Canadian ships they would relieve, ships that would now turn about and go back to Canada, either picking up an inbound convoy or hurrying to get home and go out again with another eastbound group.

The *Sturtevant* moved abreast of the Canadian corvette that was her opposite number, and the Canadian skipper picked up his bullhorn to give a quick summary of the convoy composition and the latest convoy orders. Then he said, "Goodbye and good luck," and the corvette turned on her heel and headed back to Halifax, warmth, and comfort.

The *Sturtevant* and the other American escorts settled in for the rigors of an escort mission.

Four hours on and eight hours off, the watches stretched interminably. At the end of the first hour every man on deck was soaked to the skin and freezing cold. The next three hours crawled along. Someone observed that the Germans were twice as badly off, chilled by spray and waves as well as wind and snow, and when below living in tiny cramped quarters. Yes, they were better off than the Germans, but so what? That was not much comfort.

Watch after watch, the convoy made its way toward Cape Race, where they would change course. At Cape Race they could expect the worst of conditions of wind and sea when this sort of weather blew along.

The night Convoy UK *213* reached the area southeast of the cape was typical; cold winds lashing down from Labrador, whipping the sea to froth, with the sea temperature at 33 degrees.

Ensign Sheldon Kinney was turned out of his bunk for the midwatch, to relieve Ensign Cummings. The seaman who awakened him had bad news: "The officer of the deck says to put on all the clothes you've got."

Kinney put on his uniform and peacoat and life jacket and adaptation goggles and made his way to the wardroom. In the pantry he braced himself between sink and icebox to pour coffee from a thermos. The dishes in the wardroom rattled in their racks as the destroyer lurched and rolled through the heavy seas.

He looked at the liquid that flowed into the cup and a song went through his head:

> *The coffee that they make here*
> *They say is mighty fine;*
> *It's good for cuts and bruises*
> *And tastes like iodine.*

On deck, Cummings met the ensign coming out of the wardroom. Shouting above the wind, he said, "Hurry up." He was shivering with cold as he led Ensign Kinney to the chart-house. They went through the captain's night orders together, and Cummings gave Kinney the course, speed, and navigational position of the ship, screening instructions, unexecuted orders, condition of boilers and generators, and positions of enemy submarines as known or suspected.

They moved out of the comfort of the chart-house and Kinney looked at the sea, a blend of black and gray, to port until finally he could make out the outline of the key ship in the first column. This ship was the beacon on which the destroyer officers based their night station.

Ensign Kinney touched the peak of his parka to salute, but Cummings was already down the ladder.

"I relieve you, sir," said Kinney to a back. Ensign Cummings was halfway to his bunk. The bridge and the responsibility for the ship was now all his.

Ensign Kinney looked around the darkness of the ship and toward the convoy. "The blind leading the blind," he thought.

The first hour of the watch ended. Kinney's hands were numb in the wet mittens. Salt spray stung his lips, cracked by the cold wind.

"Ship port bow," came the sudden cry of a lookout. In a second, terror gripped the voice.

"We're going to hit!"

Ensign Kinney saw a big hull bearing down on the destroyer, the strip of water between the vessels narrowing inexorably. The other ship had appeared out of the snow and the night. He shouted orders, and hearing them did not recognize his own voice:

"Full right rudder . . . all engines back . . . emergency . . . sound collision. . . . Call the Captain."

The backing turbines spun in reverse and the *Sturtevant* shuddered. The helmsman threw the weight of his body into the task of turning. The quartermaster leaped for the siren cords, and one long blast sounded. Ensign Kinney braced between the pelorus and the windscreen, waiting for the thudding and shock of collision.

The men on the bridge waited. They had done all they could do, and there was nothing more than to wait. The seconds ticked by: one, two, three, four, five—and then came the impact.

The *Sturtevant* heeled sharply to starboard as the bow of the freighter tore into her forecastle. The merchant ship pushed the destroyer before her as if it were a log. The grinding of steel hulls showered the night with sparks, illuminating the ice-covered decks and superstructure and the white foam of seawater sweeping the decks. The clash of tearing metal drowned out the fury of the gale.

For Ensign Kinney the world dissolved into two elements, noise and momentum: the crushing force of the ships as they ground together and the sparks that flew, the sound of the freighter's whistle again and again, the signal "We have been torpedoed," and then the shriek of the destroyer's siren just abaft the bridge. It sounded, and then it stuck and continued to screech.

Kinney tried to see toward the bow but the icy salt spray and snow blinded him. He heard one young signalman ask his veteran sidekick:

"Did she cut us in two? Will we sink?"

He could not hear the answer that the veteran growled out; it was drowned in the wind.

Below decks, men were thrown to the deck by the force of the impact. They picked themselves up and headed for the ladders, moving to collision quarters. Behind them the damage-control parties were battening down the doors and hatches.

Those who got to their emergency stations first waited anxiously, wondering what was going to happen next. Those who knew understood that the point of greatest danger would come when the ships parted. Would there be so gaping a wound in the *Sturtevant* that she would fill with water and sink?

Ensign Kinney looked around on the bridge for the captain but could not distinguish faces from more than a few inches distant. The captain was not on the bridge, he finally saw. Ensign Kinney still had the responsibility for the ship's welfare.

Aboard the freighter visibility was as bad as it was on the *Sturtevant*. The captain of the freighter was trying to move ahead, not knowing that the destroyer was still impaled on her bow. It seemed that she was bent on driving the destroyer under.

Ensign Kinney ordered full reverse on all engines to prevent that fate, and the freighter scraped down the port side of the destroyer and disappeared in the snowy blackness.

The destroyer stopped, and the damage-control parties began to assess the situation.

The captain appeared around from the corner of the chart-house, cursing the member of the watch who had been so kind as to seal the door of his sea cabin from outside with a dog wrench against the stormy night. He had been trapped for minutes during the noise and confusion of the collision.

The skipper's presence turned near-panic into confidence on the bridge. The captain knew his ship; if she could be saved, he would save her—that everyone knew.

With every evidence of assurance, he began the task.

A parting blow from the disappearing freighter had caved in the port side and water was pouring into the forward engine room. The black gang—the fireroom crew—turned to stop the flow of water. With each roll of the ship the vapor saturated the compartment and water spurted through broken rivet holes and struck hot machinery. The steam welled up. Men were working bilge pumps and battens to shore up the weakened side and stop the vaporizing.

On the first platform deck the plates had bulged aft in the transverse collision bulkhead of the anchor windlass room, forward of the chief petty officers' quarters. The chief boatswain's mate and his damage-control party bolstered the bulkhead. They dared not go forward to see what had happened to the bow section. That would have to wait for daylight, and they could only hope that there *was* a bow section. The merchant ship had left her calling card, the remnants of one of her lifeboats scattered atop the galley deckhouse; amid the ready ammunition boxes, some of them overturned, broken antennae, and parted rigging lay water casks, food packages, and protective clothing in a jumbled mass.

The men of the *Sturtevant* now waited for dawn. At first light the bow began to take shape. At least there was a bow. But it canted off to starboard and plates of the port side at deck level showed wide gaps. Seawater rushed in and out as the bow rose and fell. The starboard side had buckled, compressed into a sort of hinge for the dislocated plates of the bow.

With protective clothing to pad them against the buffeting against the ship, the captain and Ensign Kinney went forward. They saw that everything forward of the CPO quarters was flooded. Their fears confirmed, they scrambled back over the narrow forecastle deck and the skipper climbed back to the bridge.

Now was the time for decision. He could order the ship turned back, and perhaps make St. John's, Newfoundland. This was the best chance of survival for the crew of the *Sturtevant*. Or he could stick with the convoy. This was the best chance for the survival of the merchant ships. The decision was the captain's alone. None of the six officers and 135 men could help. He knew that they would welcome a decision to return to port, but he also knew that the convoy commander and the division commander would welcome a decision to stick with the convoy. They needed his ship.

Ensign Cummings was back on the bridge now in his capacity as communications officer.

"See if you can raise the division commander," the captain said.

Cummings hurried to the radio room and told the radioman. Over the horizon, the radioman of the USS *Roper* answered their signal. "Inform him that we will remain with the convoy," the captain said.

The word spread throughout the ship quickly, and men turned away from thoughts of Newfoundland's warmth and to the job ahead.

So they fought the sea with pumps and lumber and plugs to stanch the water from coming through the holes. But every time the ship's bow rose and fell in the surge of the sea there was that worry: Would it hold? The worry was much worse in the fastness of the night, when men could not see what was happening but could imagine dire results from every unusual noise.

The black gang had it worst. The men were constantly aware of the damage. The rivets ran, the plugs came out, the timbers buckled and had to be replaced.

The spirit was provided down there by the old Fleet Reserve chiefs. They were, said the young fellows, metal men, with "gold in their teeth and lead in their tails." But they had a proud tradition in the old four-pipers, and they knew their ship and the sea.

A hurricane passed them to the north, heading for Iceland. The crew compartments were covered with a thin mist and everything was wet. The officers and men were so tired that they slept in their jackets, stiff with salt and wet from the snow and rain after their watches topside.

Finally the convoy sighted the north coast of Ireland, and destroyers of the Royal Navy came in to take over the passage into the Irish Sea and into the western approaches to Britain. The convoy gone, the three American destroyers passed up Loch Foyle and the

Sturtevant was last in line. As the men were piped to quarters for entering port the chief boatswain's mate growled at the deck division drawn into ranks on the forecastle: "Look proud, sailors, You've been to sea."

The *Sturtevant* went into drydock at Londonderry and the British patched her up; she made her way back to the Boston Navy Yard, where a new bow was put on her. She was ready for sea again, and this time she had radar, which should prevent another collision. But four months later she struck a mine and went to the bottom in only 60 feet of water. Seventeen men of the crew were lost, but a handful survived, including Kinney and Cummings, both of whom also survived the war.

In January 1942, while the *Sturtevant* was at sea, German submarine-force commandant Admiral Karl Dönitz had sent out half a dozen U-boats, which were working the American coast, never more than two at a time in these first months. Germany had declared war on the United States just after the Pearl Harbor attack, but it took Dönitz some time to get his boats to sea, so it was late January before they began to make the assault felt seriously. By mid-February the assault was in full swing, and the beaches of the Atlantic shore were black with the oil of the sunken tankers. At first there was no convoy system along the shore, because the Americans did not have enough convoy escorts to undertake the job. Instead, a handful of destroyers of the Atlantic fleet did their best to escort deep-sea convoys heading to England and to combine that with patrol duty off the American shore. But there were not enough "tin cans" to do the job properly.

Harry W. Luessen was the son of a navy professional, a chief machinist's mate who, when Harry was born, was stationed at New Orleans. Later he was transferred to the Philadelphia Navy Yard and the family moved to Camden, New Jersey, and Harry graduated from high school in Camden in 1939. He decided to go into the navy because he was sure the war was soon coming to America. He signed up for a six-year enlistment and after boot camp was assigned as a quartermaster striker, a neophyte steersman.

On the day the Japanese were bombing Pearl Harbor Seaman Luessen was aboard the old four-stack destroyer *Jacob Jones*, heading toward Cape Cod after a convoy voyage to England. It was Luessen's second convoy duty. They heard about the Japanese strike when they were still at sea. They were ordered to go into Boston Navy Yard under full power. After refueling they went to sea immediately, to pick up a Newfoundland convoy bound for England.

The convoy trip took four weeks, and when they got back to the American shore the submarine menace off the East Coast was so serious that Admiral Ernest King reversed earlier refusals to allocate any of his Atlantic fleet destroyers for antisubmarine duty offshore. The *Jacob Jones* was assigned to antisubmarine patrol between Cape Cod and New York Harbor.

On February 22, 1942, the *Jacob Jones* pulled into the Brooklyn Navy Yard for some maintenance work. Seaman Luessen by this time had qualified as a quartermaster's mate, and a complicated life aboard the *Jacob Jones*. Because the ship was allocated two quartermasters and found itself with three, so one man had to go. They solved the problem by flipping a coin, and Quartermaster Luessen lost: He was the one who would be transferred out of the ship. So next day he was sent to the naval receiving station at Pier 92 for reassignment. The date was February 26, 1942.

Next day the *Jacob Jones* sailed from Brooklyn, her patrol area changed. This time she stood south, toward Cape May near the mouth of the Delaware River, just then a hotbed of U-boat activity.

On the morning of February 28, the *U-578* was working along the 1,000-fathom line off the coast when it spotted the World War I American destroyer. The skipper of the *U-578* fired three torpedoes. The first blew away the destroyer's bridge and killed the captain, Lieutenant Commander Hugo P. Black, and thirty men. The second torpedo sheered off the stern of the warship. The ship began to go down and the survivors launched four life rafts into the freezing sea. The water was icy and survival was chancy, particularly for men struggling in the water. Their fate was sealed a few seconds later when the sinking destroyer reached a critical depth and her depth charges blew up, killing most of the rest of the survivors. Of the crew of 162 men only eleven survived, eleven men who had been aboard and lucky Seaman Harry Luessen.

Luessen knew nothing about the sinking until many hours later when he telephoned his parents in Camden to tell them he had been transferred off his ship. Then they told him they had thought that he was dead, killed in the loss of the *Jacob Jones*. It was the greatest shock of Luessen's life and one he never forgot. Fifty years later, to the day, Luessen traveled to Cape May Coast Guard Training Center to participate in fiftieth anniversary memorial services and threw a pine wreath into the chill waters of Cold Spring Inlet.

FOUR

Disaster in the Java Sea

Lieutenant Wood and the *Preston* had been attacked on the first day of the war in the Philippines. Here is more of his story:

> *We stayed in the Philippines for a few more days and then began a withdrawal to the Netherlands East Indies. We finally went ashore for the first time since the outset of the war in Soeraboya, Java, on Christmas Eve. We conducted operations for the next month throughout the NEI, carrying out our mission of supporting the PBYs.*

One disaster followed another. The principal disaster in the Far East was the loss of the Asiatic fleet, and the symbol of the Japanese naval superiority of the time was this campaign in the Dutch East Indies, all too brief, ending in the Battle of the Java Sea.

This campaign represented the end of the old American navy. The American Asiatic fleet had become an anachronism, a fleet in name only, with a heavy cruiser for a flagship and a single carrier, the *Langley*, so ancient it was suitable only to ferry planes, not launch them for fighting.

The commander of the Asiatic fleet was Admiral Thomas C. Hart; this tale of the last days of his fleet is both his war story and the story of the end of an era.

The surface fighting element of the fleet was led by Captain Albert H. Rooks in the fleet flagship, the *Houston*. He had two light cruisers, the *Boise* and the *Marblehead*, and thirteen destroyers—all over-age coal-burners of the sort given to the British in exchange for the West Indian and other Atlantic bases. They comprised Destroyer Squadron 29, under Captain Herbert V. Wiley.

When it became apparent that the Japanese were up to something nasty and the Yangtze River Patrol had been dissolved in late November 1941, Rear Admiral William A. Glassford, the senior American naval officer in China, left for Manila. When he arrived there aboard one of his gunboats in early December, he was assigned by Admiral Hart to set up a task force and join the British and Dutch in a forlorn attempt to protect the Dutch East Indies from Japanese invasion.

Glassford's ships were sent on ahead of him to the Dutch East Indies. The *Marblehead* and four destroyers sailed on November 24 for Tacloban in Borneo. The tender *Black Hawk* and four destroyers were sent on the same day to Balikpapan. When it was learned that the Japanese task force that was to attack Malaya had sailed, they were diverted to Singapore and had just arrived there when word came of the sinking of the British battleship *Prince of Wales* and cruiser *Repulse*, by Japanese aircraft. The four American destroyers hastened to the scene to try to pick up survivors but learned that the few survivors had been picked up earlier and went back to Singapore, where they hung around for several weeks, until it became obvious that the Japanese were going to capture Singapore, and were then moved to the Indies.

Admiral Hart and the Asiatic fleet were reeling from one shock to the next. The admiral got the word in the middle of the night via a radio intercept that reported the Pearl Harbor distress call as the Japanese were attacking the Pacific fleet base: "We are under attack. Repeat, we are under attack. This is no drill. This is no drill." Had the admiral not been smart enough to have sent virtually all of his surface vessels away from the Philippines, they probably would have been sunk within a few hours, for the Japanese air forces wasted little time in hitting the Philippines and smashing the American naval base at Cavite. There was never any talk of a joint army-navy defense, because General Douglas MacArthur knew as well as Admiral Hart did that Hart's surface fleet would be wiped out immediately in any encounter with the Japanese.

After the Japanese bombed and essentially destroyed the naval facilities at Cavite on December 10, Admiral Hart sent most of his Asiatic fleet submarines south to Borneo for safety. On December 11, Admiral Hart called a conference of shipowners and agents and advised them to get out of the Philippines. He could not provide any escorts, but the ships had a good chance to escape to the south.

"But what about the Japanese?" asked the shipowners. Wouldn't they sink the ships at sea?

"The ships will be just as safe at sea—probably more so—than they will be in Manila," said Admiral Hart. He knew that the Japanese controlled the air, and soon enough would control the sea around the Philippines as well. About forty deep-sea vessels were clustered at Manila, and a number of interisland steamers as well. Within the week virtually all the ships had left Manila, carrying the passengers who were going to make their escape and with as much cargo as they could hold. They got away clean.

"We were lucky," said Admiral Hart. The Japanese had already landed at Aparri on December 10.

The Americans were lucky, but they were not in any way united in their defense efforts. Admiral Hart seemed to get information from General MacArthur's command as an afterthought. He did not learn of the decision to withdraw from Manila until December 23, and when he checked the next day, he found that it was already under way. As if to emphasize the swift progress of disaster, the office of the commander of submarines of the fleet was bombed on December 24 and on Christmas Day. If submarines were to operate at all in the Philippines it would have to be from Mariveles, on Bataan Peninsula. So the tender *Canopus* was moved there and was promptly bombed by the Japanese, killing six men.

Admiral Hart saw that the end was not very far away and that there was nothing an admiral of a fleet could do in Manila. The Japanese were marching swiftly. On Christmas Eve, Admiral Hart sent a plane south to the Dutch East Indies with his staff. The next day he planned to leave himself. Manila had been declared an open city on Christmas Day, and everybody who was going to get out had left or was leaving. The clubs were filled with anxious civilians drinking and waiting to see what the Japanese would do to them. One of his officers was methodically moving around the city, dynamiting oil-storage tanks. Admiral Hart did not get out on Christmas Day. The planes that were to take him and the rest of his staff were destroyed by Japanese bombing that day, so finally the admiral escaped in the submarine *Shark* on December 26.

Admiral Rockwell moved to Corregidor, where he and General MacArthur valiantly announced a "unified command" of the defense of the Philippines. The naval contingent consisted of the gunboats *Mindanao*, *Luzon*, and *Oahu*; the minesweepers *Tanager*, *Finch*, and *Quail*; a few tugs and a handful of yachts that could be used as patrol boats; and six PT boats of MTB Squadron 3.

The two destroyers of the fleet left in Manila on Christmas Day departed on December 27. One of them, the *Peary*, had a frighteningly close call on her way.

The *Peary* had a brand-new skipper, Lieutenant Commander John M. Bermingham, who had taken over on December 10. Admiral Hart left in such a rush he gave no orders to the destroyers. The Japanese came that day with another bombing attack aimed specifically at the destroyers and very nearly hit the *Peary*. After that, Admiral Rockwell issued orders to the *Peary* and the *Pillsbury* to get out while they still could. So on the night of December 26, the two ancient destroyers sailed. They sailed separately and the *Peary* made the island of Negros the following morning. Skipper Bermingham expected Japanese planes to be overhead at any moment so he ordered the crew to bring the ship in along the shore, where she was camouflaged with green paint and tree branches. The job was done early that morning and was finished just before five Japanese bombers passed over, heading north. Bermingham then got the wind up and moved the ship to Asia Bay, where she was camouflaged again. That afternoon more Japanese planes flew over, heading south. They did not see the destroyer.

That night the *Peary* sailed. Commander Bermingham asked for flank speed and the black gang gave him 25 knots, which was kept up until she was in the Celebes Sea the next morning. There she was found by a Japanese patrol bomber that began shadowing her and followed her all day long. The skipper had to figure that the Japanese were going to come after him soon.

Commander Bermingham's sailing instructions had included

intelligence that a Japanese cruiser and at least one submarine were standing off North Borneo. He assumed that the Japanese plane had informed its headquarters and that the word had reached these ships. So he sailed again and again made 25 knots, heading for Menado on the northeast tip of Celebes. Early in the afternoon two PBYs passed over the destroyer but did not respond to the ship's "friend or foe" challenge.

Shortly after two o'clock in the afternoon three more Japanese bombers appeared to join their shadow; they all started an attack that lasted two hours. Bermingham maneuvered his ship, and the crew fired all the machine guns whenever the planes were in range. The planes attacked alone, each coming in to drop two bombs, then to zoom away and return again.

The fourth bomber was just beginning its attack when the men of the *Peary* saw a plane low on the horizon. It came in to 500 yards, dropped one torpedo and, just afterward, another. The skipper called for all reverse power on the starboard engine, the ship swung around, and the torpedoes missed. Then a second torpedo plane came in to attack. The skipper ordered right full rudder and swung the stern out of the path of the "fish," but it was a near thing: The torpedoes passed about ten yards away along the starboard beam.

The torpedo planes tried to strafe and did hit the stack, but the machine-gunners of the ship put up such a hail of fire that the planes turned away.

It was now early evening. Commander Bermingham decided not to hole up for the night but to make a run through Banca Strait into Molucca Passage. Shortly before 6:00 P.M. the ship passed Menado. Shortly afterward three Lockheed Hudson bombers with British markings appeared. The identification challenge was made, and the men on the bridge thought they saw one of the pilots wave as if in greeting. But the other two British bombers came in for a glide-bombing attack. Bermingham told his crew to open fire, no matter if they were British, and swung the ship hard to starboard. As the ship heeled, one of the machine gunners fell overboard and was last seen swimming, wearing his life jacket, headed for an island to the port.

Each of the British planes made two attacks, dropping a 250-

shrapnel bomb on each run. The ship escaped all but the last bomb, which hit ten yards off the port propeller guard. Shrapnel flew into the steering engineering room, breaking steam pipes. The fragments killed a machine-gunner and set fire to a four-inch gun cartridge. Fireman Third Class G. A. Fryman picked the burning cartridge up and threw it overboard, where it exploded. As the two "friendly" planes pulled out of their attacks they strafed the ship, but did no further damage.

They had done enough already. The starboard engine had been damaged by the bomb, and now it was overheating. As if that were not enough trouble, the long run at high speed had consumed an enormous amount of fuel and the feed water for the boilers was growing low.

Therefore Bermingham decided to hole up for the night and put in at Maitara Island near Ternate, tied up along the reef. Again the ship was camouflaged with branches. That night the crew went ashore and got supplies of water and coal, and the next day the damage was repaired and they set out again for Ambon. But the repairs had not worked. The thrust broke down again and the ship went on her port engine alone until she reached Ambon at noon on December 31.

At Ambon Commander Bermingham discovered that the PBYs that had passed over had reported the *Peary* to be a small Japanese cruiser, moving at high speed toward Menado escorted by a Japanese bomber. Bermingham really appreciated that. Much more he appreciated the apology of the Australians, who had carried it out. "At least you fellows are better shots than the Japanese," he said.

Down in the Dutch East Indies, the American navy was suffering from too many chiefs and not enough Indians and bows and arrows. Admiral Glassford, who did not like Admiral Hart, was aboard the *Houston*, in command of the task force. Admiral H. Purnell, Hart's chief of staff, who did not like Admiral Glassford, was the de facto commander of the Asiatic fleet. Admiral Hart, who did not like Admiral Glassford either, was somewhere en route preparing to take over. So on January 1, the Americans had three commands in the Dutch East Indies to run their handful of ships.

Soon the command structure became even more complex and confused. Admiral Helfrich, the Dutch naval commander, wanted Admiral Hart to come to Batavia, while Admiral Hart wanted to stay in Surabaya. The British, losing in Malaya, were just about to set up in Batavia. And on January 10 General Sir Archibald Wavell arrived to take supreme command of all the forces in the area. Admiral Hart was made naval commander—which meant his job was primarily in Batavia, where four army, six air force, and four navy organizations were trying to function together. The result was usually confusion.

At first the attention of the high command was focused on Burma and Malaya, where the Japanese were winning all the battles and very quickly taking territory. The British were largely concerned with convoying troops to Singapore, in which the Dutch assisted them. Because of the need for ships to convoy the troops, it was impossible to put together a unified striking force large enough to stop the Japanese.

The battle for the Dutch East Indies was already lost, and everybody knew it. The reason was Japanese air superiority, established from the beginning of their operations. The Allies could never put together, from their six air forces, a strong-enough force to give air support to a naval operation.

Admiral Hart planned an attack on the Japanese at Kema using destroyers, led by the cruiser *Marblehead*, but when the ships were on the way submarines reported that no Japanese were there, so the assault was canceled.

Next the admiral planned an attack on Makassar Strait. On January 20 the Dutch reported a large convoy moving in toward Balikpapan. The only ships available for the raid were four destroyers, supported by the cruisers *Boise* and *Marblehead*. Admiral Glassford was ordered to make the attack. The attack began at Timor and moved north. On the way the *Boise* struck a reef, gashed her bottom, and had to retire from the action. She had to go to India for repairs, and thus did not participate further in the Java campaign. Admiral Glassford transferred his flag to the *Marblehead*, but engine troubles reduced her speed to fifteen knots, so the destroyers were sent in alone. Commander Talbot, in command of the four destroyers, received orders directly from Admiral Hart to attack. Talbot then issued his own orders:

> *Primary weapons torpedoes. Primary objective transports. Cruisers as necessary to accomplish mission. Endeavor launch torpedoes at close range before being discovered. Set torpedoes each tube for normal spread. Be prepared to fire single shots [as] target warrants. Will try to avoid action en route. Use own discretion in attacking independently when targets located. When troops are fired close with all guns. Use initiative and determination.*

The old destroyers performed magnificently. They got their speed up to 27 knots and held it without bursting their boilers. Just before 3:00 A.M. the ships moved toward Balikpapan. The Americans saw lights on the water, and realized they were from burning Japanese ships hit by Dutch bombers that afternoon.

The destroyer *John D. Ford* led the way, followed by the *Pope*, *Parrott*, and *Paul Jones*; they were in communiction by voice radio. Soon the column was steaming back and forth among the Japanese vessels of the convoy, firing first their torpedoes and then their guns and creating enormous confusion among the Japanese. The *John D. Ford* fired a torpedo at a Japanese destroyer, which missed, and then the *Parrott* fired several torpedoes, one of which hit something. No one was quite sure what ships they were seeing and what they were hitting, but they were hitting something. The men of *Parrott* saw a Japanese destroyer blow up and sink. The discrepancies in the logs of the destroyers were so great during this hour of action that it was hard for anyone to find out what had really happened: The number of explosions did not add up with the number of claims.

But what was known of this hour of action was that it was the most successful of the American naval actions so far. The old destroyers were performing magnificently, and they were sinking Japanese ships.

At the end of the hour the destroyers had exhausted their torpedoes and were firing their guns, the second phase of the battle. In this phase the American destroyers engaged several Japanese destroyers. But as the American ships withdrew no one was quite certain what they had accomplished.

> *It seems fairly certain [said the official combat narrative] that we sank at least five or six ships. Two of these, because of the nature of the explosions and their burning, were thought to be fuel ships. One was a destroyer, which was completely demolished, and at least two merchantmen were sunk. It is entirely possible that there were other hits unrecorded because of the poor visibility. And there seems to be no doubt that several other ships were damaged by gunfire. The commander of a Dutch submarine which was present throughout the action reported that our forces had destroyed 13 enemy ships but there is some doubt about the accuracy of this count.*

The sailors of the Allied destroyers were disappointed in their torpedo work, but the Japanese torpedo work was much worse: They scored no hits at all. So the action ended. The next day Army B–17s bombed the Japanese ships in their anchorages. The battle had not prevented the Japanese from taking Balikpapan, but it had been a definite victory—as it turned out, the only Allied naval victory against the Japanese until the Battle of Midway.

But the victory was hollow at best. "Had we been able to strike at other expeditions as effectively as in Makassar Strait, the Japanese advance might have been slowed sufficiently to permit help to arrive from the United States," wrote the author of the combat narrative.

The American command in Pearl Harbor did not know that Washington had decided there would be no help for the Asiatic fleet or the American forces in the western Pacific. The American war effort was focused on the Atlantic theater—period. The men manning the ships of the Asiatic fleet, conducting their valiant battle against enormous odds, were sacrificial lambs offered to slow the Japanese advance, with no real hope that the advance would be appreciably slowed. The men of the fleet did not know it, but they and their ships had all been made expendable on the day Prime Minister Winston Churchill convinced President Franklin Roosevelt that Adolf Hitler must come first and the struggle against Japan must be placed on hold.

By February 1, 1942, the ships of the American Asiatic fleet were beginning to show the wear and tear of war. They had been at sea almost continuously since December 8, and many of them, like the *Marblehead*, needed repairs. The Japanese net was closing around the Dutch East Indies. Malaya had fallen and the British had retreated to Singapore. The last reinforcement of troops had been delivered under a hail of Japanese fire that sank two British troop ships and damaged the USS *Wakefield*.

Admiral Hart decided that the next targets of the American naval command should be the same convoy that had been hit so hard at Makassar Strait, but when the Americans moved they found that they faced a vastly superior force of ships and that the Japanese knew they were coming. Admiral Glassford decided that the attack would fail and called it off.

On February 4, Dutch Admiral A. B. Doormann, now commanding the combined strike force of Allied vessels, ordered an attack on that big convoy, which now apparently was ready to invade Makassar, so the ships assembled. The major American vessels in the force were the *Houston* and the *Marblehead*. The Japanese found the force and began a series of air attacks in which both the *Houston* and the *Marblehead* were badly damaged. The *Houston* took one bomb that killed forty-eight and wounded twenty more and destroyed the after turret of the ship for the rest of the campaign. The *Marblehead* was hit repeatedly by bombs. One wrecked the wardroom; another lifted the main deck and bent a portion of it back, wrecked the chief petty officers' quarters, disabled the steering gear and jammed the rudder full left. She could still make 25 knots, but she steamed in a circle.

Here is the story, as written in the combat narrative:

Several times the [Dutch] Tromp *approached the* Marblehead *to take off survivors if that should become necessary, as it seemed it well might. Fires were raging fore and aft. Damage control crews and all unengaged men were busy fighting them or caring for the wounded. The executive officer had come to the bridge severely burned and his place had been taken by the gunnery officer. The damage control officer supervised the firefighting and efforts to free the rudder. By 1100 the fires were under control but arcs from broken electric cables constantly started new ones in oil-filled compartments. It was not until 1300 that the rudder angle was reduced to about nine degrees left.*

There were 70–80 casualties in addition to many minor injuries that did not take men out of action. The forward battle collecting station and dressing station had been destroyed and the amidship station was unmanable so that the wounded had to be carried aft to a makeshift station in the torpedo workshop. This was no easy task on slanting decks made slippery with oil.

The *Marblehead* was ordered to go south for repairs. The question was whether she would get back to Tjilitjap before she sank. As the combat narrative put it, it seemed that the ship was kept afloat as much by the determination of the captain and the crew as by her own buoyancy, for twenty-six of her watertight compartments were completely flooded and eight more were partly flooded.

After they got her back to Tjilitjap they found that the dockyard there was unable to repair the ship properly. In fact, they could not get all the water out of her. But they could make the ship habitable, which they did, and make some repairs. So the crippled vessel set out for home. In 148 days she sailed 9,000 miles to Ceylon and South Africa, most of the way without a rudder. About that time, Lieutenant Wood's *William B. Preston* began operating out of Darwin.

Early in February, we fell back to Darwin, Australia. We made a couple more forays to the NEI, always retiring to Darwin.

Attrition, war damage, and lack of maintenance was rapidly depleting our aircraft, but as they were rendered inoperable by whatever means, we salvaged their .50 caliber machine guns. We mounted them wherever we could. As to be expected, the ingenious American blue-jacket[s] found the best locations and fabricated fittings to secure them. Now our AA armament presented a formidable array of 29 guns. (Sounds like something from the days of sail!)

Early in February, the Japanese, regrouping from the attack on Pearl Harbor, were training their pilot replacements for those lost. Their Task group, departing the Empire, was cruising south through the Solomons and off the coast of eastern Australia, and was eventually to enter the Java sea via the Torres Straits. This operation would also support their land base forces, which by now had control of the main islands of the

NEI, and would prevent any replenishment of our beleaguered forces in the area.

Also in early February, a few ships carrying military supplies were gathering in Darwin. The destroyer Peary, severely damaged in Cavite and the cruiser Houston were the only other U.S. ships in the harbor. The Australians had a corvette and hospital ship and they, along with the merchants, made a total of about thirty ships.

On 16–18 Feb, we received reports of [an] unidentified aircraft overhead, probably scouting from Ambon, NEI 3–400 miles to the north. The presence of the Houston, severely damaged in an earlier engagement, plus the miscellaneous other ships was surely reported to the aforementioned task force. The Houston may have received intelligence that we did not, for on the evening of 18 Feb, she departed Darwin.

On the morning of 19 Feb 1942, our Captain left the ship to visit shore installations to negotiate for some aviation gasoline. We were still tending a few hardy surviving PBYs. On that same morning, Lieut T. H. Moorer (years later to be Chairman of the Joint Chiefs of Staff) manned his plane to scout east of Darwin. Since Dec 8, when at anchor, we always had steam to the main throttle, and the anchor at short stay (remember—we left one in Malalag Bay Mindanao). At about 0800 our lookouts (we had no aircraft radar) reported large formations of aircraft overhead. We knew they were not ours and so we sounded G.Q., hoisted the anchor, cut loose the boats still at the booms, ordered all engines ahead flank, and prepared to give them the best we had. In the absence of the Captain, I, as Executive Officer left my normal battle station and took command on the bridge. Their method of approach was to become familiar to us later on in the Pacific war, pressing home their attack in a 45 degree glide. The volume of fire from our AA battery of 29 guns was much more effective then [sic] when we had only 4 in the earlier attack. A few Army Air Corps pilots in P-38s, enroute to the NEI, arose to engage but they were no match for the well-trained Zero pilots. One was shot down near our ship, the attacker pursuing and continuing to attempt to gun down the pilot who had bailed out.

In the meantime, the merchant ships were prime targets. All save one was sunk, the hospital ship was bombed, but not severely, and the corvette was hit. Peary, badly damaged, never got underway. She was hit by a string of bombs and set afire from stem to stern. My recollection is that there were three survivors. Meantime, we engaged when possible. One attacker slipped through and sent two bombs (probably 100 kilos) at our *ship. One passed over the bridge and exploded in the water near the bow to starboard. The other hit us at frame 200 port side. killing everyone at the battle station to which he was normally assigned. We lost steering control, fires raged, the ship's bottom was holed and carnage was everywhere. The hole in the hull was shored and the fires put out, but we were not yet able to restore steering control. A hand crew manned the steering engine aft and desired rudder angles were sent by ship's phone from the bridge. We continued to maneuver.*

The Captain, while attempting to return to-the ship was dumped in the water by a nearby explosion. He swam to a buoy and observed the rest of the battle from there. Lt. Moorer reported the enemy task forced and shortly thereafter was shot down by their aircraft. He and his crew were rescued by a freighter. The freighter too was sunk later that day. Moorer then swam to a nearby island, reported to base via the Coastal Watchers network and later returned to Darwin.

Having regained steering control, I decided to clear the harbor, for surely the planes would soon return to pick off the survivors. We proceeded to the southwest at best speed. We could now steer from the bridge. There was one more minor skirmish, a Japanese Emily dropped a string of bombs but was not even close.

Time to assess the damage. Material-wise we could proceed. Personnel-wise, the shipmates we lost could never be replaced. We had the sad duty of preparing fifteen fatalities for burial. Their bodies were sewed in a navy blanket, their head stone a 4" shell. We hove to, and with all the respect and honor for our shipmates we could muster, we consigned their remains to the eternal sea.

On February 14, Admiral Hart gave up operational control of the Allied forces to Dutch Admiral Helfrich and headed back to the United States—the tacit admission of the Americans that as far as they were concerned the battle for the Dutch East Indies was lost. Admiral Glassford thus became senior American officer in the area; he remained at Bandoeng and moved his staff there except for Admiral Purnell, who remained at Surabaya. But that place was so heavily bombed that in mid-February the Americans moved out to Tjilatjap. The Japanese were moving fast, and on February 19 most of the American auxiliary ships were sent to various places in Australia.

The struggle went on against vastly superior Japanese forces and Japanese air power. Some odd events occurred, as on the *Parrott*, when in one battle the steering control jammed as she was making 28 knots and she swung left toward the shore; an emergency full speed astern was called, she stopped dead in the water and began to back, and a chief petty officer was thrown overboard. He swam to the Bali shore, joined up with some Dutch soldiers, and eventually reached Java and rejoined his ship.

By this time, General Wavell had become convinced of the futility of further effort, and Admiral Hart was long gone. On February 23, Wavell had orders to leave Java. He did, in a British sloop escorted by the American destroyer *Pillsbury*.

Then came the Battle of the Java Sea on February 27—fought by British, Dutch, and American ships against the Japanese, under the command of Admiral Helfrich. The conditions were impossible. Lieutenant Otto Kolb, the communications officer for U.S. Destroyer Squadron 29, was aboard the Dutch flagship *De Ruyter*. "There were no common flag signals or signal books available nor were there any tactical plans, save of a most rudimentary nature," he reported.

Bravely the Allied fleet went into action. On February 25 they had word from General MacArthur that the Japanese had assembled 100 ships at Jolo. The Allied fleet was battered and short of everything, and the major remaining American ship, the cruiser *Houston*, only had one gun turret operating. On February 26, Admiral Doorman decided to make a sweep to try to stop the Japanese advance. And so the ragged Allied force steamed out to meet the enemy. The cruisers were in the lead: the flagship *De Ruyter*, then the British *Exeter*, then the American *Houston*, then the Australian *Perth*, and the Dutch *Java*.

At four in the afternoon the Japanese were in range and began firing. "Every fourth Japanese salvo straddled the ship," said Lieutenant Commander Jacob Cooper of the destroyer *Ford*. The Japanese were good shots. The *Houston* was firing five or six salvos a minute with her one turret. "During this time two columns of smoke were observed which appeared to be hits on the enemy," said Cooper. The Allies were good shots, too, that day.

It was not long before the *Houston* took an eight-inch shell in her engine room, but the worst damage at this time was to the *Exeter*, hit in the boiler room by a shell that killed fourteen men and cut her speed to 15 knots. The Dutch destroyer *Kortenauer* was sunk, and soon the British destroyer *Electra* went down.

The battle continued that night, the *De Ruyter* and the *Java* were sunk. Soon only the *Houston* and the *Perth* remained.

On the morning of February 28, the two cruisers put in at Tandjong Priok. Nobody knew what damage the enemy had suffered and everything was conjecture. All that was known was that Admiral Helfrich intended to fight on with his greatly diminished force, now down to five battered cruisers and a handful of destroyers. One British cruiser and two destroyers left Surabaya on the twenty-eighth. An enemy force was reported and then nothing more was heard of the three ships. The cruisers *Houston* and *Perth* sailed out from Tjilatjap and nothing more was heard from them. Not until much later in the war was the story of the last sea fight of the *Houston* told.

During the night of February 28 the Japanese began to make amphibious landings on Java. The American ships had been ordered to assemble at Tjilatjap. Their situation was critical: Fuel was low, and the oiler *Pecos* had been sunk by Japanese aircraft along with the old carrier *Langley*, her deck loaded with airplanes.

On March 1, the joint command in the East Indies was dissolved. Admiral Glassford had orders from Washington to take his ships south to Australia whenever the situation warranted, so he ordered the ships to go to Exmouth Gulf in western Australia, and they began to set out. The admiral was driven to Tjilatjap and then took a plane to Australia. Most of the ships left in the American command never reached Australia, and for a long time no one knew what had happened to them. Thus came the end of the Asiatic fleet in the last battle fought by the professional sailors of the old American navy. Admiral Hart did not go to sea again. He was made chairman of the Naval General Board, and very soon he retired. The future belonged to the young, and the new American navy that was being readied for battle was made up of a hard core of professionals and many more officers and men who came into the navy for hostilities only. They had a lot to learn, but it was soon apparent that they had the enthusiasm and the spirit to learn it.

Lieutenant Wood had been promoted to lieutenant commander. He and the *Preston* survived the attack in Darwin and very soon afterwards moved to Sydney for repairs. Here is more of his story:

After repairs in Sydney, we returned to the West Coast, berthing in Perth. Along with the Childs and Heron *we served as advance base in Exmouth Gulf, our planes conducting patrols to the North and West into the Indian Ocean." [He is too modest to say so, but then-Lieutenant Commander Wood was recommended for the Navy Cross for this action—he received the Silver Star.]*

In September, I received my orders back to the States. Crossing Australia by air and then flying the Pacific in an experimental patrol craft, we flew only during daylight hours with stops in Noumea, Suva, Canton, Palomyra, and Pearl. A few days later to San Francisco and finally home to Annapolis.

Not much fanfare, as contrasted to the opening paragraph, on our return. Rationing controlled shoes, gasoline, sugar, meat, whiskey, and all manner of wearing apparel. Women were a large part of the armed services, doing men's work in ship building, aircraft manufacturing, and all the other war activities. Just as the young people of today, we found it the best place in the world to live—even though no woman looks good in cotton stockings. Incidentally, our daughter was a couple of months short of her sixth birthday.

FIVE

The Battle of the Coral Sea

C. W. Lynch left his home in Burnet, Texas, in the summer of 1941 when he was fifteen years old and went to Lampasas to enlist in the U.S. Navy, Burnet being too small to have a recruiting station. He signed up on July 18, 1941, for a six-year enlistment and was sent to Austin and from there to San Diego. After boot camp he was assigned to the aircraft carrier *Lexington* and soon found himself at Pearl Harbor. His job was seaman, which meant he swabbed decks, scraped rust, and painted, and when he was finished he swabbed decks and scraped rust and painted some more.

When the Japanese attacked Pearl Harbor, Seaman 2 c Lynch and the *Lexington* were at sea. The American reaction to the Japanese attack was faltering, caused by the interference of the politicians and the sacking of Admiral Husband E. Kimmel, the commander of the Pacific fleet. There had been a chance for a strong beginning with a counterattack on the Japanese to be timed during the Japanese Wake Island invasion attempt in December. Admiral Kimmel had set in motion a plan to use three-carrier task forces to defend Wake. But when Kimmel was abruptly dismissed and charged with dereliction of duty, his temporary replacement Admiral Pye stopped the relief forces just as they were about to engage the enemy and withdrew them to Pearl Harbor. Admiral Pye did not want to take the responsibility for risking the carriers, for if he lost even one of them, it would put his career at risk. That was the kind of thinking that dominated the American navy until Admiral Chester W. Nimitz arrived to take command of the Pacific fleet at Christmas 1941. Then things began to happen. The Japanese definitely had the initiative in the Pacific during the last days of 1941 and the spring of 1942, and were moving rapidly in the South Pacific. Their move was so rapid, in fact, and so definitely a threat to Australia, that in the early spring Admiral Ernest King, commander of the American fleet, told Nimitz he had to get some carriers down into the South Pacific to challenge the Japanese. And so two task forces were dispatched, the *Lexington* task force, under Rear Admiral Aubrey W. Fitch, and the *Yorktown* task force under Vice Admiral Frank Jack Fletcher.

In April 1942, Fletcher's task force was operating out of Noumea in New Caledonia, which was to become the center of American activity in the South Pacific. Admiral Fitch's task force was at Pearl Harbor, where it had put in for repairs and upkeep.

The Japanese were planning a new movement in the South Pacific, and the Americans knew it because they had broken the Japanese naval codes. The move was to capture Port Moresby, on the British side of the island of New Guinea, whose government the British had shared with the Dutch under mandate of the League of Nations. New Guinea had been a German colony until World War I, when the German colonial empire was wiped out in the first few months of the war. Now, the Japanese, who had already captured Dutch New Guinea, intended to take Port Moresby and then threaten Australia and other European and American possessions in the South Pacific. To double the threat, the Japanese also intended to build a string of air bases down the Solomon Islands chain toward Australia. They had already captured Rabaul, whose harbor and air base on New Britain island dominated the whole area. They also had taken Bougainville, the most populous and civilized of the Solomon Islands, and had major bases at each end. They proposed to build a major air base on Guadalcanal Island and a seaplane base across Lungga Channel on Tulagi Island, which stood just in front of the much larger New Florida.

About all this Seaman 2/c Lynch knew nothing at all, nor did most of the men who manned the ships of the two carrier task forces. The navigators knew where they were supposed to go. The black gang knew how to get there. The fliers knew from day to day what they were assigned to do. The watch officers knew their jobs, but only on the bridges of the two admirals was anything much known about the tasks of the carrier forces, and even here the information was very sketchy. What was important was that the Americans were down in the South Pacific looking for a fight, and intent on stopping the Japanese juggernaut's forward motion.

By the first of May Admiral Nimitz knew that the Japanese had a carrier force in the South Pacific too. There were actually two carrier forces in the Japanese area, one built around the light carrier *Shoho*, and another built around the two heavy fleet carriers *Zuikaku* and *Shokaku*. The *Shoho* was part of a group that was to undertake the invasion of Port Moresby. The *Zuikaku* and *Shokaku* were part of a group of covering ships that was to prevent any American interference with the Japanese plans.*

Nimitz ordered Admiral Fletcher, who was the senior admiral and thus would command the over-all American force, to go to the Coral Sea and to look for a fight there. If Seaman Lynch had known what was in Admiral Nimitz's mind he might well have decided to jump overboard. In fact, a few days later, May 4, when the *Lexington* and the *Yorktown* got into battle with Japanese forces and Seaman Lynch saw aircraft coming back to his ship all shot up, he did try to jump overboard but was physically restrained until he calmed down. All the same, from that point on Seaman Lynch was a nervous man, and the fact that he was promoted to Seaman First Class did not make any substantial difference.

In order to get ready for battle, Admiral Fletcher ordered the tanker *Neosho* to head for what he hoped was a safe area to wait for the American forces to win the battle and then join up. Unfortunately for the *Neosho* and her accompanying destroyer the *Sims*, they were found on May 7 by the Japanese carrier planes that were searching for the main elements of the fleet. The *Sims* was sunk by bombing, and the *Neosho* was left in a wrecked and half-sinking condition with many wounded men aboard.

This was a matter of which neither Admiral Fitch nor Seaman Lynch was aware because all the ships were observing radio silence. So Seaman Lynch prepared for a battle he had no desire to fight, and Admiral Fitch prepared for the moment all his career had been readying him to meet.

On the morning of May 8, 1942, the men of the *Lexington* were at battle stations at dawn, the tension so strong in the ship that every man was conscious of it. One of the pilots who had been a football player at the California Institute of Technology compared the situation to the hours just before a big football game. But then the search planes were launched, and there was nothing to be done but wait for the results; the ship secured from General Quarters and everybody waited. When you were waiting there was not much to do, so Lynch jawed with his friends, looked out at the great endless sea, and waited.

Seaman Lynch's action station was at a 20mm antiaircraft gun pod in the midsection just below the edge of the flight deck. Its crew hadn't had a lot of practice. Before the Japanese hit Pearl Harbor the big emphasis had been on saving money in the navy and so live ammunition was scarce and firing practice was such that not many of the gunners felt completely confident as they faced what might be their life's work. Seaman Lynch had never mastered the manual's way of shooting the gun: training through the crosshairs on the tip of the muzzle. He never seemed to hit anything at all. The first loader in the pod, a seaman named Wright from Peabody, Massachusetts, was a lot better shot than Lynch was, and he was the first to admit it.

That morning there was some excitement when the planes began to take off. It was about ten o'clock, and the fighters and the bombers took off and headed out. That was the end of the excitement, but the scuttlebutt had it now that something was going to happen very soon. That report, which spread like lightning throughout the ship, was the result of Captain Frederick Sherman observing to a couple of his officers on the bridge that he expected a Japanese attack on the *Lexington* to come at about eleven o'clock that morning.

About half past ten word was passed that the combat air patrol was shooting down Japanese planes. Nobody could see anything; it was happening miles away, but Lynch could see that the ships around the *Lexington* were changing their formation. He did not know that this was in direct response to Admiral Fitch's orders to the cruisers to assume their fighting pattern around the carriers to give maximum antiaircraft fire power. Then, just before eleven o'clock, Seaman Lynch saw some more fighter planes going off the *Lexington*. He did not know that this was the last of the combat air patrol and that the Japanese were very near.

They were at General Quarters again now, which meant that you had your helmet on and were manning your gun. Never mind that there didn't seem to be anything to man it against.

At about eleven-fifteen things really began to happen. Lynch saw them coming, little shapes that looked like mosquitoes a long way off but grew bigger every second. He was trying again to fire his gun by the book and he could tell that he wasn't hitting anything so he said to hell with it and began using his own system. He could tell by the tracers where they were going, so he began firing ahead of the Japanese planes as they came in and down below them a little bit. He was letting the Japanese fly into his fire, and he could sense that he was getting hits, a lot of hits. He didn't make any claims, but he saw some planes he had been firing at start to smoke and then get on fire and then smack into the sea with their wings tearing off.

Now Lynch was having a little fun and feeling good about hitting something, and the gun was going all the time, with Wright doing the loading and Lynch doing the firing.

He hardly felt the first torpedo when it hit the ship. He was too busy. But somehow somebody got it through to him that they had been hit, and then he began to notice that his balance was different. The ship was listing. It was about eleven-thirty.

The 20mm got hot, and soon the barrel was red-hot. Lynch knew something had to be done. He and Wright got some seawater and poured it on the barrel to cool it down, and took it out. Then they couldn't get the barrel back into the gun so they were out of action. He and Wright decided to go over to the other side of the ship and get a new barrel from one of the guns there. They went over, and when they started back they saw the ship was listing and that the list was getting worse.

But then at about noon the list seemed to get fixed somehow. (The *Lexington*'s damage-control parties had been doing a superhuman job after the ship took half a dozen torpedoes.) Then the attack was all over and everything quieted down on the deck. The *Lexington* landed aircraft. Everything seemed to be under control.

About halfway between twelve-thirty and one o'clock that afternoon the explosion came, and not very long after Seaman 1/c Lynch knew that the ship was in real trouble. There were a lot of fires, a lot of smoke, and a lot of men running around the decks. But everything seemed all right. Somebody went down below and got a few gallon cans of ice cream and brought it up, and many of the seamen sat on the deck with paper cups and spoons, eating ice cream.

Although Seaman Lynch did not know it, Captain Sherman and Admiral Fitch were fighting a losing battle down there, and the damage-control parties were not making it. A little after five o'clock the order came to abandon ship.

Lynch was on the flight deck, and it looked like a long, long way down. He thought about it for a while and about how he had been so eager to jump off a few days ago. There were some ropes that ran down from the deck into the water, and he slid down one of the ropes for a way, then fell off and went down, down, down. He went so far down the water got black. Later on he told a lot of lies about it, including one that he thought was a big joke: "I went so far down that the sharks were up above me, and I came up and stuck my finger up the ass of this shark, and got a free ride all the way to Sydney."

The fact was that Seaman 1/c C. W. Lynch was plenty scared, being there in the water and thinking about sharks (he did not see any), and then swimming around and wondering what he was going to do.

He did not wonder for long. The destroyer *Morris* came along, loaded with survivors, and here was one more. They threw him a line; he grabbed it and was pulled alongside, and eager hands lifted him up out of the water. He was saved.

That was all that Seaman Lynch and almost all the other American sailors in the *Yorktown* and *Lexington* task forces knew about the Battle of the Coral Sea. The Japanese claimed a victory, because they had sunk the *Lexington* and the destroyer *Sims* and the tanker *Neosho* (which they identified as a cruiser). Radio Tokyo blared a statement of victory, and Admiral Nimitz at Pearl Harbor was hard put to reply. It was not until much later that Naval Intelligence was able to put together the facts. These facts showed that the Americans had really won an important strategic victory. The strike against the Japanese seaplane base at Tulagi was exciting but not really important. The sinking of the light carrier *Shoho* in the early stages of the battle was encouraging, as was the damage done to the fleet carrier *Shokaku* and the loss of most of the carrier *Zuikaku*'s aircraft. The Americans did not then know it, but those two carriers had been scheduled to participate in the Midway battle in June and could not make it because they were laid up for repairs. If they had gone to Midway, the result of that battle might have been very different. But the real strategic victory was that the Battle of the Coral Sea caused the Japanese to abandon their effort to capture Port Moresby that spring, and following the Battle of Midway the following month they delayed the invasion again. After the Americans invaded Guadalcanal the whole Port Moresby adventure was shelved and the Japanese never again had a chance to go on the offensive. One might therefore say that Seaman Lynch and his buddies helped turn the tide against Japan those May days of 1942 when they fought their battle from the decks of the *Lexington*.

SIX

The Admiral and the Supply Clerk

Navy Supply Clerk Van Watts thought he was going off to war that December day in 1941 when he left San Diego for Puget Sound, but when he arrived on December 11 and boarded the USS *Mackinac* he discovered that first there was some waiting to be done. He and the *Mackinac* lingered on the West Coast for many a month. But finally spring found the ship in San Francisco, and on May 11, 1941, she sailed into the broad Pacific.

The *Mackinac* was a seaplane tender. Naturally enough, Watts believed that they were heading west to tend seaplanes, probably in a combat zone. Sailor Watts was going to war at last!

Well, not quite.

The *Mackinac* put in at Pearl Harbor, where it picked up Rear Admiral Richard Evelyn Byrd. Admiral Byrd was a graduate of the academy at Annapolis, but his admiral's flag had been earned in the frozen lands of the Arctic and Antarctic. The last of the great explorers of the unknown regions of the earth, his promotions after his retirement from the active navy had all been made by act of Congress.

Since Admiral Byrd was an explorer and had retired at a very early age as a line officer for medical reasons, it was not easy to find a spot for him in the naval establishment when the war came. He was too famous, and too well connected.

After Pearl Harbor Admiral Byrd had written to his friend President Roosevelt, asking for employment in the effort against the Japanese and Germans. President Roosevelt had passed the request with a favorable recommendation (which was like a presidential order) to Admiral King. Admiral King had consulted with Admiral Nimitz at Pearl Harbor. And Admiral Nimitz, with his admirable aplomb and command of the problems he faced as commander in chief of the Pacific Ocean areas, had found a first job for Admiral Byrd. Nimitz was expecting to be moving out into the Pacific, on the way to Tokyo, and he needed a survey of the various Pacific island groups to discover their suitability for air bases. Admiral Byrd was an airman, so who could be better informed? The deal was struck, and Admiral Byrd and his staff flew to Pearl Harbor, where he picked up his ship, the *Mackinac*, and sailed for the South Pacific.

The *Mackinac* had not been built to accommodate an admiral, so the admiral had to be content with the captain's cabin. The captain bumped the executive officer out of his cabin and the exec bumped the navigator. By this time they were getting out of the stateroom class and down to the two-bunk officers' quarters. Admiral Byrd had a staff of eight, only one of whom was an enlisted man, and they had to be accommodated as handsomely as possible.

The Byrd party came aboard the ship quietly—no piping over the side and no assembly of the crew. Watts was electrified when he learned who they had aboard. Admiral Byrd had been a special hero of his since Byrd had flown over the North Pole when Watts was six years old and over the South Pole when Watts was nine. As a boy he had read all of Byrd's books: *Skyward, Little America, Discovery, Exploring with Byrd*, and *Alone*, the chronicle of an adventure in which Byrd had spent several months less than ten degrees from the South Pole, making scientific observations and experiencing life alone under the most severe arctic conditions. Byrd was Watts's special hero.

Aboard the *Mackinac*, as the ship headed southwest from Pearl, Admiral Byrd did not have much to do. He spent his days reading and sunbathing. In both activities Sailor Watts had more than the usual sailor's opportunity to observe his hero, although he came far from invading the admiral's privacy. As supply clerk he doubled as ship's librarian, and every day or two he would be asked to produce some books for the admiral to read to relieve the boredom of the long sea journey. Among other works, Byrd then read Ambassador Joseph E. Davies's *Mission to Moscow* and Hitler's *Mein Kampf*. After a call from the admiral's yeoman, Sailor Watts would select a handful of books from the library shelves and carry them to the admiral's cabin, waiting in worshipful silence while Byrd decided which ones he would keep. Sometimes he kept all of them and then returned them after one or two days. Watts was itching to tell the admiral that he had read everything he wrote. Naval discipline kept his mouth shut. But one day when he delivered his books, the admiral smiled his thin-lipped smile and even ventured a pleasantry. Sailor Watts grabbed the opportunity to communicate.

"It might interest you sir," he said, "to learn that a copy of your *Alone* is in our library."

Byrd smiled the thin-lipped smile again, but said nothing.

The moment of ecstasy had ended.

But Sailor Watts's curiosity about the lofty, lonely figure in the captain's cabin had not. He took the *Mackinac*'s copy of *Alone* to his bunk and read it over for passages that might help him understand this mysterious man. He learned that Admiral Byrd's penchant for books was newfound. "There was no end to the books that I was forever promising myself to read but when it came to reading them I seemed never to have the time or the patience." Now on the thirty-one-day voyage aboard the *Mackinac*, he had both.

The admiral's other recreation was sunbathing, and every day he would go to the rangefinder platform on the bridge structure. Seaman Watts's action station was in the conning tower, just above the platform. The first day out of Pearl, Watts and a fire-control man were standing watch and watching the admiral, who paid no attention to the action-station calls since he did not have an action station or any part in the defense of the ship. He continued to take the sun.

"Look," said the fire-control man. "The admiral's turning white."

It was true, his left cheek and ear were dead white in the hot tropical sun.

"Sure," said Watts, from the depths of erudition. "He froze his face in the Antarctic. I know all about it."

Sailor Watts had consulted the pages of his new bible and found the answer on page 262. Admiral Byrd wrote in his diary there that on July 23, 1934, when he was in his South Pole shelter at 80–08 south latitude, the temperature had dropped to 73.5 degrees below zero.

" 'My left cheek was frostbitten and the flaps of the sleeping bag and even my hair were stiff from the frost of my breath.' "

"How the hell d'you know all that?" asked the fire-control man.

"It's all in his book," said Sailor Watts.

So there was a rush on the ship's library to consult *Alone*. Some of the fame rubbed off on Sailor Watts, and as the ship's expert on Admiral Byrd he had considerably more respect than he deserved.

The ship sailed on as the admiral read and sunbathed, to Palmyra, Pago Pago, Wallis, Tongatubu, Fiji, Efate, and finally Noumea. When they stopped at each of these islands, Admiral Byrd and his staff would go ashore and survey the island for its potential as a base of air operations.

When the *Mackinac* reached Pago Pago the crew was allowed shore leave while the admiral took the ship's reconnaissance aircraft on a flight to Apia, the capital of British Samoa. When he returned the ship sailed again, the admiral's party went ashore at Wallis and at Tongatubu, but Byrd and the captain decided these islands were too fragile and unspoiled to have a warship's crew foisted on them, and the ship's company remained aboard. Their next liberty was at Fiji.

Finally they reached Noumea, which, partly on the basis of Admiral Byrd's report, would become the center of American activity in the South Pacific a few months later. There Admiral Byrd and his party left the ship and flew back to Washington, where he wrote his report and submitted it to Admiral King, while the *Mackinac* was assigned to other duty in South Pacific waters, and Sailor Watts continued his efforts to become a warrant officer.

SEVEN

Blind Man's War at Midway

Sailor Ronald Veltman was one of those at the Battle of Midway. He had joined the navy in 1941 and was a "plank owner" on the commissioning crew of the carrier *Hornet*. A navy medical corpsman, he knew virtually nothing that he did not see for himself about the progress of the war, yet he was involved in some of its most famous actions. He was aboard the *Hornet* in training one spring day in 1942 when she took two B–25 medium bombers aboard and they practiced takeoffs from her flight deck. That was interesting to the men of the *Hornet* but it did not mean anything. Next thing they knew, the *Hornet* was at Alameda, California, loading sixteen B–25s and then heading into the Pacific with Admiral Halsey in the carrier *Enterprise* to stage the famous Doolittle raid on Tokyo and other cities in Japan.

What Veltman remembers was that it was a particularly foul day that April when the B–25s took off from the carrier, after the task force had been "spooked" by Japanese picket boats about 600 miles out of Tokyo. The last plane to take off was involved in an unlucky incident. An "airedale"—a plane handler—walked into one of the spinning propellers and lost his left forearm. That plane later crashed in Chinese territory; the crew was picked up by the Japanese and three members were executed by the Japanese.

At Midway, Sailor Veltman's major recollection was at the end of the battle, when all was quiet, going into the ready room of the *Hornet*'s torpedo bombing squadron and feeling the eerie silence. None of the *Hornet*'s sixteen torpedo bombers came back from the mission, and only one of the pilots survived.

The next thing Ronald Veltman knew about Midway was that it was history, and he was already far away, on his way to the South Pacific.

While Sailor C. W. Lynch was floating around in the South Seas following the sinking of the *Lexington* and Sailor Van Watts was under the thrall of Admiral Byrd on their way to the South Seas, the major drama of the war was being played out at Midway atoll in the central Pacific.

Most of the sailors, even those involved in the action, did not know much about what was going on when they sailed out of Pearl Harbor. No one then knew that Admiral Isoroku Yamamoto was accompanying the fleet to attack Midway, that the whole core of the Japanese imperial navy was involved. Admiral Ernest King suspected that the whole Midway operation was a trap and that the real objective of the Japanese was to make a landing on the West Coast of the United States. Therefore Admiral Nimitz, who suspected that the Japanese were much more likely to attack the Hawaiian Islands if they were successful at Midway, operated under two constraints. First, he had to protect Midway, and almost until the last Admiral King's intelligence from Washington was so faulty that he found it hard to believe Midway was the Japanese objective. Second, because of this King ordered that only "strong attrition tactics" be employed and that the carriers and American cruisers not be unduly risked. In other words, the Americans were running scared.

Admiral Nimitz was nearly as much in the dark as were his subordinate commanders. But Nimitz staked everything on the belief that Midway was the target, and that the Japanese would make a rendezvous of all their forces about 700 miles from Midway. So he ordered the area 700 miles west of Midway to be searched daily for enemy ships from May 31 on. But nothing was found on that day or on June 1, when a B–17 ventured 800 miles west. The navy's PBYs were also out, but they were really unsuitable for searches in which strong enemy air power might be encountered. On May 30, two PBYs made contact with two Japanese patrol planes from Wake about 500 miles from Midway and were badly shot up. The same thing happened on June 1, but this time the PBYs escaped damage.

On June 3, the PBYs located part of the Japanese force, but not the carriers. What they saw was the occupation force, merchant ships and transports making ready to take over the islands. The contact was very spotty and the island air commander sent a B–17 to follow up an army plane with a navy observer aboard. But try as the aviators might, they did not make contact with the Japanese carriers that day, and so at the end of it, neither Admiral Fletcher, who was in command of the American carrier force, nor Admiral Nimitz, who was in command of the whole operation, knew exactly what the Japanese were up to. In that they were not so very far ahead of their ship captains, who as usual were "flying blind" except for knowing that the enemy was out there and it was their job to get at them and fight.

The next morning the army B–17s found and attacked the invasion force and thought they had hit a cruiser and transport. In fact, they hit nothing. The antiaircraft fire was so heavy from the Japanese ships that they bombed from 12,000 feet and did not stick around to see any results.

On the night of June 3, a flight of four PBYs, each carrying a torpedo, left Midway on what the navy called a historic mission, the first night attack with torpedos by American planes on enemy ships. All the pilots and crew were volunteers, led by Lieutenant William Richards, executive officer of Patrol Squadron 44. They took off at 10:35 on the night of June 3. At 1:15 in the morning of June 4 they found ten ships and attacked. At first they thought one ship might be a carrier, but no such luck; it turned out to be a transport. They throttled back their engines and made a gliding attack. Lieutenant Richards dropped his torpedo first, and thought that an explosion followed. Lieutenant (jg) Daniel C. Davis attacked second, but did not like his approach and so pulled up and made another run. He dropped his torpedo from 200 yards out but saw no results. He had missed. He strafed the ship as he passed, and the ship opened fire on his plane.

Ensign Gaylord D. Propst attacked. He believed he saw the flash of a hit as he withdrew, running through antiaircraft fire. He was attacked by a Japanese fighter and escaped into the clouds.

Ensign Allan Rothenberg did not find the enemy at all and began to run low on gas, so he turned and headed back to Midway.

By the time the Midway PBYs were coming home, they were warned that the Japanese had begun their first carrier air attack on the atoll, so they set their course for the nearby island of Lisianski. Three planes landed at Laysan, and Ensign Propst landed at sea near Lisianski, out of fuel. All these volunteers had a rough time. Three of the crews, having flown from Pearl Harbor the day before and then made their attack, were delayed all day on the fourth and finally flew back to Pearl on June 5. That was the end of their battle of Midway. Ensign Propst and his crew, forced down on the water, were not picked up for fifty-three hours, and that was theirs.

Meanwhile, early on the morning of June 4 the army air force with its B–17s and medium B–26 bombers prepared to attack, as did the marine air group at Midway. At 5:45 a navy PBY found two Japanese carriers and the B–17s set out to attack them. The Japanese guns were too numerous, and although they gave the best account of themselves they could, their efforts were not very successful; several were shot down and many others were shot up. As for the navy and marine defenders of the island, they turned to and were manning their guns as the Japanese came in to drop their first bomb at 6:30. Just before that moment, some American gunners found the range and shot down one of the Japanese bombers in flames.

The Japanese dive bombers headed for the powerhouse on Eastern Island and the oil tanks near the marine dock on Sand Island. They made hits, and the smoke from the burning oil tanks interfered with the American antiaircraft gunnery. The navy PT boats opened fire with their antiaircraft guns, and at last one Japanese plane crashed some distance beyond them, so they thought they had gotten results. The gunners continued to fire although the attack was over in a few moments, but a few Zeros came in to strafe before they headed back, and the gunners fired at them.

For the moment the attack was over. The American planes came in to land, and it was found that of the twenty-seven marine fighters that had taken off fifteen were missing and seven were badly damaged. They claimed forty-three Japanese planes, plus an unknown number supposed to have been shot down by the missing pilots, but that was entirely overblown. Putting two and two together and getting six, the defenders claimed that they must have shot down an enormous number of Japanese planes, because the bombing was so light.

What the survivors had learned was that the Japanese had a great fighter plane in the Zero. All VMF pilots of various degrees of experience and capability were awed by the performance of the Zero I Sento Ki fighter, claiming that it had 20 percent more speed, climb, and maneuverability than did the F2A–3 or the F4F–3. The only way our pilots could have shaken them off was to dive at speeds better than 400 knots or to use cloud cover.

As the navy commander looked around him that morning after the first Japanese attack, he realized that the damage to Midway had been severe. Almost all structures above the ground had been destroyed or badly damaged. The powerhouse had been hit, the hangar destroyed, and the gasoline system had been damaged so that from this point on refueling had to be done by hand. This made it very difficult to get planes in the air in a hurry. What the Japanese had not done was hit the runways, apparently planning on using them later in the day.

After this first Japanese attack, the island's attack planes—army, marine, and navy—all went to hit the Japanese carrier fleet. The army B–26s went first but had no luck and suffered heavy losses. The survivors claimed several torpedo hits, but these were false.

The six navy TBFs commanded by Lieutenant Fieberling made an attack at the same time as the B–26s. Of this flight only one plane returned to Midway, making a landing with one wheel still up. The surviving pilot was Ensign Albert K. Ernest, and he was so confused by the events of the flight, the heavy attack by the fighters, and his own desperate attempt to survive that he could give no account of the attack. That was Ensign Ernest's Midway battle. That of the army and the marine pilots was nearly as confused.

The successful attack on the enemy came from the American carriers. The Japanese were as confused as the Americans about the fighting as it progressed and had no clear idea of the number of American carriers involved.

What could be learned at this point at Pearl Harbor was meager and grim. The Midway air forces had shot their bolt and failed to stop the Japanese; that much was clear. Although extravagant claims for planes shot down and ships damaged were made, the total, even if accepted, indicated no serious damage to the enemy's striking power. These were hours of great worry at Pearl Harbor; Admiral Nimitz with his great calm and apparent confidence refused to panic. He was waiting.

That morning, as far as any of the Americans knew, only two Japanese carriers were involved: That was all that they had sighted. But Admiral Raymond Spruance was sure there must be more carriers involved, from the numbers of planes reported.

After the Americans planes were launched from the *Hornet* and the *Enterprise*, the Japanese carriers changed course, and thus the American scout bombers failed to find them. The men on the bridge of the *Enterprise* knew, but radio silence was being maintained so the pilots could not be informed. The *Hornet*'s ten fighters in the air exhausted their fuel and all landed in the sea before they reached Midway. Eight of the ten pilots were rescued. All but two of the dive bombers made it back to the *Hornet*. Thirteen of them first landed at Midway, two in the lagoon.

Lieutenant Commander John Waldron's Torpedo 8 left the *Hornet* and moved at low altitude toward the enemy. The torpedo planes became separated from the fighter cover. They found the enemy carriers and attacked. Not one of the planes survived the attack, and only one pilot, Ensign George H. Gay, made it back to represent Torpedo 8. He dropped his torpedo and erroneously claimed a hit on the carrier *Kaga*, and then his plane went into the water near the *Akagi*. He hid under a floating seat cushion and did not inflate his life raft because he was so close to the enemy that he was afraid he would be picked up or strafed. Thus he was the only real witness to the fate of those two carriers. In fact, Ensign Gay was the only American who saw very much of the Battle of Midway. He saw the dive bombers of the *Enterprise* and *Yorktown* when they came in and attacked from high altitude, surprising the Japanese fighters, which had come down low to destroy Torpedo 8. If it had been planned that way it could not have worked any better. The other two torpedo squadrons also attacked, but none of them did any damage to the Japanese fleet. That failure was a rude commentary on the American's torpedo and attack system at that point in the war, but it worked in a way never anticipated. In effect, the Americans feinted with a low punch, sacrificed the *Hornet* Torpedo Squadron and most of the other two apparently to no avail, but in so doing made it possible for the dive bombers to be deadly effective. It couldn't have been more advantageous, for the American dive bombers were the most effective aircraft the U.S. Navy possessed at this point in the war.

When the Japanese carrier planes attacked, the only carrier they found was the *Yorktown*, and only eight of their attack planes succeeded in getting through the American fighter screen. One bomber put his bomb into the *Yorktown* aft of the Number 2 elevator. Another scored a near miss close to the fantail that started fires on the ship. Then three more bombers came in and two scored near misses, while the third made a hit on the starboard side of the carrier as the plane crashed into the sea. The seventh plane dropped a bomb that hit the Number 1 elevator and then crashed into the sea. The last plane barely missed on the starboard side. The Japanese attack had been very successful in terms of the eight planes that penetrated the screen. Repairs to the bomb damage seemed to be under control by noon. In the afternoon another attack put two torpedoes into the *Yorktown*. All the lights went out. The ship's list increased to 26 degrees, and without power the flooding of compartments could not be accomplished. The ship's commanding officer, Captain R. P. Buckmaster, believed the vessel might capsize at any moment. Just before three o'clock orders were given to abandon ship and almost all the men went off. After an inspection the captain also left the ship. Aboard the *Yorktown* the damage was seen as very serious and the ship considered lost.

On Midway, the defenders had little idea of what was going on. To Captain Logan Ramsay, the island's air defense officer, the future looked desperate.

"At this time things looked very black," he wrote. Most of the reports had not been received. As far as Captain Ramsay and the defenders of Midway knew, one Japanese carrier had been damaged by the army (untrue). "The losses of the marine air group were so heavy that it appeared the attack had been broken up before reaching the convoy. The *Yorktown* had been hit. Three enemy carriers appeared to be left to deal with the American force. It appeared that it was quite possible that we would be under heavy bombardment from surface vessels before sunset."

So grim did the situation look on Midway that afternoon that arrangements had been made to evacuate nonessential personnel to Pearl Harbor along with some of the aircraft.

Then came the news that the pilots of the American carriers had sunk three of the Japanese carriers. Even so, work on Midway went very slowly, particularly hampered by the breakdown of the gasoline storage and fueling system. Finally four B–17s went out to attack late in the day and found one Japanese carrier burning and a "battleship" also damaged. They attacked a cruiser and two other B–17s later attacked and claimed to have damaged a cruiser and a transport.

And they encountered another group of B–17s, just coming in from Hawaii, that had been ordered to attack before landing. That evening, six remaining dive bombers on Midway tried another attack but did not find any Japanese and returned to Midway without enemy contact. That evening after dark, the PT boats also set out to attack but did not find the enemy either. They headed back to Midway, arriving the next day.

So the Battle of Midway ended, finally, with four Japanese carriers destroyed. During the next two days the fleets milled about, each set of commanders trying to make up their minds whether to take strong action against the enemy; in the end, neither did. Since the Americans were constrained by their prebattle orders from Admiral King not to put the carriers at unnecessary risk, Admiral Spruance made no real effort to find and destroy the rest of the enemy fleet.

The Japanese were constrained by Admiral Nagumo's loss of all his fleet carriers. All that remained at the disposal of Admiral

Yamamoto was one light carrier with his part of the fleet and two light carriers that could be hurried down from the Aleutians invasion force, plus some land-based air from Wake. Admiral Yamamoto was so unsure of the performance of Admiral Nagumo, which was at its usual timid level, that he first ordered and then canceled a night surface attack against the Americans, thus forfeiting any possible chance of pulling a victory out of the defeat. In all this, both fleets suffered from very bad communications.

After the day's battle, Admiral Spruance made no real effort to pursue the enemy. He really did not have much of an idea of what then comprised the enemy.

"I did not feel justified," he wrote.

> *In risking a night encounter with possibly superior enemy forces, but on the other hand, I did not want to be too far from Midway when the enemy might approach Midway in the morning. I wished to have a position from which either to follow surviving enemy forces or to break up a landing attack on Midway. At this time the possibility of the enemy having a fifth fleet carrier somewhere in the area, possibly with his occupation force or else to the north, still existed.*

At two o'clock in the morning a report from the submarine *Tambor* indicated a large number of hitherto unknown ships in the area 90 miles west of Midway. This suggested a landing attempt to Admiral Spruance, so he went into a defensive posture, moving the fleet to a position to repel a landing.

This was the main Yamamoto force of the Combined Fleet, which until this point the Americans did not know was at sea.

At Pearl Harbor Admiral Nimitz did not know exactly what was happening either. When the carrier *Saratoga* appeared at Pearl Harbor and was dispatched to the scene and then turned for a time toward the Aleutians, the Americans lost a chance to make ultimate use of their three carriers in the area to destroy the Aleutians invasion force. And so the battle that had started with so much rumbling died to a mere rustle as both fleets backed off.

Admiral Fletcher, who was so unsure of himself that he had turned tactical command over to Admiral Spruance, did not make any real effort to save the carrier *Yorktown*. The degree of damage had been overestimated. The ship remained afloat all night, but nothing was done then to save her. Fletcher ordered a watch kept on her, but the burden of his orders was to not work on the vessel but to sink it if the Japanese tried to board.

On Midway that night of June 4, Captain Ramsay still worried about invasion. The worry was increased at about one-thirty when a Japanese submarine surfaced offshore and shelled Midway. There was no damage, but it put the wind up. The rest of the hours of darkness were spent worrying about the possibility of attack.

On June 5, what was left of the Midway air force attacked the Japanese, who were definitely now seen to be withdrawing, and some of the planes reported doing damage to ships. Although army, navy, and marine aircraft claimed hits on heavy cruisers, no one was quite sure how many cruisers were involved. Actually the cruisers *Mikuma* and *Mogami* were the ones, with one of them sunk and the other seriously damaged before the fight ended. But this was not known anywhere until survivors from the sunken *Mikuma* were rescued by Americans later. The next day the Midway planes attacked again and claimed to sink a ship, but what they had done was attack the U.S. submarine *Grayling*, which crash-dived but came up again later.

All during the battle an enormous amount of confusion was engendered by the differing tales of the pilots involved. On June 6, for example, Lieutenant Clarence Dickson of the *Enterprise*'s Scouting Six Squadron reported that the *Hornet* group first attacked a cruiser and that the *Enterprise* group attacked another group of ships. But the fact, as ascertained much later, was that the two ships were in the same group and that pilots of both carriers attacked them both.

The Pacific fleet intelligence officers and staff and Admiral Nimitz later tried to sort out all the claims to determine what had really happened. It was quite a job, as can be seen from notes to the battle prepared at Pearl Harbor:

In these footnotes it was suggested that the Hornet *and the* Enterprise *were not attacking the same group of enemy ships. It appears that both the* Mogami *and the* Mikuma *were in the group attacked by the* Enterprise *at noon and that it was the* Mogami *which fled burning and streaming oil accompanied by two destroyers. If this analysis is correct, the heavy cruiser left gutted and abandoned by the* Hornet's *second attack was not the* Mogami, *though it may have been of the* Mogami *class.*

This would mean, too, that more enemy ships were damaged than was previously supposed. So long as it was believed that both [the] Hornet *and* Enterprise *were attacking the same group, it was assumed that one attack merely added to the damage already inflicted by the other, and it had to be assumed that the other enemy group escaped without damage when the Midway planes failed to find it. The view here advanced means that both groups came under attack and received serious damage.*

It seems probable that the ship photographed by the Enterprise *planes was the cruiser left gutted and abandoned by the* Hornet's *last attacks, in fact that was the only ship left in such a condition. The fact that the pilots of the photographic planes saw a cruiser and a destroyer fleeing westward confirms this, for there had been a smaller cruiser with the one left dead by the* Hornet.

But as we have seen, it could not have been the Mogami, *for the* Mogami *had not been in this group, but in the group attacked by the* Enterprise *at noon. Far from being left "gutted and abandoned," she had been seen shortly after noon, damaged and burning, it is true, but proceeding westward under her own power at 10 knots. She was not, therefore, sunk as reported, but almost certainly returned damaged to Japan. It seems probable, however, that we did sink the ship photographed, which may have been of the same class.*

So how many cruisers were sunk? The Americans did not know, but the answer was one.

In the final analysis, in such matters, the admirals and captains were often no better off in terms of knowing what was happening in a battle than the men below deck.

In the Midway battle the sinking of the *Yorktown* proved to be an object lesson to the American navy; the errors that led to its destruction were never again repeated.

The ship was abandoned after the second attack on the afternoon of June 4. That night she was virtually abandoned by her fleet, with the cruisers *Vincennes* and *Pensacola* moving off to join Admiral

Spruance's force and only the destroyer *Hughes* standing by to see that the Japanese did not capture the *Yorktown* before she sank. Everybody expected her to sink.

The intention was to transfer survivors from the destroyers to the cruiser *Portland*, which would go to Pearl Harbor to deliver them on land. The *Astoria* and several destroyers would then return to look at the *Yorktown* with an eye to salvaging her. All this was countermanded from Pearl Harbor by Admiral Nimitz, who dispatched the destroyer *Fulton* to pick up the survivors. By also sending the minesweeper *Vireo* from Pearl Harbor, Nimitz gave some indication of his displeasure with Fletcher for leaving the carrier so abruptly. Fortunately, during the long night the Japanese had not found the crippled and virtually abandoned carrier with its single escort.

Captain Buckmaster and 180 officers and key men then decided that they had been premature and started back to the *Yorktown* with three destroyers, while the rest of Admiral Fletcher's task force joined up with the *Saratoga*, which was ordered to go after the Aleutians force.

On the morning of June 5, the *Hughes* rescued from the *Yorktown* two wounded men who had been overlooked in the hasty departure from the ship. She also picked up a *Yorktown* fighter pilot who had tried to come back to his carrier but had had to land in the sea near it.

By one o'clock in the afternoon the *Vireo* had arrived on the scene, taken the *Yorktown* under tow, and headed for Pearl Harbor at three knots. The load proved too heavy for her, and she was barely able to keep the tow going or move at all.

During the afternoon Nimitz sent the destroyers *Gwin* and *Monaghan* to join the group. They put a salvage party from the *Gwin* aboard that afternoon. Admiral Nimitz had now definitely decided that the *Yorktown* would be salvaged and he sent the destroyers *Hammann*, *Balch*, and *Benham* to join up, which they did at about two o'clock in the morning. About two hours later, at first light, Captain Buckmaster and his officers and men arrived and were transferred back to the ship where the *Gwin* men were already working.

At 6:00 A.M. the *Hammann* was ordered to lie off the *Yorktown* starboard bow to supply firefighting water and foam and to supply power for pumps. To do this she had to secure to the carrier.

By afternoon much progress had been made. A fire in the rag storeroom had been put out. The water level in the engine room had been reduced, and the third-deck water had been lowered by three feet. Two starboard fuel tanks had been flooded to reduce the list, which had been reduced two degrees.

But all these efforts had been too late. A Japanese submarine had found the crippled cruiser, and now she acted. Four torpedo wakes were seen at 1:35. The destroyers around the carrier gave the alarm, but there was nothing else they could do. The *Hammann* went to General Quarters. Its gunnery officer, Lieutenant Charles Hartigan, ordered the machine-gunners to fire on the torpedoes and try to explode them. The captain of the *Hammann* called for emergency power on the inboard engine to try to pull clear of the *Yorktown* before the torpedoes hit. The first passed under the *Hammann* and hit on the side of the *Yorktown*. The debris showered down on carrier and destroyer, stunning many of the men. The second torpedo struck in the *Hammann*'s Number 2 fireroom and broke the ship's back. The *Hammann* began to settle by the bow; the order was given to abandon ship. Two torpedoes hit the *Yorktown* below the island structure. Landing gear of planes collapsed on deck, men were thrown into the water or against bulkheads. The hole in the side flooded the starboard fireroom and the list decreased.

The *Hammann* sank in less than four minutes, but most of the crew managed to escape. One of those who did not was Torpedo-man B. M. Kimbrel, who checked the torpedoes and depth charges to be sure they were on safe so they would not explode underwater. But a minute after the stern went down came an underwater explosion that killed many men in the water. It was caused either by a torpedo or depth charges going off.

Destroyers rescued survivors and other destroyers looked for the submarine. They did not find it, although they thought they did. They spoke of seeing heavy oil from depth-charge attacks. But at 6:45 that evening the submarine surfaced on the horizon. The *Monaghan* and the *Hughes* set off in pursuit and five-inch guns were heard firing later, but the submarine escaped.

Still the *Yorktown* did not sink, and although the salvage parties were taken off for the night it was decided to try further salvage efforts the next day. This was a reversal of position on the part of Admiral Fletcher, who had once abandoned his flagship. But it came too late. The three torpedoes of the submarine had sprung doors and weakened bulkheads. At 3:30 in the morning it was noted that the list was increasing and a half-hour later the *Yorktown* turned over on her port side and sank in 18,000 feet of water.

So the Battle of Midway ended, an American victory. After it was all over Admiral Nimitz gave credit for the victory largely to the intelligence people who had brought him the news of the enemy's intentions. Everybody concerned at high level had some comments to make about the battle, ranging from frank admission of American inferiority to the Japanese in aircraft, both fighters and bombers, to a claim that "in a duel between carriers, the side which is able to strike the first blow against any carriers whose planes are on board wins."

This was an odd way of explaining the victory, but both Admiral Fletcher and Admiral Spruance made this statement. The fact was that the Americans managed to catch the Japanese with their planes on board through sheer luck and the failure in Japanese intelligence which kept them from knowing how many American planes and and carriers were engaged. The matter of the planes being on board was sheer circumstance, caused by Admiral Nagumo's decision to switch from high-explosive bombs to armor-piercing bombs and torpedoes for his second strike, when he belatedly learned that he faced American carriers. But in the future no carrier commander could plan on catching the enemy with his decks full. Indeed, at the time Admiral Nagumo was aware of the potential danger but comforted himself with the belief that the enemy was nowhere near, a matter that was a result of a basic failure of his own—due to overconfidence he did not send out his planes in serious search that morning. He had beaten the enemy at Pearl Harbor, at Trincomalee, at Darwin, and he had become a victim of Japan's victory disease. Intelligence, that of the Americans, aimed with the broken Japanese codes, that of the Japanese with their carelessness and arrogance born of victory, and other such matters affected the outcome of the Midway battle, but the principal one was luck. The Americans had the good luck to find the Japanese fleet first, and the good luck to send their courageous pilots in their inferior torpedo bombers in first to be decimated, so that their much more effective dive bombers could go into action virtually unimpeded by attack from what were then the best fighter planes in the Pacific. Yes, intelligence and luck won the battle of Midway for the American navy that day, and most of the sailors engaged in the struggle had no idea of what it was all about or what was happening.

EIGHT

A Destroyer Is Born

During the last few months of peace, when navy regulars were holding things together with one hand and trying to build a new hostilities-only navy with the other hand, Lieutenant Eugene Alexander Barham, of the Annapolis class of 1935, was assigned to a series of World War I four-stack destroyers being refurbished to become destroyer transports and seaplane tenders in this new war. He and his wife lived in a small hotel on Geary Street in San Francisco. It was a very pleasant existence for a sailor.

Two days after the Japanese attack on Pearl Harbor, Lieutenant Barham received orders to report to Bethlehem Shipbuilding Company's California facility, where the *Laffey* was being put together. He was to take over as engineering officer of the new destroyer when she was commissioned. A few days later he reported to Lieutenant Commander William E. Hank, the new captain of the *Laffey*, who had been stationed at the academy when Barham was a cadet. It is an indication of the tough discipline at the academy in those days that Commander Hank went out of his way now to assure Lieutenant Barham that there were no hard feelings, and all the leaning he had done on Barham in academy days was only for the good of the service. A little skeptical, Barham accepted the assurances of good will, but soon enough found that they were real.

At the same time, Lieutenant William Doyle was ordered to the ship as executive officer and Ensign Thomas Evins was ordered on board as torpedo officer.

The crew was moved to the *Laffey* detail at the Twelfth Naval District Receiving Station on Yerba Buena Island. From there it was a few minutes to downtown San Francisco and the watering holes: Shaker's, Manuel's, Streets of Paris, Chez Paris—favorites of the *Laffey* sailors, where beer was a quarter of a dollar a bottle and no head count was kept at reveille.

But at the shipyard the officers and men of the *Laffey* ran into problems. The *Laffey* had been built to operate with high-pressure steam lines that had to be steam-tight—made of one solid un-welded piece (a welded pipe in this situation might burst under pressure at a critical moment). During the process of getting the ship ready to go, a shipfitter from the construction crew, who appar-ently had more conscience than the company men, warned Lieuten-ant Barham one day that he ought to look at one particular piece of pipe. Next day, Barham had the piece stripped and examined; it had been welded and then glossed to conceal that fact. Now suspect-ing the company men of lying, Lieutenant Barham had all the lines stripped down and discovered a number of lines that had been improperly treated and installed. This was the company's way of speeding up the work. It could have cost the lives of the crew of the *Laffey*. The shipbuilders denied that this had been done, but the proof was there. All defective pieces had to be replaced by steam-tight lines.

There was another problem—the evaporators would not bring the salinity of the water down to the standards needed for the boilers. Barham and the engineering crew tried to get this fixed, but somehow the shipbuilders never did it. So on March 31, 1942, with some problems remaining, the *Laffey* was put into commission and readied to go to war.

Their first job was to take the battleship *Nevada* to Bremerton Navy Yard for repairs after the Pearl Harbor attack. When they went to meet the battleship, the *Laffey* came up like a puppy dog, all speed and frenzy. As Barham put it: "We rushed up with a proud 'Here we are!'," the newest destroyer in the fleet. So in-tent were they on creating a good impression that everything was just too fast, and then two depth charges dropped off the racks.

No harm was done, but the captain and crew of the *Laffey* felt like two cents.

Since the shipyard had not given them evaporators that would work for the ship, the crew had to fix them. This was a trial-and-error process, but the engineering gang did the job, and by the time the ship left the West Coast for the war, it was done, and the hand-built evaporators served faithfully.

The spring of 1942 was no time for naval niceties, and the men of the *Laffey* did not have the luxury of a shakedown cruise to get the gremlins out of their ship and learn its habits. Theirs would be on-the-job training.

For a lot of the crew it was the first on-the-job training of any kind. About forty of the 200 crewmen were new recruits about seventeen years old, and some only sixteen.

John Jenkins, Seaman First Class, had come aboard and been assigned to the laundry officer. On one of the trial runs, Captain Hank decided to take the *Laffey* out past the Golden Gate Bridge and see how she would respond to some speed running. Pork chops were served, which was the signal that they were going to sea. They got outside and the captain ordered General Quarters. At that time S1/c Jenkins was on duty doing the officers' laundry. His battle station was at the Number 4 20mm gun mount. He had been at his post for only fifteen minutes when the repair party reported smoke coming from the laundry porthole. Jenkins was ordered to report there. When he opened the laundry door he saw catastrophe in front of him. Nothing had been secured before going to sea. Two twenty-five-gallon containers of raw bleach had capsized on the deck and one large drum of soap powder had fallen into the mess. The officers' clothing had been bundled up in the overhead and had fallen to the deck where the bleach had burned it up.

"I thought Lieutenant Vrba [the laundry officer] was going to jump overboard," said Jenkins. Some of the officers had only the clothing on their backs. Jenkins offered to pay for the new tailoring that would have to be done out of his pay, but Lieutenant Vrba said the losses would be made up by the profits from the candy and soft drink machines.

The laundry did not represent the only damage that day. In the galley pots and pans and dishes were thrown all over the galley deck and the dinner somehow got destroyed. Since most of the men were seasick on the high-speed run, that turned out to be the least of the tragedies.

Then they were back ashore, at Mare Island Navy Yard, where they loaded ammunition and torpedoes, and as S1/c Jenkins recalled, all the "rich petty officers" got married. They were making seventy-eight dollars a month in those days, and when they went ashore they ate steak and eggs for breakfast. High livers!

Soon the ship was ordered to Puget Sound. When they arrived at the Bremerton Navy Yard the captain had a very hard time docking the ship. The process took two hours of backing and filling, and ultimately they asked for a tug and were brought alongside at dark. In the beginning, Lieutenant Barham had offered the captain some advice about ship-handling in close quarters. He wanted to use minimal power. But the captain would not listen, and continued to ring up full astern and full ahead and endanger everything around him.

It had become clear and would be well illustrated in the future, that Captain Hank was not a proficient ship-handler, and let the surrounding vessels avast and belay. This was true only when he was docking; at sea Hank handled the ship masterfully, and there was no cause for complaint.

Soon enough the *Laffey* sailed for San Diego to join the *Saratoga*, which was now going back to sea. She was tied up at North Island, fitting out for the Pacific with a new air group. So the *Laffey* waited, and the air group got aboard the carrier, and the ships cleared for Pearl Harbor. When they arrived, they learned about the Battle of Midway, which had just ended. But they did not learn quickly. As Ensign Evins put it:

> *You should not assume that I had any idea of what was going on. In time of war, soldiers and sailors, whatever their rank or position, are given practically no information at all, unless there is a need for them to*

know. Although the captain of a warship has an operations order that covers his immediate assignment, he knows very little about the strategy that brought him there, nor how his ship will be used to further that strategy. His officers know considerably less and the enlisted men, who know almost nothing at all, pass along all sorts of wild rumors.

So the *Laffey* arrived at Pearl. They saw enormous activity around them and hadn't the slightest clue as to what it was all about. Then the task group was ordered to fuel and provision in two hours and head for Midway. The captain told them nothing but that a battle was in progress near Midway and they were escorting the *Saratoga* under forced draft to try to get her into the fight. Actually, Admiral Nimitz was expecting more trouble from the Japanese after the original battle of Midway had been won. The Japanese were supposed to be bringing their carrier force down from the Aleutians to renew the fight.

But, as it turned out, it was all a false alarm, and all they learned about that battle was what Americans were reading in the newspapers, that four Japanese carriers were sunk and that the *Yorktown* was lost on the American side. They also learned that a couple of destroyers had stood by the *Yorktown* until she sank and then they milled around, finally joining the *Saratoga* group and returning with it to Pearl Harbor.

Ensign Evins was dismayed. He thought the Pacific War had ended before he even had a chance to get into it.

Back in Pearl Harbor, the *Laffey* stayed just a few days and then was assigned to the force being led out by Admiral R. H. McMorris in the cruiser *Chester*. But before they got to sea, the *Laffey* began to get a reputation of its own.

A dog came aboard and before the captain found out about it the dog had a name; Chafing Gear. The awkward moment when the captain discovered the dog was surmounted. The captain liked dogs, and before they cleared port Chafing Gear had made the whole ship into his private doghouse.

The *Laffey* was moored next next to another destroyer. Laundryman Jenkins had acquired a number of special clients for his laundry service, men who were willing to pay him to wash and dry and press their laundry. It got to be a business on the side, and one day he enlisted the laundryman of the neighboring destroyer to do some finish work for him. But during the following night the other destroyer was moved to another berth, and the next morning Jenkings discovered it was two miles away.

He asked the officer of the deck for a boat to drop him off while on other missions and then pick him and the laundry up later. He was eager to get this over with because that afternoon a beer party and baseball game were being staged by the carrier *Saratoga* and the *Laffey* men were invited.

When Jenkins reached the other destroyer, he discovered that the work had not been done, and after getting a lot of promises, he decided to swim back to his ship and stripped down to his skivvies and went over the side. He did not want to miss that ball game.

He had swum about a mile and was halfway back to the ship when Admiral McMorris' barge pulled alongside and the coxswain asked where he was going. He replied that he was going back to his ship. A brass boathook was broken out and lifted him into the barge and the barge headed for the *Laffey*. As the barge approached the ship, Jenkins could see that something like a Chinese fire drill had erupted on deck. When the officer of the deck saw the barge approaching, he notified the captain, and everyone aboard began scurrying to get into their whites.

In his skivvies, Laundryman Jenkins marched up the gangway and met Commander Hank, who was tying his necktie. The admiral followed and reported that he was giving a seagoing hitchhiker a ride home. He looked around the ship and left, apparently in the best of humor. But the officer of the deck, whose sense of humor was foreshortened, requested that Jenkins be put on report for holding an unauthorized swimming party and being out of uniform. Skipper Hank looked at the OOD and said "Forget it."

The laundry was recovered, but Jenkins did not make it to the ball game.

After the ship sailed, the captain turned toward the South Pacific. Captain Hank was supposed to tie up alongside the *Chester* en route, and in maneuvering the captain called for emergency full astern. He got it, and ran onto a coral reef, damaging the propeller. In peacetime, this action would have cost him his ship and wrecked his record, but this was war, and all that happened is that the *Laffey* had to run back to Pearl Harbor for a new propeller and would be further delayed in getting into the war.

When they got to Pearl the drydock was ready and they were in and out in a matter of hours. The crew had one night of liberty. Ensign Evins ended up sleeping on the beach at Waikiki next to a bundle of barbed wire put there to be strung to hinder Japanese troops trying to invade the island.

Next day the *Laffey* sailed one more time, in company with other warships. Obviously someone had read Captain Hank off for the grounding incident, because shortly after sailing he called Ensign Evins to his cabin and told him that unless they fired a satisfactory gunnery practice, he was going to be relieved of command. He asked Evins to take charge of the practice and do the rangefinding, although this was far from his job as torpedo officer. The pair had served aboard the destroyer *Hull*, where Hank had been gunnery officer and Evins his assistant, and Hank knew that Evins possessed a peculiar attribute that made of him a human rangefinder of great accuracy: He had steroscopic vision. Evins took over the rangefinding, the *Laffey* performance was very good and so, although the *Laffey* gun crew had not had time so far to learn the ropes, the ship did well in the gunnery and Skipper Hank's bacon was saved.

The *Laffey* was assigned to convoy three tankers to a point south of Hawaii on the Equator. The ship had the crossing-of-the-line ceremony with King Neptune in charge and all the shenanigans that went with it. They met a large task force headed for the South Pacific and refueled three cruisers and several new destroyers, and then the task force headed off to the southwest. Later the *Laffey* crew learned that those ships were part of the invasion force bound for Guadalcanal. At that time they knew so little about the South Pacific that Lieutenant Barham thought Guadalcanal was like the Suez.

The trip across the Pacific was boring. Sailor James Moore recalled that his big problem was his laundry. He accommodated himself to the crowded conditions in the ship, but he hated trying to untangle his laundry, which came back from the ship's laundry in a wrinkled, matted mass of dungarees, skivvies, and socks. So Sailor Moore made a highly unofficial deal with Laundryman Jenkins: He joined the laundry club. He would pay two dollars a week to have the laundryman pick up his dirty laundry and wash it, press it, and deliver it to his bunk. From that point on Sailor Moore had no complaints.

On the voyage across the Pacific the men of the *Laffey* grew thirsty. Some whiskey had been smuggled aboard in defiance of the regulations laid down in the First World War by the secretary of the navy that American ships would be dry ships. (They never were except officially.) But that whiskey did not last long. Some of the engineers built a still from spare parts. It was located in the forward engine-room bilges. From the southerners on the crew everyone learned how to produce alcohol, and they did. During inspections once in a while an officer would find a gallon or two of the brew and throw it over the side, but more of it went down the throats of the crew.

There were other ways of satisfying thirst. Some crewmen filled the water breakers in the life rafts with raisins, yeast, and sugar. This produced a drink known as Raisin Jack. The problem was replenishing the supply, because every week regulations called for a tasting inspection of the water in the life-raft water breakers, and so the water had to be replaced or the Raisin Jack was discovered. Some of the cooks had a recipe for Apricot Nectar, which might have been made of apricots but was certainly not nectar. The men had to hold their noses to drink it, but they did. It had an effect something like that of castor oil.

The *Laffey* sailed along, and finally on August 28, 1942, she arrived in the war zone at Efate in the New Hebrides Islands.

NINE

The Laffey *in Battle*

Destroyer *Laffey* arrived in the South Pacific three weeks after the First Marine Division had invaded Guadalcanal. These were rough and uneasy days. It was apparent that the United States Navy had not fought a war for a very long time. The watch system called for four hours on and eight hours off, except that the man who started the 1600 watch got off at 1800 and then got back on watch at 2400 hours, midnight. The routine was a stay at sea for most of the week, come into port at dusk, fuel and provision all night, and sail with the morning tide. In addition to watch-standing, all the officers and men did a full day's work during daylight hours in their specialty and got up half an hour before sunrise to stand General Quarters. As the British put it, if they were going to fight the American navy, they would let them stay at sea for two months, after which the Americans would be too exhausted to fight anybody.

Naval reservist Thomas Evins recalled the days: "The truth is, the U.S. Navy had never had to fight anybody since the days of John Paul Jones, and had no earthly idea how to conduct a real ship-to-ship campaign. The navy certainly didn't learn to do it while I was at sea."

By the time the *Laffey* arrived on the South Pacific scene the American level of incompetence had been demonstrated. The first example was the immediate flight from the scene of action after the Guadalcanal invasion by Vice Admiral Frank Jack Fletcher's three aircraft carriers that accompanied the invasion, thus forcing Rear Admiral Richmond Kelly Turner's transports to abandon the marines on Guadalcanal with minimal supplies. This dereliction brought about the battle of Savo Island in which the Japanese sank the cruisers *Quincy, Astoria, Vincennes,* and the Australian *Canberra* without losing a ship. Then came the battle of the Eastern Solomons in which the Japanese carrier *Ryujo* was sunk and the American carrier *Enterprise* was damaged. From the beginning the Japanese navy seemed to win all the battles. As Admiral Matome Ugaki, chief of staff to admiral Yamamoto's Combined Fleet, put it, "We keep sinking their ships and they keep sending in more and more . . ."

Soon after the Guadalcanal invasion the Americans began to gain control of the air over the island during the daytime hours. The Japanese had a long way to come from Rabaul, and by the time they arrived at Guadalcanal with their bombers and fighters, they were low on fuel and had very little time to engage the Americans. So the Americans controlled the daylight air. But at night it was a different story, and almost every night the Tokyo Express came down "the slot" of the Solomons, to deliver troops and supplies to the Japanese forces and to bombard Henderson Field and the American installations. When the American ships met the Japanese in these early days, it almost always turned out to be a Japanese victory. As Ensign Evins wrote: "We confidently believed that our radar equipment and five-inch thirty-eight guns were superior to anything the Japanese had. Indeed they were; it was bad American tactics that canceled any advantage we might have taken from the superiority of our equipment."

The *Laffey* joined up and began operating with Task Force 18 out of Noumea, a force commanded by Rear Admiral Leigh Noyes that included the carrier *Wasp*. Every day the *Laffey* was involved in convoy work, escorting carriers and battleships in what seemed to the *Laffey* crew pointless parading between Espiritu Santo and Guadalcanal.

In September the *Laffey* was part of the destroyer escort of the *Wasp*, which was supplying air cover for the transports that reinforced the marines on Guadalcanal. At midday on September 15, Sailor Richard Hale was in the mess room finishing lunch when his ship was jarred by two explosions. Because of their experience in the beginning of their cruises, he thought at first that the *Laffey* had accidentally dropped another pair of depth charges. But then the call to General Quarters came and he hurried to his battle station. He came up onto the bridge on the starboard side and could see that the *Wasp* was on fire and sending up great clouds of black smoke. He soon learned that she had been torpedoed by a Japanese submarine.

The black smoke was largely the result of fire in the gasoline-storage areas. The fires spread to her hangar deck and then the planes, Ammunition, bombs, and torpedoes began to explode. She began to list, and then Hale saw the crew begin to abandon ship, sliding down the listing hull and jumping off the decks into the water. Destroyers, including the *Laffey*, began to put their boats over the side to start the rescue.

Ensign David Sterrett was in command of one of the motor whaleboats sent out on rescue patrol: "We'd gotten both our boats over the side and into action as quickly as we could. The sea was not flat, but it was not a stormy day. Still, when you load a motor whaleboat with thirty men, you've got to watch to see that they don't pull the boat over."

That lesson was driven home by the sight of the motor whale-boat of another destroyer that was floating upside down and empty. Someone had not been careful enough.

The men of the *Wasp* had trouble getting through the burning oil on the water to get to the boats. The *Laffey*'s boats went alongside on the lee side, picked up all the men they could find, and then met the other rescue boats, which were upwind of them about three miles. They went back to the ship and put their rescue men aboard, then went out again for another search. They searched all afternoon and rescued more than 200 men, many of them badly burned and almost all of them covered with fuel oil.

As the afternoon wore along, the chop on the sea surface became strong, and it was harder for the men manning the boats to see survivors in the water. Those who stuck together in groups were easier to spot than individuals. The *Laffey* boats kept searching until darkness fell and it became apparent that they were not going to get all the men.

Ensign Evins remarked: "I have no idea how many died cursing us for our inability to see them when they were within yards of the ship."

After the rescue was over, the destroyers found that they had nearly 2,000 men aboard of the total crew of 2,200 of the *Wasp*. Some of the men must have died in the explosions and fires on the ship, so not so many of them suffered the death of the abandoned.

As night came down the destroyers headed for Espiritu Santo, leaving the *Wasp* still burning in the night, a beacon for the Japanese. The next afternoon they reached Espiritu Santo and put the survivors aboard the cruisers there. The *Laffey* left some of her survivors and then made a fast trip to Noumea, where the rest were unloaded.

The *Laffey* was then ordered to move to its assigned anchorage, and once again Captain Hank was the victim of his bad ship-handling. The standard procedure when moving away from a larger vessel was to back off. The captain decided to go ahead. The propellers pulled the water away from the interval between the ships; they closed quickly and the anchor of the cruiser caught the destroyer's plating on the port side and ripped a ten-foot hole. There was no other damage and no casualties. The only excitement was for the chief commissary steward, who made it a habit to sleep during the day and stay up all night. He was sleeping when he was awakened by the impact, and outside his cabin saw the ocean where a bulkhead had been before.

Again Skipper Hank escaped with his skin because it was wartime. He asked for an extra week's time for repairs, which would include fixing the feed pumps and scaling the evaporators. It was granted. During the week the crew hoped to have liberty, but Noumea was off limits and the only place they were allowed to go was a small island that, after the liberty party landed, the men discovered was a leper colony. It was a very brief shore leave.

Not to be deprived by the matter of regulations, some of the seamen aboard the *Laffey* borrowed a rowboat and rowed into Noumea. They changed out of navy clothes to protect the guilty and spent several days having an extended party. Search parties were sent ashore from the ship to find them, but they never did. The most likely place they could have holed up was the Pink House, Noumea's most famous whorehouse. But military personnel were denied access to the Pink House, and when Chief Walter Harold Coleman tried to scale the fence around the brothel to see if his men were inside, he cut his hands on the broken glass barrier set in the top of the wall and had to be rushed back to the ship for treatment.

Eventually the "shore party" came to an end and the miscreants returned to the *Laffey* before she sailed.

That week was anything but restful for the rest of the crew. The ship's garbage was a problem. It could not be dumped in the harbor, by the rules set down by Admiral Robert Ghormley, the commander of U.S. forces in the South Pacific, and had to be transported to land and then trucked to garbage dumps outside Noumea. This sort of work was usually performed by recruits and men who had been busted in rating, but suddenly the OOD found all the chiefs volunteering for the task. It gave them a chance to get ashore for a few hours and do a little serious drinking and go to the beach.

Aboard the *Laffey* as they lay in Noumea harbor, there was no news at all about the war in the Solomons, so close by, but plenty of scuttlebutt. The origin was in the communications division, whose radio operators listened in to the traffic in the area and tried to make some sense of it. Sometimes they came up with truth, and many times they came up with their own conjecture. The mixture was about half and half, just enough to confuse the whole ship. The ship heard that the Japanese had sunk three cruisers in a night battle off Guadalcanal and that the Tokyo Express ran nightly into Guadalcanal, carrying Japanese troops and reinforcing supplies.

But the *Laffey* was still on the fringes of the battle of Guadalcanal and most of the news was bad news.

On the day that the *Wasp* was sunk, that same Japanese submarine had put a torpedo into the battleship *North Carolina*, forcing it to go back for repairs. The battleship *South Dakota* ran aground on a coral reef at Tongatubu. The carrier *Saratoga* caught another torpedo late in August. The men of the *Laffey* learned all this bad news over a period of time, but they did not learn any bad news about the enemy. As far as they were concerned the Japanese seemed almost invincible. As Lieutenant Eugene Barham said, it was scary to contemplate this handful of American ships in the South Pacific taking on the whole Japanese fleet.

Morale wasn't helped any by the supply situation. Sailors in the American navy were used to very good food and lots of it. But now in the crisis of the Guadalcanal campaign, the men of the *Laffey* suddenly found the variety of their food highly restricted. "It seemed for a while that red beans were the main item in our diet," said Lieutenant Barham.

When the *Laffey* was repaired and ready to sail again, she was assigned to a newly created task force. Task Force 64, under command of Rear Admiral Norman Scott. This force was made up of the heavy cruisers *San Francisco* and *Salt Lake City* and the light cruisers *Boise* and *Helena*. Five destroyers were assigned, under Captain R. G. Tobin, commander of Destroyer Squadron 12. They were his flagship, the *Farenholt*, the *Buchanan*, the *Laffey*, the *Duncan*, and the *McCalla*. These ships had not previously been operating together and there was no time for a shakedown. The task force was assigned to go up to Guadalcanal and stop the Japanese forces that came down "the slot" every night from Rabaul to Cape Esperance to supply the Japanese. After a false start in which they had tried to win control of Guadalcanal by sending a battalion to fight the 30,000 marines, the Japanese army had been steadily reinforcing their position.

By the end of September the Japanese had sent 26,000 troops and a naval force of 3,500 men to Guadalcanal. The soldiers were mostly highly trained infantrymen, many of them from the China theater. The naval force was largely responsible for communication with Admiral Yamamoto's Combined Fleet and liaison to try to coordinate army and navy attacks on the island. Most of the Guadalcanal operations for the Japanese originated in Rabaul or at the Shortlands destroyer base off the southern end of Bougainville.

Task Force 64 headed up to Guadalcanal on October 7, toward Rennel Island. They were two days en route and then they worked around the southern end of Guadalcanal for two more days, looking for the Japanese coming down "the slot." The task force was informed by Ghormley's headquarters to be on the lookout for signal lights at night. The Australians had coastwatchers on the island who would signal the coming of enemy ships.

On the third afternoon, October 11, 1942, the *Laffey* was informed that American scout planes had sighted a Japanese force coming down "the slot," about 200 miles from Guadalcanal. Admiral Scott led the task force around the western end of Guadalcanal, then to Cape Esperance, where they could cover the entry to Savo Island. That evening the signals had been received and the word passed that an enemy force was near their position off Cape Esperance. Task Force 64 got ready to fight, and so did the *Hornet* task force, which moved to the west of Guadalcanal, while another task force built around the battleship *Washington* moved to the east of Malaita.

Three cruisers of Japanese Cruiser Division 6, the *Aoba, Furutake*, and *Kinugasa*, were heading toward Lunga Point with the destroyers *Fubuki* and *Murakumo* for a bombardment mission. They were commanded by Rear Admiral Aritomo Goto. Behind them came the seaplane carriers *Nisshin* and *Chitose*, with six destroyers. They were carrying troops and supplies to reinforce the Japanese in Guadalcanal.

The Americans knew that a force was coming, but not much more. The air intelligence had underestimated the size of the Japanese force and the exact timing. So the cruiser force managed to run down "the slot" unmolested and by evening was approaching Savo Island.

Just before 11:30 the cruiser *Helena* made the first radar contact with the Japanese, but for some reason let fifteen minutes go by before reporting it. The gear was functioning all right, but the people were not. The ship had new radar equipment, and apparently the captain did not trust it, so the contact was meaningless. Admiral Scott knew of the approach of the enemy at 11:30 when a *San Francisco* search plane sighted enemy ships approaching Cape Esperance.

At that time the American ships were steaming northeast in a column, with the *Farenholt* out front, followed by the *Duncan, Laffey, San Francisco, Boise, Salt Lake City, Helena, Buchanan,* and *McCalla.*

Admiral Scott ordered the courses reversed so he could block the passage between Savo Island and Cape Esperance.

The admiral ordered the ships to swing left to course 230 degrees, and the order was voiced over the talk between ship speaking system. The cruisers executed swiftly, and so did the rear destroyers *Buchanan* and *McCalla*. But the leading destroyers, *Farenholt*, *Duncan*, and *Laffey*, which were supposed to swing out and make a separate column and then regain the head of the column, hesitated and ended up swinging late and falling into the rear of the southbound cruiser column—an error on the part of the squadron commander. Trying to undo it, he led the three destroyers in a high-speed race on the starboard flank of the cruisers, but they had gotten out of their place of protection of the cruisers, and it was too late. They were on the starboard side of the cruiser column when the *Helena* suddenly opened fire on a target she had tracked by radar 5,000 yards to starboard. This meant the cruiser was firing over the three destroyers, and they were liable to get hit either by the *Boise* or the return fire from the enemy.

The *Duncan* sheared out of the line astern of the *Farenholt* and headed west, following a radar contact. The *Laffey* followed the *Farenholt*.

The Japanese were heading straight for Savo Island when Admiral Scott executed the sharp turn, and they headed straight toward the Americans, which let the Americans cross their T—bringing all their guns to bear on the enemy at the same time. The American ships sent out a broadside. The *Aoba* was hit. The *Furutake* was hit, as was the destroyer *Murakama*. Then, because Admiral Scott was concerned lest the three erring destroyers be hit by American fire, he ordered the ships to cease firing. Some of the American captains did not get the word and continued to fire.

Admiral Goto swung his ships to the right, intending to reverse course, but instead they came around, each under the fire of the American vessels in turn. As the *Aoba* turned, a salvo wrecked her bridge and mortally wounded Admiral Goto.

Admiral Scott was now delayed trying to find his three errant destroyers, but when they responded to recognition signals and he saw them on the right of the column, he began firing again.

Ensign Thomas Evins was on the top of the pilot house at his battle station. After the *Laffey* made her 180-degree turn and ended up out of the column, the first thing he saw was a Japanese destroyer on a course opposite and parallel to the *Laffey*'s. The Japanese ship was so close that he could see sailors running up and down the decks in the glare of the American searchlights. The *Laffey* opened fire with her guns but did not fire any torpedoes, which were supposed to be saved for heavier targets.

Evins saw the American cruisers opening fire and then being lit up by their own muzzle flashes, giving the Japanese a very good point of aim. But when the Japanese fired, there was no muzzle flash, just a flicker of blue flame from the barrels of their guns. The Japanese were using flashless cordite powder, which was much more sensible.

Being surprised as they were, the Japanese quickly turned away, but not before Ensign Evins saw that they had inflicted heavy damage on the cruiser *Boise*.

Sailor Richard Hale was stationed inside one of the five-inch gun mounts of the *Laffey*. Here is his account of the battle:

>*Boats, our gun captain, had the earphones on in communication with the gunnery officer in the director. Boats yelled out to us to lock on the director. I pushed the firing switch to my trigger into the locked position with my thumb, but I forgot to change the prism on my gunsight to one of the darker lenses; I still had the clear lens for daylight use in place when the first shot was fired. The blast was so brilliant I was almost blinded. I quickly changed the lens setting to dark, and my vision gradually returned. After we got off a few rounds, we had a hang fire, so Boats yelled at me to kick it off. I stomped the foot pedal hard. The firing pin worked well, the recoil slammed the mount, and the empty brass case went flying back to the scuttle. We had a man with long asbestos gloves whose job it was to catch the brass casings and guide them through the scuttle to the deck outside the mount. But we were firing so fast he kept missing them.*
>
>*The target was soon on fire. The range was short enough that I could follow the trajectory of our shells by the tracers in them, and when I saw one hit their Number Two mount, I yelled out and our gun crew cheered. After we ceased fire, Boats opened the hatch so we could get some air. We could see ships burning back on our starboard quarter.*

When dawn came the men of the *Laffey* were on their way back at high speed to Espiritu Santo, full of themselves and victory. They wanted to paint a destroyer and cruiser symbol on the side of their mount to show the world that the *Laffey* was a real fighting ship. They felt as if they had almost won the war already and that the rest was going to be easy. Their ship had been in battle and had not been scratched, although she fired 500 rounds of ammunition. They claimed to have set fire to a *Mogami*-type cruiser and another ship.

So the battle of Cape Esperance was regarded by the Americans as a victory, although they did not stop the Japanese from resupplying their forces and they lost the destroyer *Duncan*, the *Farenholt* managed just to limp home, and the *Boise* was hit hard. Ensign Evins watched the next day as the *Boise* buried her dead at sea. He counted 106 bodies slipped under an American flag and over the side of the cruiser as they returned toward Espiritu Santo.

That was October 12, 1942. From that point, all through October the *Laffey* continued to operate around Guadalcanal, often being refueled at sea as it moved back and forth from the supply zone at Espiritu Santo to the combat zone of Guadalcanal. Rations were short, and Sailor John Jenkins recalled that all they got to eat was beans and rice except for the occasional visit to a cruiser, when they would come away with a can of ice cream.

Sailor Richard Hale recalled that the food went from bad to worse and that everything the British were saying about the idiocy of American naval ship operations was proving to be correct.

In what would be the fall of the year—in Guadalcanal it was hot and tropical—the days dawned early in the southern latitudes, and the sailors had to be at General Quarters from half an hour before sunrise until half an hour after sunrise. So a man who drew the twelve-to-four watch and then had to stand General Quarters went all night without sleep. When they were around Guadalcanal, a nervous captain kept them at battle stations for as long as three days running. So by the end of the month, the men of the *Laffey* were numb with exhaustion. If there had been anyone around to measure their efficiency ratings he would have been in for a dreadful shock. Days and weeks of poor nutrition and overwork had made them into zombies, as Hale remembered it.

The men of the *Laffey* were also learning respect for Japanese seamanship and torpedo marksmanship. On the night of October 20, Sailor Hale was standing watch on the port bridge, screening the cruiser force, which was moving along in bright moonlight. They were keeping station at 2,000 yards off the cruiser *Chester*. Hale was looking at the *Chester* in the moonlight, thinking what a beautiful ship she was when suddenly he saw a brilliant flash and then an explosion. A Japanese submarine had come up and torpedoed the *Chester* under their watching eyes. She survived, but had to go back to America for repairs.

Such incidents, and the general feeling that the Japanese were winning all the battles, played hob with American morale. Admiral Ghormley, who had not had any enthusiasm for the whole Guadalcanal adventure, had never been able to generate any, and his defeatism affected the fleet and the whole operation in the South Pacific. Had it not been for the determination of General Alexander Vandegrift and his marines, the whole invasion would have gone down the drain because of the navy's failures to maintain adequate logistics and protect the supply lines. In October Admiral Nimitz visited Guadalcanal and was appalled at the state of morale and Admiral Ghormley's attitude; Ghormley had never even made a trip to the island to see what was going on. Returning to Pearl Harbor, Nimitz decided that a change had to be made immediately if the American effort was to survive, so he brought forth Vice Admiral William F. Halsey and gave him the Guadalcanal job. The change probably saved the invasion from the disaster toward which it was heading.

On October 22, Halsey met with Vandegrift, Admiral Turner, and several other generals. In view of the performance to date there was only one question: Could the Americans hold Guadalcanal? Vandegrift said he could hold if he was supplied. Turner said he could supply if he was protected. Halsey said he would do everything possible to protect the supply ships and get planes to Guadalcanal, and the others believed him because that is the sort of track record that Admiral Halsey had. Morale, which had been on the bottom, suddenly began to rise. Marines, navy, and army suddenly began to believe they could win this war after all. With no fanfare, on October 22, Admiral Halsey had weathered an enormous crisis in confidence and immediately began to turn the war in the South Pacific around.

On October 26, Sailor Ronald Veltman's carrier *Hornet* was off Guadalcanal near Santa Cruz. For weeks she had been showing the flag and changing positions in the South Pacific to give the Japanese the idea that the Americans had several carriers in the area, when actually, with the *Enterprise* laid up for repair, *Hornet* was the only one. But now, with the *Enterprise* back in commission, the American carriers were looking for a fight, as Admiral Halsey had ordered. All the linoleum had been ripped from the decks, and the paint on the bulkheads had been chipped to prevent fires.

On the day they met the Japanese, Sailor Veltman went to his action station between the flight and hangar decks in the plotting area. When the bombing of the carrier by Japanese planes began, he lay down next to the ready-room door; suddenly the door burst open and flames gushed out. He helped to fight the fires, as long as possible. The ship began to take a heavy list. A Japanese plane smashed into the signal bridge and the flames killed most of those there, including a pair of twins who were quartermasters on the ship. One of the twins saw his brother engulfed in flames and rushed to help. He, too, was entombed in the flaming bridge area. Veltman saw a Japanese torpedo bomber go through the forward elevator pit, but the torpedo did not explode. Veltman remembered seeing a torpedo bomber coming right at him, and a fighter, and then he hit the deck, and did not remember much for a while.

They tried valiantly to save the *Hornet*. Veltman won a citation from Admiral Halsey for his work in firefighting and with the wounded. It was a rough day. The *Northampton* got her under tow, but the tow line parted and they could not fix it in the worsening weather of the late afternoon.

Then it was time to abandon ship. Sailor Veltman's buddy, Bill Good, announced then that he could not swim.

"You go down ahead of me," said Veltman. "Take two of the five-inch shell canisters for flotation, and I will put my feet under your arms and you use your feet, and I will paddle."

So they got into the water by sliding down a line and getting rope burns, and then when they positioned themselves Veltman saw that Good was using his feet as if he were riding a bicycle. That was soon corrected, and eventually they were picked up by the destroyer *Anderson*, then transferred to the cruiser *Pensacola* and were saved.

TEN

Guadalcanal

In the middle of 1942 the U.S. Navy was recognizing some of the problems it was to have in fighting a war in the Pacific by the frantic enlistment of construction specialists who could turn rock and coral sand into air and naval bases. That summer, the Sixth Construction Battalion was put together, a thousand Seabees, fresh from their stateside occupations, put into uniform, made an integral part of the United States Navy, and sent to the South Pacific. Only one of the 1,000 men of the battalion was regular navy, Mark H. Jordan, who retired finally as a captain.

When the Japanese expansion became a recognizable threat to Australia in the summer of 1942, with the planned extension of air bases to dominate the lower Solomon Islands, Admiral Ernest King drew a line and insisted that the Japanese expansion be stopped at Guadalcanal. The invasion was first scheduled for early 1943, but when Admiral King discovered how far along the Japanese plans had gotten, it was quickly moved up to August 1942. The U.S. First Marine Division, under Major General Alexander A. Vandegrift, landed on Guadalcanal in the early hours of August 7, 1942. Four days later the Sixth Battalion of the Seabees arrived at Espiritu Santo. On August 25, Lieutenant Commander Paul Blundon, commanding officer of the Sixth Seabees, flew into Guadalcanal.

Soon, some of the Sixth Seabees were sent to Guadalcanal on the transports *Betelgeuse* and *Fomelhaut*, and then a third contingent aboard the transport *Fuller*. Here, based on the diary kept by Chief Petty Officer Mike O'Dea of Louisville, Kentucky, is an account of the war as it was fought on Guadalcanal.

On September 1, the men of Companies A and D arrived on the *Fomelhaut* and the *Betelgeuse* at Lunga Point. The next day they took over the construction of Henderson Field from the First Engineer Battalion of the marines. The Japanese, they found, had planned a 3,800-foot runway but had left an uncompleted section in the middle. The marines had already done enough work in this section to make the field usable for fighters. But the flat cross section gave no slope for drainage and the strip was graded but not surfaced. Therefore when it rained, the field became a mudhole, and operational losses from accidents on takeoff and landing were matching those of combat. The first job of the Seabees was to move dirt. They were interrupted at 11:00 A.M. by a lone Japanese plane that made an ineffectual bombing attack.

On September 4, 1942, six chief petty officers and twenty Seabees boarded the steamship *Fuller* at Espiritu Santo and sailed for Guadalcanal. Then knew so little about it that in the diary he was keeping Chief O'Dea called the place Solomon Island.

On September 7, the ship arrived at Lunga Roads at eight o'clock in the morning and three hours later the Seabees were ashore. They got instructions from the marines and set up their camp near the airfield. They could see that they had their work cut out for them, because six planes crashed that day while trying to land on the muddy field. One burned up completely.

On September 8, they reported to Commander Blundon, made a tour of the five square miles of the island inside the marine perimeter, and mapped out the work that was to be done.

The job was to keep the field operating and to extend it to 5,000 feet or more for heavy-bomber operation. They were also to grade it for drainage and to surface it for permanent operation. While one force was to tackle the maintenance job, another was to start the felling of hundreds of coconut trees on the old Lever Brothers plantation to clear the way for extension of the field. First they had to get a power shovel brought in. Then they had to have a steel Marston mat. These supplies were on the way, but they were not yet on Guadalcanal.

The next day the Seabees began to get a taste of the bombing of the Japanese planes from Rabaul. Chief O'Dea spent part of the day—most of it, it seemed at the time—in a slit trench while the Japanese planes bombed and strafed the airfield and the marine installations. In the trench he met an air corps captain from his hometown of Louisville.

All this was prelude: The following day the Japanese planes were back working over the field. There were three air raids that day. In one of them the Japanese bombers hit the marine camp and killed seventeen marines just 300 yards from the Seabee camp.

On September 12, the Japanese bombers were above as usual but on this day something new was added. The Tokyo Express came down "the slot" and shelled Henderson Field and the marine camp. Japanese troops advanced toward Henderson Field from the hills, but were stopped by the marines at a point three-quarters of a mile from the Seabee camp. The marines had moved their artillery, 75 mm and 105mm pieces, to a point 300 feet from the Seabee camp. For the next twenty-four hours they fired continuously. Chief O'Dea and his buddies sat outside their tent and watched the shooting that night.

The Japanese had been steadily reinforcing their army forces on Guadalcanal and Lieutenant General Haruyoshi Hyukatake, commander of the Seventeenth Army, had landed at Tassafaronga, preparing to stage a major assault on Henderson Field. It was made on September 12, led by General Kawaguchi's 325th Brigade, and the fighting centered around the eminence called Bloody Ridge. The key to the American successful defense was those artillery pieces that kept the Seabees up nights.

The fighting continued fiercely on September 13. Six Japanese fighter planes came over the Seabee camp at 6:00 P.M. while the navy men were eating chow and two of them dived directly into the marine machine guns, dropped several bombs, and then flew out to sea. All day long the sky was full of Japanese planes and the Tokyo Express came down "the slot" again that night. But the carrier *Wasp* flew aircraft reinforcements to the Cactus Air Force on Guadalcanal that day, and they made a big difference in the defense. On the night of the fifteenth and sixteenth the Japanese attacks petered out, and the navy brought in six transports with the Seventh Marines to reinforce the island. That raised the number of defenders to 23,000, and—like the Japanese—they were well supplied with food and ammunition. The Japanese at this stage had plenty of rice and canned meat and fish and their clothing and equipment was rather better adapted to the jungle conditions they faced than the marines' equipment. But the arrival of the Seventh Marines tended to even the odds on Guadalcanal.

On September 17, the Tokyo Express ran again, and a Japanese cruiser shelled Henderson Field and the Seabee camp. Chief O'Dea spent part of the night in a slit trench. The next day was largely spent down on the beach unloading the six transports. For three days the Japanese naval and air forces were unusually active, bombing the marines and the field, and the cruisers coming to shell. On the twenty-first one bomb dropped about twenty-five feet from Chief O'Dea and shook him up.

> 22nd. *Several doctors arrived via plane. Made trip around island with doctors and Commander Blundon in jeep, visited Jap prisoners, 87 on island at present time.*
> 23rd. *Rather quiet day, no bombing. Marines moving forward.*
> 24th. *One destroyer and transport anchored in harbor. Mostly supplies from Hebrides. But no mail.*

On September 25, the steel mat arrived and the Seabees could start making a real surface that would stand up better than the dirt and gravel. The Seabees also began improving the amenities at Guadalcanal. They took over the Japanese power plant and repaired the electrical system. They put the Tojo Ice Company back into business and increased the ice output. The Seabees used Japanese steel beams to make a piledriver and built "Douglas Bridge" across the Lunga River. In a month the marines would be able to move guns and heavy equipment across the river.

The mail came two days later, as did 150 men from Espiritu Santo to swell the Seabee battalion. The chaplain, Father Gehrig, arrived too and mass was said on the island on Sunday the twenty-seventh for the first time in three weeks. The Japanese staged an air raid and killed several marines, but of the twenty-seven bombers and their accompanying Zero fighters, the marines destroyed twenty-three bombers and one Zero, by Chief O'Dea's survey.

The bombing continued nearly every day and the narrow escape was commonplace. On the twenty-eighth a bomb hit twenty-five feet from O'Dea and Commander Blundon. That day there were three air raids.

On October 1, the Seabees moved to a new and safer campsite (or it was supposed to be), but that night they were bombed twice and one Seabee was badly burned. Another ten Seabees arrived from Espiritu Santo, but they did not bring the earthmoving equipment the Seabees were expecting for work on the airfield.

All this while the Japanese kept bombing and sending their bombardment ships down "the slot." Some nights were worse than others, like September 3, when Chief O'Dea spent three hours in a foxhole. But the next night there was no air raid.

The Cactus Air Force was growing stronger all the time. On October 4, twenty B–17s arrived after a mission in the area, and the next day the marines began a ground offensive to clear the Japanese out of the Henderson Field area and stop their harassing artillery fire on the field. In the next few days they did so and by October 8 the Japanese had been pressed out of the hills around Henderson.

October 8, sixty of the Seabees moved over to Tulagi to work. On October 9, 450 more Seabees came in from the New Hebrides.

The Seabees had the idea that the land forces on Guadalcanal were being used as bait to draw the Japanese naval forces into a trap. The trap was sprung on October 11 at the battle of Cape Esperance, in which the Americans lost a destroyer and had two cruisers and another destroyer damaged. But the Japanese lost a cruiser and a destroyer, and had two other cruisers damaged. That was one of the *Laffey*'s fights and she contributed to the damage to the enemy.

ELEVEN

Guadalcanal—the Struggle

The second week of October was a bad one for the Seabees. More men came over from Tulagi. The traffic on the beach was very heavy—and that attracted many Japanese air raids, three or four times a day. They were shelled by a Japanese battleship and stayed in their foxholes all that night. One Seabee was killed and seven were wounded near O'Dea's tent. On the nights of October 13 and 14 Chief O'Dea got no sleep at all.

One 14-inch shell made a direct hit on a foxhole, killed Chief Machinist's Mate Henry Thompson, and trapped seven Seabees. The Seabees nearby got out of their foxholes and dug the survivors out.

Another tragedy that night was the hit on the gas dump by a Japanese bomb that blew up 5,000 precious gallons of gas.

The Japanese brought in heavy artillery, and from that point on the marines and Seabees were constantly harassed by a gun they called Pistol Pete and other artillery pieces from the jungle even as the cruisers and battleships fired from offshore.

"These last four days can be explained as just plain Hell!" Chief O'Dea wrote. "Bombed, shelled, and shot at from the hills by Japs during the past 96 hours. Several of my buddies killed. Eight were killed and 10 injured from dive bombers about 5:30 P.M.—unloading gas."

The Seabees were also building tunnels on Guadalcanal. The first tunnel was built near the Pagoda, a Japanese building that was used as the control tower of Henderson Field until it became obvious that the Pagoda was a guide in bombing runs. Then the control facilities were moved into Pagoda Tunnel and the building was torn down.

Tunnel Number 2 was the naval communications center of the island. Tunnel Number 3 was a command post. Number 4 was a center for an intelligence unit of Japanese-language specialists who monitored Japanese broadcasts.

In spite of the air raids and the bombardments and Pistol Pete, the Seabees labored mightily on the airfield. They had to. On the thirteenth and fourteenth the Japanese bombers and warships put fifty-three holes in the airfield in forty-eight hours besides wrecking many aircraft. In those two days every man turned to, to keep the field going, many of them using their helmets to scoop earth because there were not enough shovels. Noon chow on the thirteenth was not served until darkness had stopped the work.

The Japanese were preparing for a new major offensive to try to capture Henderson Field. They used battleships for bombardment these days, and the bombing increased again.

On October 16, a Japanese bomb struck the stern of the destroyer *McFarlane*, which had been rushed to Guadalcanal with aviation fuel and the gasoline barge alongside was blown sky-high. Eight of the eighteen Seabees aboard were killed, a ninth man died of burns, and all the others were wounded.

"Bombed again today," Chief O'Dea wrote on October 17. "Conditions don't look so good today. Several injured." On October 19, he wrote, "The last few days we have gone through the next thing to Hell!"

The harassment made it apparent that the marines needed another airfield on Guadalcanal. At that time, Henderson Field was not tenable. There was a grassy field about a mile to the east of Henderson and the Seabees set to, cutting sagebrush, leveling hummocks, and filling low spots. They built Fighter Field One, and fighter-plane operations were largely transferred there. Then work was started on Fighter Field Two on the western perimeter of the beachhead. Pistol Pete moved in on this construction and so it was stopped temporarily.

On the October 19, O'Dea noted another big air raid with many marines killed, and intense heat. "It has really been tough going here of late." The next day he reported that several Seabees were killed by a 75mm Japanese gun.

The Seabees had also begun work on Fighter Field Three, but it got too hot in that area in the southeast corner of the beachhead.

By October 21, the Seabees were kept in their foxholes all day as the Japanese mounted a new offensive along the Matanikau River and the southern marine perimeter. The fighting was raging only two miles from the Seabee camp and they heard machine guns rattling all night long.

When the fighting slacked a little the Seabees found that it had overrun that area where they had been working on Fighter Field Three. The Seventh Marines and the 164th Infantry held the area, but the Seabees decided to stop activity until it quieted down there.

On the morning of October 26, Chief O'Dea made several trips to the front lines and saw a large number of dead Japanese soldiers. The big news of the twenty-sixth was a rumor that the marines had finally "got" Pistol Pete, the artillery piece on the slope of the mountain that had cost so many marine and Seabee casualties. But it turned out to be a false report and two days later Pistol Pete was harassing them again. The Seabees were suffering a crisis in morale: They had been under constant fire for six weeks, and their nerves were ragged. They wanted the marines to hurry and get Pistol Pete. "They better hurry and get that Jap. There is such a thing as hell on earth and we have sure been through it in the last six weeks."

TWELVE

The End of the Laffey

October 22, 1942, was the day of decision at Guadalcanal.

On that day marine General Alexander Vandegrift flew to Noumea to meet Admiral William "Bull" Halsey and decide what was to be done. Many conflicting signals had been given by the various staffs involved and until the arrival of Halsey there had been a general air of uncertainty and defeat. But Halsey had come in full of fighting spirit. One of his first acts was to hang up over the entry Noumea harbor this sign:

KILL JAPS, KILL JAPS AND KILL MORE JAPS.

What Halsey wanted to know was whether the people he had to work with had enough fighting spirit to last the course. So in came Vandegrift and General Harmon, the army air force commander, and General Patch, the army commander, and Admiral Turner and General Holcomb, commander of the Marine Corps, who happened to be in the area on a fact-finding tour.

Halsey opened the meeting with his key question: Could they hold? General Vandegrift said they could hold if he got the support he needed. Everyone else at that meeting also felt that the troops could hold. (Those who felt otherwise had quietly been eased out of the picture already.)

Within two weeks, General Vandegrift began to get a new sort of support from Noumea. On November 9, four troop transports carrying the 182nd Army Infantry left Noumea in a convoy under command of Admiral Turner. Later that same day Admiral Scott left with a convoy of supplies. On November 10, Admiral Callaghan left with a force of five cruisers and ten destroyers.

Admiral Scott arrived first at Guadalcanal and began unloading troops. Admiral Turner arrived on November 12 and began unloading while the *Laffey* and other destroyers screened the operation a few miles offshore. For nearly two days the transports lay off the beach and landing boats put to shore with men and supplies. That is why Chief O'Dea and the men of the Seabees were spending so much time on the beach, working with the landing operations.

Meanwhile two of the American cruisers and a destroyer worked over the Japanese shore positions and wrecked many of the Japanese landing craft and barges.

When the coastwatchers reported a force of bombers on their way from Rabaul and the strike was confirmed by radar, all the ships in the Guadalcanal roads got under way. Ensign Evins described the scene:

> *The afternoons are usually hot nine degrees south of the Equator, and this day was no exception. All the destroyers in our force had been at General Quarters for two days; half of the men were now snatching a few minutes' sleep near their guns while the others stood by ready to rouse them at a moment's notice. Word had just come that we could expect an attack by enemy torpedo planes.*

Ensign Evins roused his men and looked around him. All the ships seemed to have come suddenly to life. The cruisers were training their eight-inch guns to cover the sector from which the attack was expected. The destroyers were moving with boiling wakes to get into position for defense. Aboard the *Laffey* the lookouts strained to get a glimpse of the enemy. The horizon was bright, the sky cloudless. They could see the Japanese coming, little dots moving down from the north. The range closed rapidly. Someone counted nineteen twin-engined Betty bombers. They fanned out to attack from all angles. At Henderson Field, eight fighter pilots scrambled from VMF 112 and attacked the Japanese bombers from 30,000 feet.

Sailor Hale was in his gun mount and the bo'sun told them to lock on the incoming specks and close the hatch—in other words, it was time to stop rubbernecking and get to work. They locked on and the hydraulic controls of the turret swung them around; Hale could see the specks in the crosshairs of his sight.

Almost immediately the gun commenced firing, and a few moments later it was hard to tell what were aircraft and what were shell bursts out in front of them. The director locked on one plane and stayed on it. Just before the Japanese plane splashed, Hale saw an F4F coming through the American antiaircraft fire to take on the Betty. He thought the pilot had a lot of guts.

Ensign Evins looked at a sky full of black antiaircraft bursts and what seemed to be an orange-and-black wall of shrapnel between the ships and the enemy planes. The Japanese planes came on, although their number was growing fewer, and here and there he saw one splash.

Finally there were only three bombers left. One crossed the bow of the *Laffey* and streams of tracers poured into the plane from the ship and the destroyer ahead of her. The Japanese plane was smoking and gliding downward. The pilot steered for the *San Francisco* and crashed his plane into the stern of the cruiser. Ensign Evins could see the impact knock one sailor off into the water.

One of the lookouts of the *Laffey* reported a man swimming off the starboard beam a few hundred yards out, and the ship maneuvered toward him. Every gun was trained in his direction. The executive officer on the ridge had a submachine gun aimed at the swimmer.

The swimmer began to shout: "Don't shoot. I'm an American." He was hauled aboard the destroyer and reported that he was a sailor from the *San Francisco* and had jumped off the fantail as that Japanese plane had hit the stern of the ship.

The water around the *Laffey* seemed to be alive with torpedoes. One seemed to be heading straight for the ship, but it exploded short. Another missed the bow of the ship.

Then it was all over. The surviving Japanese planes were gone. Ensign Evins looked around. Not a ship except the *San Francisco* had been hit. The fight was over. The transports returned to anchorage and resumed unloading. The order from Halsey was that the force would stay in position and get those supplies to the marines, so Admiral Scott's force and Admiral Callaghan's force remained in the channel.

Now came reports that a large force of Japanese warships was moving toward Guadalcanal. Admiral Halsey had the word and he ordered up Admiral Willis Lee's two new battleships, the *Washington* and the *South Dakota*, to head for Guadalcanal.

So the *Laffey* stayed on General Quarters and on duty off Guadalcanal. Most of the time they were about a mile offshore that night. They had opened the side hatch to get some air, and as night came on they smelled the sweet smell of the island flowers. Years later Sailor Hale smelled it again in Miami and learned that it was jasmine.

The destroyer formed a screen around the transports that night and headed for the open sea south through Sealark Channel. As the transports cleared, they were herded back to Espiritu Santo. Admiral Callaghan was eager to have a crack at the enemy and had reports that he would be facing two battleships.

Coming down on Guadalcanal was Admiral Hiroaki Abe with the battleships *Hiei* and *Kirishima*, a light cruiser, and eleven destroyers, with the mission of smashing the Lunga perimeter with bombardment. He was not looking for or expecting a surface engagement with American naval vessels.

The American force moved toward "the slot." It was a dark night, no moon at all, and so black it was difficult to make out the mountain that rose up from the sea.

Soon the clocks turned the hour and it was the morning of Friday, November 13. There were thirteen ships in the American task force. Was this a sign of something? asked the superstitious.

The task force was traveling in a single column, with the *Cushing*, *Laffey*, *Sterett*, and *O'Bannon* out front, the five cruisers *Atlanta*, *San Francisco*, *Portland*, *Helena*, and *Juneau* in a line, and four more destroyers, the *Aaron Ward*, *Barton*, *Monssen*, and *Fletcher* in the rear. The column strung out for six miles.

The men of the *Laffey* considered themselves old hands at this game. They had fought the battle of Cape Esperance without a scratch. They were as confident as they could be.

Lieutenant Barham had the feeling that nothing was going to happen. Probably it would all turn out to be a false alarm. So they waited and steamed ahead into the blackness of the night.

Captain Hank was feeling the loneliness of command that night.

He sent for Lieutenant Barham to come to the bridge. When the lieutenant arrived, the captain wanted to talk. Where was the battle plan? There wasn't any. Hank hadn't the slightest idea what was going on in the minds of the two flag officers, Admiral Callaghan in the *San Francisco* and Admiral Scott in the *Atlanta*.

They did not have a battle plan because Halsey had not had time to figure out quite what was going on at Guadalcanal, but he sent his forces out to find the enemy and fight nevertheless, following his gut reaction and the Nelsonian theory that any captain who engaged the enemy could not be wrong.

But the problem was, and it was apparent on the bridge of the *Laffey*, that the flag officers were inexperienced and did not know their ships (which had been assembled on virtually a moment's notice) or their men or their capabilities. Captain Hank and Engineer Barham noted that the *Fletcher*, the newest destroyer in the force, was the last ship in the column when she should have been first, because she had the most modern radar system of them all.

The two officers agreed it was going to be a long night.

But at least Captain Hank generated a feeling of confidence, and gave Lieutenant Barham the feeling that he would somehow get them out of any scrape the admiral got them into this night.

After a half-hour of conversation on the bridge, Lieutenant Barham went back to his engine room and put on his headphones that connected him to the bridge. This was the commnand circuit and the captain's talker; the chief fireman, Sailor Lester Murphy, in the fire room, and Sailor James Patterson in the after engine room, were all on the circuit with him.

Soon the captain's talker relayed a radar contact by the *Helena* at 30,000 yards. The destroyer *Cushing* had asked permission to make a torpedo attack but it was denied. All ships were ordered to stay in a column.

Below, in the engineering spaces, the air was calm. Everyone had his job, and they were all kept busy with them. No one was sitting around and waiting for something to happen.

"But," as Lieutenant Barham noted, "going into battle, the confined spaces of the engine rooms and fire room were not the most desirable places to be. Being below the water line, and surrounded by steam pipes that are deadly when ruptured, naturally gives one pause to think. But all of us below, and the rest of the *Laffey*'s crew, were ready and willing."

Ensign Evins was at his battle station topside. Suddenly he saw something looming out of the murk. It looked like two torpedoes, bright wakes going across the bow of the *Cushing* from port to starboard. He spoke to the talker, who was at his elbow. They seemed to be 3,000 yards out.

Ensign Evins turned to the torpedo operator to tell him to train on them, but the operator had already done so. They got the torpedo battery ready to fire on the third Japanese ship in line, which looked like a cruiser. The Japanese ships began to cross the bow of the *Laffey*, and Evins was ready to fire.

But the captain would not give permission to fire.

The range closed, and the lead Japanese ship was only about 1,000 yards away. The three Japanese ships suddenly turned on their searchlights and illuminated the entire column of American ships. The American ships then opened fire. The Number 2 gun was firing so rapidly that Ensign Evins, near the mouth, was not conscious of any separate firing but of a constant roar.

The Japanese destroyer was hit by many shells and disappeared. The *Laffey* had fired a hundred five-inch shells and 500 twenty-millimeter shells into the Japanese ship area.

The *Cushing* was hit and burning. She pulled out of the column. The *Laffey* then became the lead ship in the line.

Two large Japanese ships came out of the shadow of Guadalcanal. The *Laffey* was headed between them.

Ensign Evins was ready to ask permission to fire torpedoes when the talker shouted, "Fire torpedoes to port." Evins turned and saw the battleship *Hiei* only a thousand yards away. The tubes were readjusted, taking about a minute, and the spread of five torpedoes was fired. They never saw what happened to them.

Below, Lieutenant Barham was confused by the signals coming from the bridge. First he got an emergency full astern, which he answered. All burners were full open. The steam pressure was holding fine.

Immediately afterward came a contradictory order, emergency full ahead. Barham grabbed the forward throttle and opened it as another man closed the stern throttle; the same was happening in the after engine room. The *Laffey* seemed to leap ahead, and the battleship passed astern, "only by twenty feet," Barham said.

Ensign Sterrett on deck said he was sure the Japanese battleship was going to cut the *Laffey* in two.

They were very lucky. The *Hiei* missed the *Laffey* by a few feet, and her guns were up and could not be depressed in time for her to fire on the destroyer immediately. Not with her big guns, but her small guns could bear. The 20mm gunner near John Jenkins was hit and hanging lifeless in his harness. Jenkins raised the gun and emptied the 20mm clip into the side of the *Hiei*, aiming for the square portholes. And somebody else was hitting the *Hiei*. As they raced across her bow, the men of the *Laffey* saw the pagoda superstructure of the battleship topple and fall onto the main battery like a collapsing erector set.

The men of the *Laffey* took credit for knocking down the superstructure and for killing most of Admiral Abe's personal staff and for the decision that the admiral made to disengage from the American force.

When the *Laffey* went full ahead to cross in front of the battleship, she became separated from the American column. Japanese ships were on both sides of her and astern as well. The Japanese were zeroing in on her, and she was trying to escape. She had been designed for a top speed of 37.5 knots but just then was making more than 40 knots. She could not take that long. The feed-pump impellers were starting to burn.

The *Laffey* was raked by the Japanese machine-gun fire from the battleship but soon cleared, and the range opened to 2,000 yards. The *Laffey* made for Savo Island to escape, but as she approached the island two large Japanese destroyers appeared out of the shadows on the port bow and came at her at about 25 knots.

The first destroyer crossed ahead and the second was the object of the *Laffey*'s interest. The other destroyer illuminated the *Laffey* with its searchlight and all three ships opened fire. *Laffey* hit the destroyer on the bow and it started to burn. Its searchlight went out. Ensign Evins was about to climb up the superstructure to the bridge when the Japanese turned their lights on the *Laffey*. The world burst into brilliance as star shells exploded overhead. The next moment, Ensign Evins was hanging onto a stanchion for dear life, trying to keep himself from being thrown off the ship. The *Laffey* seemed to pitch into the air and then dive for the bottom. Tons of water poured down her superstructure and every man on deck was drenched.

In the forward engine room the engineers felt an enormous explosion and the shafts began to run away. They closed the throttles and the fire rooms pulled the burners. The propellers were gone.

The chiefs got everybody out of the lower levels of the engine and fire rooms and they just made it. By the time Machninst's Mate 1 c James Moore got to the upper level it was filled with steam.

The temperature inside the ship began to rise, and the engineers knew there was a serious leak in the forward engine room. The fire mains were broken, so they had water from the main injection on the floor plates. Lieutenant Barham ordered everybody out of the engineering spaces, and when he did so the water on the floor plates was already beginning to boil.

After Barham supervised the evacuation of the engine spaces he checked the hatches to see that they had been cleared and made a turn around the deck. The torpedo hit on the fantail had blown the stern off the ship, including the propellers and the rudder, and folded the Number 4 gun onto Number 3.

There had been a hit on the bridge, and the Number 2 gun was knocked out. Hits admidship had wrecked the workshops. A Japanese destroyer nearby exploded, and the *Laffey* drifted by the wreckage. Gun Number 1 ceased firing as all power was lost.

At about this time the *Laffey* took a hit from a large shell that passed through both sides of the ship but did not explode on board. Another shell passed through the ship and exploded on the other side. The blue dye in the water indicated that this hit came from the *San Francisco*, because the Japanese ships did not carry blue dye.

They were dead in the water when the cruiser *Nagara* came

down on them, and she was close enough for them to see the crew working the guns and searchlights. The *Nagara* illuminated another ship and started firing.

Lieutenant Barham walked around the deck. Several fires endangered the ship. The damage-control party was trying to get one big fire under control in the after-handling room, but there was no water from the fire mains. All systems were out. The men had to use the gasoline pump and a bucket brigade. They used empty five-inch shell casings for buckets.

It was obvious to Barham that the *Laffey* was not salvageable and that in any sort of heavy sea she would break in half. That information had to be gotten to the captain.

In the meantime there was plenty to be done. The Number 4 gun was bent in half and most of the men in the turret had been killed, but the fuse-setter was sitting in his cubbyhole with the shell hoist bent over him. The remains of the turret were filled with thick, oily smoke. He had to be rescued with a cutting torch. But they did not have a torch, and they didn't have enough men available to try to drag him out. There was nothing they could do for him except hand him a gas mask so he could have a few breaths of air before the smoke overcame him.

The ladders to the bridge had all been destroyed, but Barham managed to get to the bridge. He told Captain Hank that the stern had been blown entirely off and the steam lines were damaged beyond repair, that the ship was broken in half, and that they could not control the fires. Captain Hank said he did not intend to leave his ship.

The captain and Lieutenant Barham had a brief acrimonious discussion about this. He said, "Just get me going and I'll get us out of this."

There was no way to get the ship going again.

The lieutenant repeated what he had said before about the ship. She was dead in the water, really dead.

Hank could not accept that. Lieutenant Barham gave up and asked for permission to put the rafts and boats into the water. The captain gave him permission. Barham started to the main deck when the captain gave the order to abandon ship. It was 2:40 in the morning.

Ensign Evins was working on the Number 4 gun mount to try to save some men who were still alive in there, inside the splinter shield. He crawled up the deck and into the mount and helped evacuate the wounded to the one dressing station on the ship. He saw one man who had both legs broken but was still conscious. The fire was burning beneath the deck to which he was pinned. Two torpedomen were working to free him, but the decks were getting hot. Just as the order came to abandon ship the torpedo men got him free and the man was strapped to a stretcher and put in a liferaft. The last Evins saw of the man and his rescuers was when he slipped over the side and swam to his own raft. Their names later appeared on the list of casualties.

Some men reacted in strange ways. One officer was in charge of the after repair party when he was told to abandon ship. He pulled out his .45 pistol and threatened to shoot anyone who left the ship. One man told him the captain had given the order. The officer said he didn't care. He gave permission to put four wounded men over the side. Someone behind him then jumped over. The officer turned and took a shot at him, and when his back was turned EM3 Robert Wallace jumped over the side. When he came up from the water he was black from oil. He found a liferaft and looked over at the *Laffey* burning. The officer with the pistol was just jumping over the side.

As the men began to abandon the *Laffey* the hulk was drifting about five miles south of Savo Island. The wounded were being put over the side in rafts. Lieutenant Barham was in charge of the swimming party. He looked up toward the bridge. Captain Hank came down to a lower level and said to him, "Go on over if you're ready."

Barham asked if the captain was coming.

"I'm coming, chief, just as soon as everyone is off the ship." He even made sure that the dog, Chafing Gear, got into a boat.

Lieutenant Barham gave the order and they all jumped off the starboard side and began swimming away from the ship.

Lieutenant Ratcliff made a search for survivors and completed it. The only men left aboard were those beyond help, the doctor, who had gone to the sick bay for the last patient, the captain, Lieutenant Bergman, Ensign Sterrett, and himself. Ratcliff was on the opposite side of the ship from the captain and the others.

Seaman First Class John Jenkins noticed that his life jacket was completely torn away in front. He threw it off and jumped into the water. He began swimming away from the bow. He wanted to keep the ship in sight, so he swam on his back.

Ensign Sterrett went forward to avoid the heat of the burning ship and brought some mattresses from the officers' staterooms to put over into the life rafts. He was in no hurry to get off the ship because he remembered that the *Duncan* in the battle the night before had stayed afloat until the following morning. He thought that if he could stay on board longer, he might avoid the sharks that now had a fearsome reputation in Guadalcanal waters, so well had they been fed for so long. He was standing on the break in the forecastle looking around. The ship was pretty well cleared. He could not see anyone else aboard. The fire was burning hot and fast in the after end. Just then the captain came around the port side forward, passed Sterrett, said something to him, and took a few steps toward the starboard side. Just then the ship blew up.

Ensign Sterrett knew that the magazines had exploded. The decks were ripped off and the air was full of flying steel. The flame reached all the way to where Sterrett was standing; the shock knocked him against a bulkhead. He thought he would stay there awhile, but then the ship took a sharp list to starboard and started to slip, and he knew it was time to get off.

He went forward down the port side; by the time he reached the forecastle deck he was sliding. A piece of metal banged him on the shoulder, knocked him down but did not hurt him. He went over the side with a life jacket, without a helmet.

Barham was about 50 yards from the ship when it exploded. Debris fell everywhere, and he saw watertight doors and big chunks of metal flying high into the air. He turned and watched as the *Laffey*'s bow went up and the ship slid under the water. When the *Laffey* sank it was suddenly very dark. He looked around and did not see anyone. He called out, but there was no answer. He was completely alone.

THIRTEEN

Winning the Battle

In the three/day naval battle that followed the sinking of the *Laffey*, the Japanese lost two battleships, the *Hiei* and the *Kirishima*. The battle was noteworthy because it ended the Japanese attempt to resupply their forces on Guadalcanal in quantity and marked the turn of the tide in naval affairs. The Japanese had been forced onto the defensive on the sea as well as on the land and in the air.

From the shore, Chief O'Dea and the Seabees and marines could see ships burning, six at one time, and many mangled bodies washed up on the island shore, Japanese and American. On November 14, the shore was shelled by a Japanese cruiser for an hour and a half.

In those three days, the marines and Seabees had witnessed more excitement than O'Dea ever hoped to see again.

> *The Japs are determined to take this island back under any conditions. This is now the third day of the sea and air battle and may last a few more days. No sleep for forty-eight hours and have been on the go all the time, really tired. Sat up and talked with aviators all night.*
>
> *Sunday, November 15. All church services canceled. The Japanese warships attacked again at 6:00 A.M. Shells from Japanese guns hit fifty feet from me. Four Japanese ships landed troops on the beach. I was forced to jump from the jeep several times as large 100-pound shells from Japanese guns hit within 75 feet. But planes have been arriving, and three airports are now going at full speed. Never saw so many planes in action. We will never let the Japs have it again. The aviators had been doing a marvelous job. Our B–24 bombers sank five Japanese ships loaded with troops.*

Finally on the night of November 15, life quieted down, and Chief O'Dea got a good night's sleep. Next morning he was ordered to stay around camp and he spent the day doing nothing but resting.

By this time Henderson Field was prepared for heavy duty with several hundred thousand square feet of Marston matting in place and many protective revetments built up to shelter aircraft. They were all needed. Henderson had become a very busy place, with elements of the army air forces joined by various naval fighter and bomber squadrons and marine air squadrons, all rushed to the Solomons to stem the Japanese attempt to capture the island and its airfield. On November 16, the Seabees got some help. The First Marine Aviation Engineers arrived to take over airfield construction. So the Sixth Seabees were assigned to road and bridge building.

FOURTEEN

The Remains of the Laffey

Lieutenant Barham's feeling of being totally alone was soon dissipated. He heard the sound of a motor on the water close by, and reached in his pocket, found his flashlight, and pointed it toward the sound. In a minute or two the boat reached him, and he heaved himself in. It was one of the *Laffey* whaleboats, damaged but still seaworthy.

In the boat the lieutenant found Chief Quartermaster Francis Paul, a gunner's mate with his arm badly wounded, and a fireman. They were all in shock. Barham got back into the water and engaged the pintle and gudgeon on the rudder and took over as coxswain. He set out to find the liferafts and take them in tow. By daybreak he had rounded up all but two rafts and was in voice contact with all of them.

Tom Evins had been wounded in the right arm and had a shrapnel hole in his back that worried him more. He got onto a liferaft and then into the Barham boat.

Robert Wallace couldn't swim, but somebody hauled him onto a raft, and soon it was hooked up to Lieutenant Barham's motor whaleboat.

Richard Hale spent the night on a cork liferaft which he found after the *Laffey* went down.

John Jenkins was in the water all night. He and several other men heard whaleboats but could not find them, and they did not want to be picked up by the Japanese who were all around. They stayed in the water, floating on their backs and trapping air in their dungaree shirts. At dawn they found a liferaft, and when they ascertained that the voices they heard were American they swam toward the raft. It was full of wounded, so they hung onto the edges. They started singing and sang all the songs anyone could remember, from "Deep in the Heart of Texas" to hymns.

After day dawned, Jenkins and friends watched as the cruiser *Portland*, which was disabled and using her boats as tugs, opened fire on a Japanese light cruiser. The third salvo hit the cruiser and in a minute or less she went down. This happened about three miles from where Jenkins and his people were located. They started to cheer when they saw it. They were afraid of sharks but they were not attacked perhaps because the enormous explosion of the *Laffey* had frightened them all out of the area.

Ensign Sterrett was probably the last man off the *Laffey*, and he swam around after the shock wore off and in about twenty minutes he came across one of the mattresses he had thrown overboard and he climbed aboard and rode it.

The water was like glass that night. Sterrett watched ships burning on the horizon, and occasionally heard a ship blow up and go down. He heard men shouting in two languages and trying to get together. He was happy on his mattress and stayed where he was for an hour. But when the survivors of the *Laffey* indicated they were moving off he sang out and was rescued. He got onto a raft, and they all started toward Tulagi, with Lieutenant Barham in charge of the tow.

They were not getting very far very fast, about one knot an hour. They passed the *Cushing*, dead in the water but not sunk. Lieutenant Barham went aboard and briefly thought about trying to get her going, but he had too much responsibility and no one was able to help him so he gave up the idea.

After they left the *Cushing* a young black man swam over and hoisted himself into the boat. He had been swimming for hours. He was from the *San Francisco*. He didn't say anything more. Fifteen minutes later, Barham looked at him to see if he needed attention. The man was dead.

The sun finally rose and marine Higgins boats came out from the shore and rescued them.

Lieutenant Barham jumped ashore from the Higgins boat when

it reached the naval facility on Guadalcanal and promptly fell flat on his face.

Ensign Evins had a more hairy experience. He was lying on the bottom of the landing craft and the coxswain of the boat and the man on the .50-caliber machine gun in the bow saw some Japanese swimming around and wanted to go shoot them up, but their passengers finally dissuaded them. The next thing Ensign Evins remembered he was lying on a bunk in the First Marine Hospital looking at the ceiling, which was made of Japanese shipping crates with Japanese calligraphy. The doctors were busy with the gravest cases brought ashore, so Evins and the other wounded got a dose of sulfa, a shot of antitetanus, and a minibottle of bourbon.

The men who were not wounded were taken by truck to the Tenaru River to try to wash the fuel oil off. They stripped and washed in the sand but the water was cold and the soap did not remove the oil. Finally they went to the diesel station, where the Seabees had rigged a hot shower from the cooling water discharge and they got clean again.

The marines gave them khaki clothing, shoes, and underwear, and army-issue mess kits.

The evacuation of the wounded began the next day and Richard Hale and Ensign Sterrett were flown out by C–47 transport to Espiritu Santo. The others were given tents and cots and told to set up camp seaward of Henderson Field. There were a thousand survivors in the camp, but Lieutenant Barham was still the senior officer present. The marines arranged for a hot-food line in the camp.

There were plenty of bunkers and foxholes around the area, which came in handy because the Japanese were still shelling Henderson Field. They came for the first two nights after the men of the *Laffey* got there, and shells were flying overhead. The battle of Guadalcanal was still being fought.

Rumor had it that the Japanese were gearing up for another big push on land to take the island. Many of the survivors drew arms and ammunition just in case. The sailors were worried and trigger-happy, and the marines around them got scared. The marine colonel came to Lieutenant Barham as senior naval officer and showed him where the marines were dug in.

"The Japanese are over there," he said, pointing. "But frankly, Lieutenant, we are a damned sight more scared of your people with their guns then we are of the Japanese." Lieutenant Barham got busy and got the rifles and ammunition turned in to the supply officer and organized ammunition resupply teams to help the marines instead of shooting at them in case the Japanese came in.

The men needed something to do, so Lieutenant Barham organized them into working teams, and they went to the beach and helped the Seabees unload the transports as they came in. When a shortage of aircraft fuel developed and a lot of fifty-gallon drums had to be moved over from Florida Island, the men of the *Laffey* stood waist-deep in the water, and when the drums were dropped off the landing craft into the water, they would roll them onto the beach and into trucks, which took them to Henderson Field.

All this happened in three days. On November 16, Lieutenant Barham managed to find a typewriter and sat down to report the loss of the *Laffey* to the Secretary of the Navy, as was required.

The survivors remained on Guadalcanal for a month. Finally the transport *Barnett* came in. When she was in the harbor, the USS *Alchiba* also arrived, and after the survivors of the *Laffey* were loaded aboard the *Barnett*, the two ships came under attack from a submarine that had gotten into the harbor. The *Alchiba* was hit, and the captain immediately beached her because she was loaded with gasoline for Henderson Field. The *Barnett* beat a hasty retreat out of the harbor and headed for Espiritu Santo, with the *Laffey* survivors aboard.

When the ship got to Espiritu Santo, reassignment of the men began.* Lieutenant Barham was asked his preference; he said he wanted to go back to the United States and get a new destroyer. He was ordered to Kearney, New Jersey, to become executive officer of the USS *Dashiell*, which was about to be commissioned.

Meanwhile, many more Seabees were coming into action, most of them destined for the Pacific. Alfred G. Don was one of them. Here is his story:

---

* Of the other survivors, Ensign Evins and some of the other wounded were invalided out of the service and Evins became a successful attorney. Most of the rest went on to distinguished naval careers, and several of them retired as captains. Lieutenant Barham retired as rear admiral.

Like most, I entered the service not knowing one thing about it. Then too, I was already married with one son. However, I wanted to do my part. I knew nothing about the SEABEES until a Chief Petty Officer at the Philadelphia Recruiting Station, sitting at his desk, dressed in dress blues with gold hash marks from shoulder to hand, sat me down, asked some questions, found that I had some construction background and it was then that he recommended that I seek enlistment into the SEABEES.

Even then, I didn't even know what it meant to be a SEABEE. Especially so, when it came to being assigned a rating commensurate to your past experience. When the interviewing Civil Engineer Corps officer said to me that he would like to give me a Second Class Water-tender rating, however, I was quite young and a Fireman First Class would be sufficient. I said, "OK with me." What I would have given to know then what I know now that I should have made him give me the Second Class Watertender rating. So much for my first-ever dealings with the Navy, and in particular, the SEABEE Recruiting Program.

Onward—by train from Philadelphia to Camp Perry, Virginia for the so-called SEABEE boot camp training. My first taste of military training—A Marine DI shouting to all disembarking civilian dressed boots to fall in, line up, and be double-quick about it. Of course, the language was concise and clear—expressions most fitting for us newly acquired members of a military organization. These expressions were to carry forth on a daily basis for reasons at that time hard to comprehend. However, as our days in boot camp were drawing to a close, those expressions were finally understood and eventually became reasonable if one was to survive the rest of his time in service.

Between medical shots, close order drill, mess cooking, compound duty watches, hospital detail, and finally a three hour wait (under the blazing Virginia sun) standing at parade rest in dress whites waiting for a personnel inspection by the Station Commander, then known or called "Pig Farm" Captain WARE, CEC, USN to appear. He showed us how much he liked us SEABEES graduating from his Camp. He flew by, standing ramrod straight in the back of his command car traveling at about 35MPH, taking all the hand salutes that were rendered to him. So much for our last days at Camp Perry.

Hot dog!! 60 hours of special leave before reporting back to Camp Perry for further assignment. Lucky me, I was placed in a holding Company doing about 2 weeks of mess cooking. Now this assignment was one of fond memories. Up at 4 A.M., off to the galley for muster, eat *breakfast and stand by for 6 A.M. breakfast to feed the rest of the troops on-board. With me and 6 other SEABEES assigned to the so-called "pot wrestling detail." This entailed a steady grind of scraping left-over food off of all pots and pans before deep sinking them for cleaning and drying. This duty ran the whole day through—4 A.M. to after 9 P.M. before being able to return to the barracks for a shower, a short letter home, and in the sack. So it went for the rest of those 2 weeks. Finally, a draft of us left by train across country to the main SEABEE base at Port Hueneme, California. A week of additional military training and additional gear. Once again, on board a train heading south to Camp Pendleton, a Marine Corps base. There, we were placed into competing Companies, trained by Marine DI's. If you have never been in a competition of any type, this was quite an experience. Each Company competing was judged on their input and output which not only included close-order drill, but mastery of all type of weapons and explosives. Best of all, the 10–15 mile weekly force marches with full pack and one canteen of water to carry you through that day. Why the competition? Not only to get us SEABEES in good physical condition and being able to master the weapons, we learned to work as a team, both physically and mentally. Would you believe what an additional carrot being dangled in our faces for putting forth our best efforts? "A 48 hour pass to Hollywood" . . . for the best of all competing Companies. Not only did we suffer and finally make the grade, along came the movie makers from Hollywood. Yep, they started to shoot the "Fighting SEABEES" with John Wayne and so forth. Some of the SEABEES were offered a chance to be extras in the movie. Playing both the good guys and the bad old Japanese. They were offered $5.00 a day as much as they paid the other civilian extras in those days. Oh no, we didn't even get a chance to enjoy getting the extra funds and spending it, we were told by the SEABEE Commander in Charge that we were already receiving our pay (about 21 dollars a month) big deal, eh!*

As for the construction skills being up-graded, they finally placed SEABEES into classes that taught automotive and construction operation and maintenance, others into electricans type of powerline and telephone installation and so on. I was assigned to pontoon class. We learned the difference between an "A" and a "B" angle, what the word "jewelry" meant in this type of building pontoon causeways, barges, etc. I did learn how to launch a string of pontoons as well. I consider myself fortunate of not having to remain in this type training for too long. We again, boarded busses and headed further south to Camp Elliot, San

Diego, California for another go of training. This training cycle was of something very different, in that they assigned us SEABEES to use all the wood scrapes in building a "Mock City" for use by the Marines to train in how to recognize booby traps within a house, and as well, how to place these booby traps. While on this detail, we were treated to another Hollywood feature being made. This time it was John PAYNE and Susan Hayward in the movie Pride of The Marines. *Wow! We were all star-struck just watching those stars doing their thing all day long. Takes and retakes you wouldn't believe, I felt sorry for the Marines that had to crawl on the ground right through mud holes and having live ammunition flying over their heads about 18 inches high. A few lifted their butts too high crawling under the wire entanglements and ended up being carried off to the Base Dispensary for treatment. This shoot lasted about 3–4 days in our area. Once over, we had to get back to the job of building more houses etc.*

Our big day arrived—marched on-board a Pacific bound banana boat known as the "Del F. Brazil" How many remember being sea-sick? You bet I can. I thought for the first three days underway, I would never survive. However, I came around and enjoyed the next 27 days zig-zagging across the Pacific to our first stop—New Caledonia. I am getting a little ahead of myself at this juncture. When the ship was ready to cross the 180th Meridian, there was a ritual that all good seamen follow. We were known as "pollywags" and therefore, needed to be treated to a ritual of some doings before we could be known as "shellbacks" after crossing this Meridian. Of course, once you became a "Shellback" and ever traveled over the Meridian again, you could become a part of the group causing great pain on the new "Pollywags." As always, never came close again to the Meridian to get my licks in . . .

Underway after spending a day at a recreation beach run by the French since New Caledonia is a French posession. A great swim and a few beers after being dried out for the 30 day trip getting over to New Caledonia. Back on-board, underway for Esperito [sic] Santos, New Hebrides. Spent a week there visiting with many of the SEABEE Battalions already at work there. They took on additional supplies and onward to Guadalcanal. Yep, a replacement into the 25th Naval Construction Battalion which was located at Teterc Beach. Once again, found myself mess cooking. This time it was back to "pot wrestling" my past experience at Camp Perry must have been given out upon my arrival at the 25th camp. However, time went by fairly quick. I did learn to eat and like dehydrated food. Our cooks had a way of camouflaging these food stuffs to where they did become palatable. To this day, I can't bring myself to eat "Spam," "Vienna Sausage," or New Zealand "mutton." We had spam in the blanket, out of the blanket, in tomato sauce and the same with Vienna sausages. As for the mutton, that was stinking before cooking, during cooking, and even after being doused with spices, it was still greasy and hard to get past one's nose. But, we survived. I must say, our cooks made the best "Raisinjack" in the camp area. Once in a while, we would not get some fruit for desert, or oatmeal for breakfast, because those ingredients were the makings for the "Rasinjack." Finally, with mess cooking finished, I was assigned to transportation.

As the engineering Battalion for the 3rd Marine Division, our job was to maintain their camp area, roads into and out of, as well as our own areas. My job was one of driving a dump truck going to the riverbed to have gravel placed in the bed for spreading on the roads camp areas, and in particular, the supply dumps. As one knows of the tropics, rain and more rain can be dumped on you in a short span of time. By having these roads, camp areas, and supply areas covered with gravel, rather than just graded earth, we could travel during these rainy days without too much difficulty.

FIFTEEN

Landing in North Africa

In order to forestall an invasion of Africa by Germany and Italy, [which] if successful would constitute a direct threat to America across the comparatively narrow sea from western Africa, a powerful American force equipped with adequate weapons of modern warfare and under American command is today landing on the Mediterranean and Atlantic coasts of the French colonies in Africa.

So President Franklin D. Roosevelt announced on Sunday, November 8, 1942, that the Americans had joined the war in Europe against Hitler and Mussolini.

The war had not gone exactly as the Allies had expected. The Americans were already deeply engaged in the Solomon Islands, as a result of the new set of Japanese movements in the summer of 1942. But now they had come to the European theater as well.

The American landings were in Algeria and Morocco. The Morocco expedition was called the Western Task Force and was under command of Rear Admiral Henry K. Hewitt.

The principal objective of the western expeditionary force was the city of Casablanca. The key to Casablanca was the town of Media at the mouth of the Sebou River, on the southern bank. The city and the bank of the river were guarded by two batteries of guns.

Major General George S. Patton, Jr., would lead the Sixth and Ninth army divisions in the attack on the shore. So the United States was preparing to launch its second amphibious invasion of an enemy shore. The first, at Guadalcanal, had been relatively simple, because the Japanese had been surprised and the major fighting at the beginning had taken place on the islands of Gavutu and Tulagi, across the sound from Guadalcanal. The major American forces had gotten ashore virtually unopposed. The same could not be expected in Africa, and was not. The training for amphibious operations had been as complete as the state-of-the-art in 1942 would permit, but it left a lot to be desired. The navy was not really prepared for amphibious operations yet.

One of the key elements in the navy assault on Casablanca was Bill LeBaron's ship, the cruiser *Wichita*, which opened fire on the Casablanca defenses at 7:51 that morning. Everything went well until 11:42, when the *Wichita* was hit by a shell that injured fourteen men. Bill LeBaron was not one of them.

Hours before the guns began to fire, navy Lieutenant Mark Starkweather and a navy underwater demolition team were in action. They left the transport *George Clymer* at 3:30 that morning in a Higgins boat, the current state-of-the-war landing craft. Starkweather, Lieutenant James Darrock, and fifteen men were in the boat, and all around them were stacked their weapons, wire-cutting equipment, and explosive charges. This team had been very hastily recruited when some of the requirements of the North African invasion began to beckon, very hastily trained, and given the name Combat Demolition Unit. Their task this morning was to cut a cable-and-boom arrangement inside the mouth of the Sebou River. General Patton wanted Port Layautey and its airfield, and this boom was protecting it and preventing the American landing forces from coming ashore here.

Lieutenant Starkweather and his men were salvage experts who had helped raise sunken ships from Pearl Harbor after the Japanese attack on December 7, 1941. Only two months earlier the invasion planners had realized that they needed demolition experts. Who knew what sort of underwater obstacles the French might have erected to prevent landings on their shore? So Starkweather and his men were assembled and told about the boom and net arrangements that they would have to destroy. They were given a quick course in cable-cutting, demolition, and command tactics. Then they had been flown to England to join the Western Task Force.

Photographs and maps of the area showed the boom, overlooked by the stone Casbah fortress, which housed some big pieces of artillery, from 75mm to 155mm guns of the coastal battery.

No one knew quite what to expect. The fortress was manned by Vichy French troops. Would they fight? Or would they do as President Roosevelt had called on them to do, and turn against the Germans and fight with the Allies?

General Patton was very nervous about the whole operation. The capture of the airfield behind Port Layautey was very important to him, and it had to be done before the French had a chance to destroy the installations.

As the combat demolition team pulled away from the *George Clymer*, a strong wind was blowing and the rain was coming down hard. The sea was rough and impeded the progress of their blunt-nosed landing craft. Worst was the ground swell for which this area was famous. Just after leaving the transport area, the boat was caught on the top of a thirty-foot swell that was just starting to break. The wave snatched at the boat and accelerated its progress, carrying it straight between the jetties at the river mouth.

The coxswain struggled with the wheel and ran up full power to prevent the craft from being pooped, caught by water rushing over the stern and sunk. The landing craft raced ahead and was seen by the French, who fired a red flare.

The coxswain regained control of the landing craft and the boat reached the calmer waters inside the river mouth. The coxswain then steered along the south side of the river, toward the boom. There was no sound from the enemy, and Lieutenant Starkweather began to believe that they had not been seen after all. Then the shooting started. The first fire came from heavy machine guns, but it was far short of the Higgins boat. But then the defenders turned on searchlights, which began to sweep the river. The lights moved toward the boat, and suddenly it was illuminated.

The coxswain pushed the throttle home and began to zigzag in an attempt to lose the lights. The 75mm guns of the fortress opened up and shells began to fall around the boat, sending up tall columns of water. Then one of the American destroyers outside the mouth of the river began firing on the Casbah, and the fort turned its attention to the destroyer. Still the searchlights kept the boat in their glare, which meant that the element of surprise was completely gone. Lieutenant Starkweather ordered the coxswain to get out of there, and the coxswain swung the boat toward the river mouth. They came out of the river and into the fierce Atlantic swell once again, and the boat bucketed and rolled in the heavy surf. In the violent pitching the men lost their grips on what they had been hanging onto and were thrown about the boat. Lieutenant Starkweather was thrown head-first into the coming of the cockpit and injured his face. One sailor was flung onto the equipment in the bottom of the boat and broke both ankles. The rest of the sailors suffered cuts and bruises.

Once the boat got through the surf and the river mouth, the seas quieted and all the coxswain had to do was negotiate the heavy swell on the way back to the *George Clymer*. By the time they arrived, the assault troops had already made their major landing, some distance from the mouth of the river. No one had anticipated the difficulties the amphibious force encountered, and it took nearly two days to get the troops and equipment ashore. At the end of those two days the airfield was still in enemy hands, and General Patton was perturbed. He needed that airfield and he needed it in a hurry.

By ten o'clock on the morning of D-day a beachhead had been established south of the river mouth but from that point the progress was slow. The troops of the Casbah were the French Foreign Legion, and they fought vigorously. An attempt that first day to run up the river was made by the cruiser *Dallas*, but she encountered such fierce fire from the shore batteries that she turned about and went out of the river again.

The soldiers scheduled to make the assault on the airfield were a detachment of Rangers aboard the *Dallas*, but they had to wait until that boom and net could be destroyed, so they waited as the battle raged on the beaches. The *Dallas*, meanwhile, was busy firing on the forts and beaches.

General Patton ordered another attempt to cut the boom on the night of November 9, and Lieutenant Starkweather and his crew set out once more from the *George Clymer*. They boarded their landing craft just after midnight. This time they carried two light machine guns as well as their other equipment, two rubber boats, and a large incendiary bomb.

The sea, they found, was running higher than it had on their first attempt.

The destroyer assigned to give covering fire if they needed it was having difficulty remaining on station near the river mouth, twisting and turning in the wind.

Lieutenant Starkweather and his crew hid behind the gunwales of their landing craft while the coxswain stood erect, concentrating on the waves and the course he had to follow.

The problem was to watch for a break in the wave pattern and scoot through the gap before the high seas came up again. The coxswain had learned on the previous day and now he managed to catch one of the smaller series of waves. From the boat he could see the dark outline of the jetty on the south bank of the river, but not the one on the north. The boat approached the jetty, and passed within thirty yards. Lieutenant Starkweather waited nervously for the warning flare that would again bring the searchlights probing and gunfire. The coxswain throttled back to muffle the sound of the engines. A sialor in the bow served as lookout and passed back whispered instructions to the coxswain.

Soon they located the heavy boom cable and the net below it. A line of small boats was strung across the harbor mouth, and the cable and net were suspended from the boats. Above the boom was a small wire that was very taut. Lieutenant Starkweather suspected it was a warning device, and he warned his men not to touch the wire until the last moment.

The demolition men worked swiftly on the cable. Some of them went into the water. Others worked from the landing craft, installing a series of explosives on one portion of the boom. Their primary cutting tool was an explosive cable-cutter. In training it had not always worked properly, so the team had brought along extra explosives just in case. Now they installed hundreds of pounds of backup charges. They worked in the shadow of the fortress, waiting nervously for that moment when the searchlights would come on again and the machine guns would begin to clatter.

Two men stood by the machine guns, but they had the safety catches in, for Lieutenant Starkweather had forbidden them to fire without his orders. They waited nervously while the men in the water fixed the charges. Some charges were then placed on the small taut cable; the cutter charge on the main cable was fired and blew up with an enormously satisfying roar. There was no response from the shore, but when the taut cable was blown, immediately the searchlights began to work from the fortress and guns began to fire.

The boats supporting the heavy boom now began drifting downstream, carrying with them the greatest part of the boom. The job was done. All the demolition team had to do now was to get out alive if possible.

Starkweather gave the order to the machine gunners to fire and they began shooting at the searchlights. One of the machine guns knocked out two searchlights, after which the searchlights were turned off. But mortar flares began to shoot off overhead and the gunners from the Casbah were firing. Shells started to hit the landing craft. The machine guns fired, men with tommy guns began firing, and soon every man was using some sort of weapon against the enemy—to what end, no one knew. Lieutenant Starkweather ordered the men to stop firing, maybe that would make them less of a target. It seemed to work, because the hail of enemy fire suddenly slowed.

The landing craft zigzagged as it raced toward the open sea and safety. It began to take on water from the shellholes. The coxswain ordered the men to throw over the side everything possible to lighten the boat, and they began jettisoning equipment. First went hundreds of pounds of explosives, then the rubber boats. And then the giant incendiary bomb went over too. Finally the light machine guns were thrown overboard.

Water was still coming into the craft, and almost every man was bailing as they raced to the mouth of the river. But then they hit the surf line and the waves came crashing over the boat. Every man had to hold on for dear life. Their escorting destroyer was in position and fired at the Casbah to divert the gunners. The coxswain raced on and got through the breakers, now concerned lest the boat fall apart underneath them from the pounding of the sea. Just outside the river mouth, the landing craft came up to the destroyer, whose skipper now maneuvered to guide the landing craft back to the transport. In half an hour they were alongside the *George Clymer*, and they were taken aboard, their Higgins boat hauled after them. When they were safely aboard the transport they began counting the holes: thirteen from large projectiles and many from small-arms fire.

When the word that the boom was broken reached the cruiser *Dallas*, she got under way and entered the mouth of the river, crashed through what remained of the boom defenses, and steamed into Port Lyautey. The assault troops moved ashore under the protective fire of the cruiser and the battleship *Texas*. The *Dallas* grounded on the bottom, which was not as deep as the charts showed, but although she dragged several times she never stuck fast, and her Rangers landed and began the fight for the airfield. They ran into machine-gun fire but still moved steadily toward the airfield, and within a few hours the soldiers had secured the airfield.

Admiral Kelly, the naval commander, then issued a statement aimed at the French, announcing the attack on the fort at Medina and the capture of Port Lyautey and the airfield and calling on the French to stop resisting. But the broadcast met with no response, so the Americans continued to advance on Casablanca. At eleven o'clock in the morning the first American planes landed at the Port Lyautey airfield. Meanwhile the army troops were isolating the Casbah with the support of the cruiser *Savannah*.

"The final attack," according to an army memorandum, "had touches of *Beau Geste* about it, the attack employing the most modern weapons against a 1918 enemy defending a walled fort. Notwithstanding the fact that the attack disposed of a highly mechanized task force, the older weapons were not outmoded."

Throughout the day, the soldiers attacked, supported by planes from the airfield and the *Sangamon*, an escort carrier. They ran into heavy antiaircraft fire, but the carrier stayed on station until sunset, when it retired to the west. On the afternoon of November 10, the army captured the Casbah, and at 4:00 A.M. on November 11, General Lucian Truscott, the commander, issued a cease-fire order.

Armistice negotiations had begun; that night the Allies announced that hostilities in French Morocco had ceased.

So the first amphibious operation of the underwater demolition teams had succeeded, although raggedly. In the next few months the UDTs would receive hurried training, both for operations in the Pacific and in the European theater. There would be more ragged performances at Sicily, but the demolition men were learning all the time. What they were looking forward to as 1943 moved along was the day when they would invade Hitler's Fortress Europe.

SIXTEEN

Guadalcanal Secured

On November 17, twenty-one B–17 bombers landed and twelve B–24s came in. They would be operating out of Guadalcanal for a time. They were planning a raid on Bougainville for the next day.

On November 18, Chief O'Dea listened to a radio broadcast by President Roosevelt, praising all concerned for the victorious outcome of the naval battle of Guadalcanal. The next day Commander Blundon made a short speech to the Sixth Seabee Battalion at five o'clock at the Seabee camp, and said that they would be leaving the island in December for a rest on New Caledonia.

Life on Guadalcanal slowed down then. They finished the bridging of the Ilu River in eighteen days and built a main highway across the east and west boundaries of the expanded beachhead, the Malimbiu River, and the Matanikau. They put up two tanks for high-octane gas with a 420,000-gallon capacity each. They ran a pipeline to deep water for a tanker connection. They bridged the Matanikau even when the mortars were still pounding within range of the building.

Over on Tulagi the detachment of Seabees had built a crane on Government Wharf. They built a pontoon drydock for the newly arrived PT boats, and the crane was used to extract a "hot" torpedo that had stuck in a tube. The PT skipper complained about the difficulty in navigating around the coral reefs. The Seabees obliged by blasting channels through the coral for the PT boats.

There was much paperwork to catch up on, and new men coming in to be trained to take over the battalion's responsibilities. Supply ships were coming regularly, and Chief O'Dea was instructing new men in beach unloading. The mail was beginning to catch up—a little. O'Dea got two letters, dated September 25 and 27, from the States.

On the November 24, the Sixth Seabee Battalion took over road construction on the island. One couldn't say that it was quiet yet— several marines were killed near the Seabee camp in an air raid on November 25. Now Solomon Islanders were being brought in to form labor battalions. Four hundred came in on November 25.

It was apparent that the Japanese had not given up. Every day they raided and every night they raided to keep the Americans from getting decent sleep. And the attrition was growing. Admiral Greenman, the senior naval officer, was taken out of the island on a stretcher by plane, victim of the climate and the strain.

November 26 was Thanksgiving. It was celebrated with a Japanese air raid at 3:30 in the morning.

On November 27, Chief O'Dea left for Florida Island, across the Lunga Channel behind Tulagi Island. That night their cargo ship, the USS *Alchiba*, loaded with ammunition and supplies, was hit by a submarine in the channel and started to burn.

The next few days were marked by air raids and rain, plenty of rain. They were also marked by the naval battle of Tassafaronga, in which Admiral Tanaka with his supply destroyers routed a superior American naval force, at the cost of one destroyer sunk as well as one American cruiser sunk and three damaged very seriously. On the shore this meant no sleep again as the man watched the gun flashes.

During the next few nights there were several engagements as Tanaka tried vainly to supply the Japanese forces on Guadalcanal with drums of food and medicine and ammunition thrown into the sea. The Americans had achieved air superiority and were able to interdict the Japanese supply service.

On November 30, in one of the naval battles the cruiser *Minneapolis* limped in to Tulagi, her bow shot off. The Seabees pitched in to make emergency repairs.

On December 3, the Eighteenth Seabee Battalion arrived at Koie Point, which meant the Sixth Seabees would be moving out shortly. So would the exhausted First Marine Division, which had been continuously in action since the first week of August.

Admiral Aubrey W. Fitch came to Guadalcanal to take over as commander of the air forces in the Solomons area, and Chief O'Dea spent December 6 showing him around the various Seabee construction projects.

On December 8, the Seabees said farewell to General Vandegrift and the First Marines and hello to the new army command that was taking over the island.

Commander Blunden came down with malaria and Chief O'Dea took over the management of the 450 Solomon Islanders who worked for the Seabees now. Daily life became more relaxed. On the afternoon of December 10, Chief O'Dea went for a swim in water that had not long before been full of dead bodies. He had a chance to realize that the scenery of Guadalcanal was "really lovely."

The rain continued. More of the eighteenth Seabee Battalion came to Guadalcanal. Just when Chief O'Dea was beginning to think the war was over, the Japanese ran another series of air raids, but these days the Japanese planes raided nervously, mostly at night, and not very effectively. Ships were continuously arriving and departing from the harbor despite the occasional air raids. The mail was coming in more regularly. But every time that Chief O'Dea began to get the idea that it was all over, something happened to remind him that Guadalcanal was still a battle zone. On December 20, he went up front to select new road and bridge locations and was caught in Japanese artillery fire several times. He found dead Japanese lying all around. He did not notice that most of them had died of starvation.

On December 21, Commander Frye of the Twenty-Sixth Seabee Battalion arrived. This battalion was their official relief, and the Sixth Seabees knew they would be leaving soon.

O'Dea went down to the refrigerator plant with Commander Blunden and Commander Frye. While they were there at four o'clock in the afternoon, an ammunition truck exploded a hundred feet away from them, killing and injuring a large number of men. The truck was blown to pieces, and two Seabees were killed. Arms, legs, and other body parts were scattered around the area. The rain began to come down as they tried to help the wounded. To add to the carnage a Japanese plane came over and dropped eight bombs.

On Christmas Eve they were getting ready to leave the island soon. O'Dea went to a Christmas service and sang carols. He could still hear shooting in the hills. The Japanese were still out there; the men were always potentially under fire and would remain so as long as the Japanese remained on the island.

Guadalcanal was becoming very civilized. There was a movie at the Seabee camp, *All Through the Night*. But there was also another air raid.

December 27, the bulk of the Twenty-sixth Seabee Battalion arrived on Guadalcanal and on December 28 Commander Blunden was ordered to leave the island with his men on January 5 aboard the USS *Leggett*.

The air raids continued as O'Dea and the other Seabees instructed their successors in the various jobs.

On January 4, the Seabees of the Sixth Battalion were up at 4:30 A.M., and at 6:00 marched to the cemetery dressed in white uniforms and paid tribute to the men they were leaving behind on the island. Father Gehrig said mass and Chief O'Dea served as acolyte. They were getting ready to pull out.

January 5, as they prepared to leave, they went through another air raid alert. 1:00 P.M. they were aboard ship and the ship sailed full of the Sixth Seabees, and nuns, priests, and refugees from Bougainville. What impressed Chief O'Dea most was the excellence of the food. He had almost forgotten navy chow in the months on Guadalcanal.

> *The 26th Battalion Band was at the beach to see us sail, playing patriotic songs. We were leaving the Island of Hell but had completed our original task of chasing or killing the Japs from this island. The island is now secure, but of course we cannot remain to enjoy the freedom of this island since we have a bigger job ahead of us. After a few weeks' rest we will be after the Japs again, even if we must go as far east as Tokyo. They will never again dominate these islands, after we have once landed.*

SEVENTEEN

The Wreck of the 709

While the Guadalcanal campaign was at its hot and sticky height, the fall of 1942, halfway across the world in a grim and icy winter other American sailors were facing quite a different sort of danger. They were the men of USS *SC 709*, a subchaser operating out of New England and Canada.

SC 709 was a wooden vessel, commissioned at Elizabeth City, North Carolina, in November 1942. She was 120 feet long and had a beam of 20 feet. She carried one three-inch gun forward and two 20mm guns and 20-depth charges, sound gear, and radar.

In the fall of 1942 the *709* operated out of Portland, Maine, but in January 1943 she received orders to operate from Argentia, Newfoundland. She left Portland on the afternoon of January 15. The sailing was easy and uneventful that first day, and the second, but on the afternoon of January 16 a snowstorm began and about an hour later the temperature took a drop and ice began to form on the superstructure. The skipper understood the problem very well. His ship was not built to carry a heavy deck load. He and Chief Petty Officer Harry Luessen, the assistant navigator and quartermaster, conferred about what was to be done. They decided to make for the nearest port of refuge, Halifax harbor. The course was set for Halifax.

But when the *709* arrived, she found the antisubmarine nets in place and the harbor closed. By radio she asked permission to enter.

Permission was denied. Didn't they know there was a war on?

The skipper headed back out to sea, not knowing quite how to escape the obvious dangers of this storm to the little vessel.

Studying the Nova Scotia chart, the captain found that the only ice-free port shown was Louisbourg. The *709* headed there. That night the storm grew worse, and the seas broke high above the little craft, and the ice built up steadily on the superstructure. The crew worked to lighten the ship, particularly at the stern. They needed to jettison their depth charges, but the ice imprisoned them.

By seven o'clock in the morning of January 17 visibility had been reduced to little over a hundred feet. There was no way of taking a fix in this storm, so they guided by dead reckoning, Assistant Navigator Luessen and the captain headed for Louisbourg. According to their reckoning they should sight the harbor at eleven o'clock that morning. Near that hour one lookout spotted a church steeple and some ships moored in the harbor. But then came the discovery that on their present course they could not enter the harbor; the course would have to be changed. When they tried to change course Luessen and the skipper discovered that their ship had become unnavigable because of the ice. Suction had been lost on the starboard engine, and the rudder would not move. All that could be done was to drive ahead, and this meant she would go up on the beach just off the entrance to the harbor. Despite every attempt, the ship would not respond, and she drove ahead, onto the shoal between Rockford Point and Battery Island.

After the *709* hit, she began to fill. Everyone was forced up on deck and to the starboard side of the vessel. Some of the men, who had been on watch, were dressed for the storm. Some had been routed out of their bunks and had grabbed whatever they could to shelter them from the cold.

The sea pounded the ship, driving her toward deep water, but soon she filled enough so that she grounded firmly on the bottom and then the waves and wind began to subside, and she was stuck fast, her twenty-six-man crew in danger of freezing to death in the ice.

The grounding of the *709* had been noticed by the pilot's station at Louisbourg, and the Canadian navy station had been notified. Coxswain Hyacinthe Pottie of the Royal Canadian navy harbor craft at Louisbourg had tried to rescue the Americans, but the storm was still fierce and the wind so high that the harbor craft could not reach them. They couldn't even fire a line to the ship.

Some of the Louisbourg fishing fleet decided to try to give a helping hand. They got a tug to break a path through the ice for their boats. Then they brought their shallow-draft fishing boats through the shallow water and took off the men of the *709* that afternoon at about two o'clock.

When they got to the ship they found that they had come just in time. The crew were using blankets, pillows, and mattresses to try to protect themselves from the cold, and not all of them were doing very well. One man's feet had frozen and swollen so badly that they burst his boots. Others had frozen fingers and cheeks. Some of the men of the crew could no longer move when the rescuers came.

The crew was taken off and to the Canadian Legion Hall at Louisbourg. There the Red Cross had set up emergency facilities. They were stripped of their frozen clothing and wrapped in blankets and fed soup and coffee. As they came around, they were taken to the air force hospital at Victoria Park in Sydney Nova Scotia. One man lost several fingers, and two men lost a foot from frostbite. But not a man was lost in one of the worst storms in the region that winter, because of the fishermen of Louisbourg.

EIGHTEEN

A LeBaron Goes West

In the fall of 1942 Sailor Jack LeBaron's ship, the netlayer USS *Holly*, was hailed into Boston Naval Shipyard for improvements to help her cope with the submarine menace in the Atlantic and to upgrade her firepower with more guns.

Most of the crew was replaced, particularly all the veteran chief petty officers, who were coming up to retirement age or whose specialties seemed to be needed elsewhere. Their old skipper had been a Harvard man and a yachtsman, but now they got a new skipper, a ninety-day wonder who had left a job as lingerie sales-man at a Boston department store to join the service. As soon as the crew was replaced and the work on the ship was done, in a typical naval maneuver she was assigned not to the Atlantic waters but to the Pacific fleet and ordered to make her way west through the Panama Canal. So late in December 1942, the *Holly* headed south and west.

The first port of call was New York City, where the ship arrived on the afternoon of December 31. Sailor LeBaron was lucky enough to get shore leave and spent the one night, New Year's Eve, in Times Square. Next day the ship sailed for Miami. Theoretically they were on watch for submarines on the way south, but all they saw were a few oil slicks, which could have meant anything at all. It was just as well; the crew was so green they would just have gotten in trouble had they found a U-boat. The chief and only signalman, for exam-ple, was still trying to master Morse code. Sailor LeBaron was in training for gunner's mate, but since he had learned semaphore as a Boy Scout, he decided to keep up his skill by second-guessing the signalman. Soon enough LeBaron discovered he knew more about signaling than the signalman.

Miami was again a one-night stand and then they headed for Jamaica. There everyone had shore leave and was introduced to Jamaica rum. For many members of the crew of the *Holly* this meant shore leave would be a very short conscious experience. Sailor Le-Baron managed to avoid the worst evils of drink, however, and spent the later hours of the evening in a *maison de joie* with three other sailors and four cooperative young women.

Too soon they left Jamaica, headed for Panama and a convoy that was going to run to the South Pacific. In Panama the *Holly* made a name for herself. When the ship arrived off Panama and they could see the shore. It was very easy to see the entry to the locks, and this, of course, was where the skipper set his heading.

As the *Holly* stood in toward the shore, a flurry of signals came from various points ashore. The signalman was trying, not very successfully, to read the messages and interpret them for the captain of the ship.

The closer in they came the more intense the signaling grew. LeBaron noticed and dropped what he was doing to read the message.

"You are headed into a minefield," it said. By that time the *Holly* was apparently in the middle of the minefield, because the messages stopped. They managed to get in safely. What the naval commander at Panama had to say to the captain of the *Holly* was not shared with Sailor LeBaron.

The *Holly* stopped over for several days as the convoy was assembled—not much of a convoy, but representative of the U.S. Navy's capabilities of the time, short on destroyers and with the new destroyer escorts not yet coming into service in any numbers. The convoy was made up of two destroyers and a large number of merchant ships.

They headed toward Australia, zigzagging all the way, and when they crossed the Equator held the Father Neptune ceremony, although there was only one shellback aboard the *Holly* at the point that they crossed the line.

After thirty days at sea the *Holly* dropped out of the convoy at

Bora Bora, Tahiti, which was a navy supply base. They were not allowed to go ashore, perhaps to protect the natives. But the Tahitians came to the ship in their canoes to sell grass mats and other local products.

From Bora Bora the *Holly* sailed for Pago Pago. Again the skipper was niggardly with shore leave, which earned him the sobriquet "Captain Bligh" from the crew. Then they made Suva in the Fijis, where Sailor LeBaron was introduced to warm English beer. Next they went to Espiritu Santo, and here the *Holly* got to work laying antisubmarine nets around the harbor.

The only recreation allowed the men of the *Holly* (and other American sailors on American ships) was a trip every two weeks to a small island in the harbor, which had a softball field and one basketball goal stuck on a coconut palm. This was a strictly navy recreation area. Here the sailors went to unwind after two weeks of sea duty. Quite simply, they went to get drunk. And almost all of them did.

On arrival at the island each man was given a case of beer. The shore party was told that no beer could be brought back to the ship. Three hours later the shore party would end and the boat came back to pick them up. Then the fun began. The crew members would weave down to the little pier, trying to show one another how sober they were, many of them falling off the deck having to be fished out of the water. When the boats started back, they gave an impression that the coxswains were all drunk too. But there was reason for this waving and bobbing of the boats. When a man fell overboard, the coxswain would make a 180-degree turn and the crew would pick the sailor out of the water. Then another 180-degree turn was necessary to return to course. Every few feet, as the boats returned to the ship, men kept falling out.

It was not a very happy time and the *Holly* was not a very happy ship. Virtually every man aboard had an application for transfer at all times. All applications were refused, except one; a man named Spaulding finally got transferred out, to a destroyer, and later went down with the ship when she was sunk in the Solomons. The other sailors just kept applying for transfer, which kept being turned down.

Except for the beer parties there was virtually no relief from routine for the men of the *Holly*. However, one bit of the routine in a way offered its own reward: assignment to the laundry detail. There was no laundry aboard the ship and no water for washing clothes, which left the fastidious the single option of washing their clothes with saltwater soap, which had the appearance and texture of a piece of salt pork. But once in a while, as when the wardroom linen needed washing, the dinghy would be sent up a freshwater stream that emptied into the bay. Just getting the smell of clean clothes and having a chance to do laundry in fresh water was worth the assignment.

The officers lived an entirely different existence. Most of them went to the officers' club ashore every night of the week. As time went on the animosity between officers and enlisted men increased, and particularly the men's antipathy to the captain grew very strong. One night when the skipper returned to the ship from the club, on the way to his cabin he tripped and somehow ended up over the side. He swore that there had been helping hands and called on the sailor who had the gangway watch for evidence. The sailor said he hadn't seen anything at all.

The captain thought about the matter for a while and decided his life was in danger. He called in the carpenter's mate and ordered him to carve a .45-caliber automatic pistol out of wood. It was made and painted black. The captain then retrieved the .45 assigned to the gangway watch, which was the only firearm issued aboard the ship, and replaced it with the wooden pistol.

Word got around the ship, and soon had permeated the whole Espiritu Santo naval establishment. A few days afterward the *Holly* was out at work, putting down nets with a sister ship and the captain was on the bridge surveying the operation. The bow of the sister ship suddenly nudged the bow of the *Holly*, and at the same time the men of the other ship passed across to the men on the forecastle of the *Holly* a homemade bow and arrow. Everyone on both vessels saw it, and the *Holly* erupted in laughter that could be very well heard on the bridge. The skipper suddenly disappeared from sight. The next day the issue .45 automatic pistol was again given to the sailor on the gangway watch.

WWII AMPHIBIOUS FORCE

Seal of the Naval Beach Battalions and other amphibious forces. Worn on the left shoulder of uniform (Courtesy: Clifford Legerton).

Clifford Legerton of the U.S. Navy 8th Beach Battalion. His battalion landed in Southern France in 1944.

Unloading the 36th U.S. Army division on Green Beach and Quarry Beach in Southern France on August 15, 1944 (Courtesy: Clifford Legerton).

Moving across the invasion beach in southern France on D Day, August 15, 1944 (Courtesy: Clifford Legerton).

Chow time at the English villa at St. Raphael, in southern France. This villa was taken over by Platoon C-7 of the 8th Naval Beach Battalion (Courtesy: Clifford Legerton).

Seabees of the 25th NCB on Bougainville. After the 3rd Marine Division landed at Empress Augusta Bay, the Seabees came in to build the airfields that would isolate Rabaul (Courtesy: Alfred G. Don).

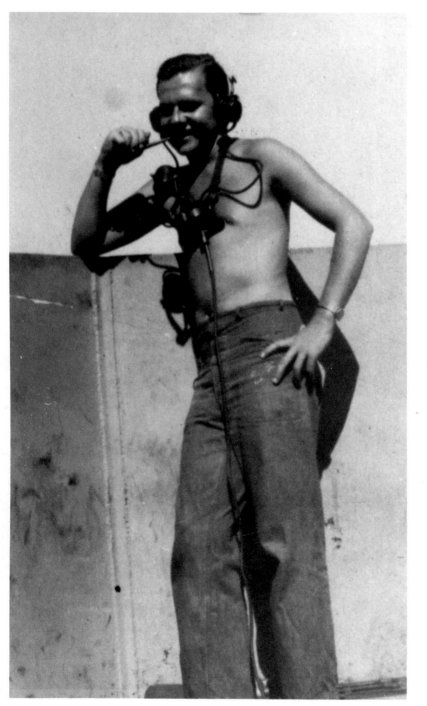

Sailor Bill Askin on duty aboard his LST (Courtesy: Bill Askin).

Ted, Allan, and Jack LeBaron (left to right) with their mother and two friends. The photo was taken on a rare occasion during the war when three of the four LeBaron brothers were home in Waterbury, Connecticut, on leave.

Bill LeBaron. He served in the cruiser *Wichita* during the war and saw action in the Pacific and in the European Theater of Operations.

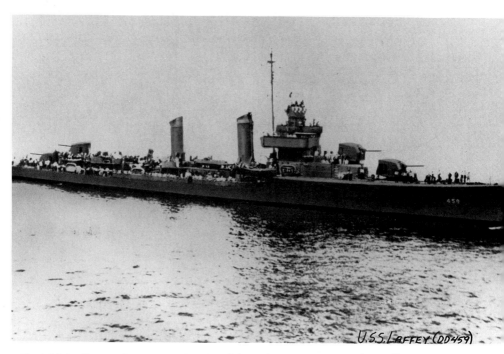

The USS *Laffey*, as she appeared in Guadalcanal waters in 1942. The *Laffey* served in several major naval engagements before she was sunk (Courtesy: Rear Admiral E. A. Barham).

Seabees did everything from stevedoring to road building in the Pacific. These are members of the 119th Seabee Battalion at Milne Bay on New Guinea (Courtesy: William Casey).

USS PC 554
ATLANTIC CONVOY
1943

JSS Patrol Craft 554 on Atlantic convoy (Courtesy: George Atterbury and Harry Ayres, Jr.).

Seabee Mike O'Dea (driver) in a jeep on Guadalcanal (Courtesy: Mike O'Dea).

Aboard the carrier *Hornet*. Left to Right: Roger Balcombe, ARM 2/c radioman, Roy Eddington, Chief Machinists' Mate, the gunner, and David Mangum, Aviation Pilot First Class. A few days after this photo was taken Balcombe was killed (Courtesy: David Wheeler Mangum).

7 bomber on Henderson field, Guadalcanal (Courtesy: e O'Dea).

Seabees at the ice plant captured from the Japanese on Guadalcanal (Courtesy: Mike O'Dea).

Front line trench on Guadalcanal (Courtesy: Mike O'Dea).

Henderson Field, Guadalcanal. This was what the Americans and Japanese were fighting for (Courtesy: Mike O'Dea).

Pier at the submarine base at Pearl Harbor. The submarine is the *Argonaut*, which has just returned after participating in the raid on Makin island by Carlson's Raiders.

submarine rescues a downed U.S. airman in the East China Sea.

Japanese POWs rescued by an American submarine land at Pearl Harbor.

Lieutenant Roy Davenport receives the Navy Cross after the second patrol of the USS *Silverside*
Admiral Charles Lockwood, commander of submarines in the Pacific Fleet, is presenting the mec

A view of Japan's famous volcano Mt. Fuji through the periscope of
the USS *Trepang.*

fter lookout aboard the USS *Haddock*.

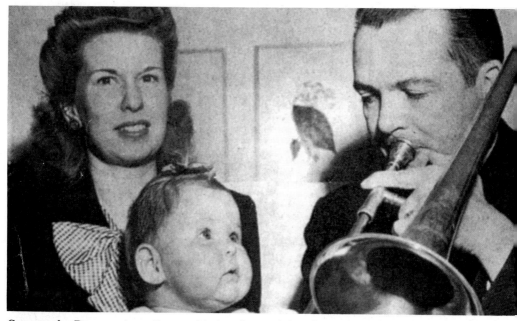

Commander Davenport practices on his trombone while ashore with his wife and daughter.

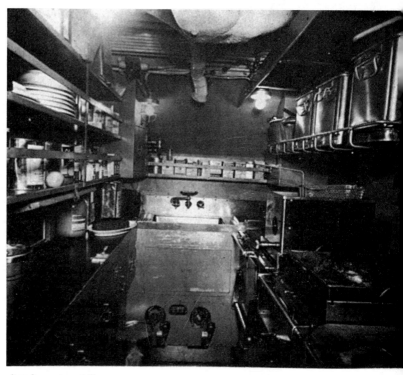

A submarine galley.

ilor looking over his mail and eating a fresh apple after a long cruise aboard a submarine.

The launching of the submarine *Trepang* at Mare Island, California.

NINETEEN

Sailor Lynch Takes Time Off

After Sl/c C. W. Lynch was plucked from the waters near the exploding carrier *Lexington* in the Coral Sea on May 8, 1942, he and other survivors were dropped off at Tongatubu, where they spent some time, and then they stopped at other South Seas ports. Eventually they got to New Caledonia just in time for fireworks: an ammunition dump loaded with 18,000 bombs blew up. The survivors got transportation home aboard the new carrier *Langley* and when they arrived in California, Lynch decided he needed six months' leave instead of the sixty days allocated by the navy.

Lynch's experience on the *Lexington* left him with a deep and abiding reluctance to go back to sea, and the best way to avoid it seemed to be not to report for duty. So he worked in a restaurant for a time and also traveled around some. Then he was picked up by the Shore Patrol in the Chicago area. He was so far AWOL that everyone he met in the brig assured him he would get a general court-martial and probably be shot for desertion. He was scheduled to be returned to Boston (where his original orders had sent him) but the navy obviously was in no hurry to deal with his case. He waited.

TWENTY

The Answer to the U-Boats

The launching of a number of escort carriers turned the war around in the North Atlantic in 1943. Admiral Dönitz had started his U-boat campaign against America in the winter of 1942, and it had been very successful for three months—until British and American forces assembled enough escorts and planes to slow the campaign—but that year the really effective brake was put on by Hitler, who forced Dönitz to divert many of his submarines to the Mediterranean. By 1943, when the Germans were ready again to assault the American shore in strength, the escort carriers had begun operations with convoys and they made all the difference in the world.

Perhaps the most famous of the escort carriers, and among the first, was the USS *Bogue*. That little ship and its squadron, VC-9, began operations on February 20, 1943. On March 10, Lieutenant McAuslan became the first *Bogue* flier to sight a U-boat, just two miles from the convoy in which the *Bogue* was traveling. He attacked, but his depth charges would not release and the submarine dived and got away. All day long planes searched for the U-boat without success, but the skipper of the *Bogue* was sure the U-boat was following the convoy, because these were the days of the wolf-pack attacks in mid-Atlantic. On March 11, Lieutenant Roberts was preparing to land on the carrier when he saw a swirl of water two miles astern of the carrier. He turned and made an attack, but saw nothing further.

The first cruise ended without event, but on the second cruise, on April 28, 1943, Lieutenant Santee sighted a surfaced submarine and attacked. There were no conclusive results, but the convoy was not attacked on that run. On May 21, the action really began, when Lieutenant Commander Drane bombed a submarine on the surface. The next day Lieutenant Kuhn damaged another U-boat. Then three more pilots reported attacks on U-boats within a circle of 100 miles. Two of the pilots sank one U-boat and fifteen survivors were picked up. Between June 4 and June 12, *Bogue* planes made seven definite attacks on submarines, sinking one, probably sinking another, and damaging a third. On the next cruise, which ended in July, they sank a U-boat and damaged another on the way to Casablanca. VC-9 then left the *Bogue* for other service but the carrier continued on the North Atlantic run and became famous for its sinkings of German U-boats.

VC-9 then transferred to the USS *Card,* another escort carrier, and on September 23, 1943, began a cruise in which ten attacks were made on U-boats in four weeks' time. Evidence indicated four sinkings.

There was plenty of opportunity in this heyday of the wolfpacks. On one flight Lieutenant Sterns sighted five surfaced enemy submarines. He attacked one and sank it. The other four U-boats submerged and escaped before other planes could arrive on the scene.

But the escort carriers and the destroyers and escorts formed themselves into hunter-killer teams that became so effective in sinking enemy submarines that by the middle of 1943 the U-boat threat was largely dissipated and the U-boats went basically on the defensive, not to make another serious threat to the Allied lifeline until 1945, when two new U-boat types were developed, along with the snorkel underwater breathing mechanism. But by that time the Allies were closing in on Germany on the land and the war ended before the new U-boat menace had time to develop.

TWENTY-ONE

Chicago Is a Sailor's Town

On Monday, March 15, 1943, the day after Allan LeBaron's seventeenth birthday, he went to the navy recruiting substation in Burlington, Vermont, and opted to join his three brothers in the naval service. Within the week he had been installed at the Naval Training Center in Sampson, New York. By this time the navy was able to give its new sailors real training before sending them to service. Allan LeBaron even managed to get back to Vermont to graduate with his high school class in June.

After several weeks he was transferred to the Naval Air Technical Training Center at Navy Pier, Chicago, for a twenty-one-week course that would change him into an aviation metalsmith.

Not only LeBaron's three brothers, but also his father and his brother-in-law were all in the navy, and all but his brother-in-law were overseas already. Brother Ted, after surviving the Pearl Harbor attack, had gone on to Australia, where his PBY had been shot down on patrol. The crew had been picked up, and then the rescue vessel had been bombed and sunk. But Ted LeBaron had survived. So the youngest member of this navy family had some traditions to live up to.

Among the first things to interest him at Chicago were the two lake steamers converted to become training carriers, the *Wolverine* and the *Sable*. One was a stern-wheeled craft and the other a side-wheeler, but they both had flight decks, on which thousands of young Americans qualified in carrier landings.

Young LeBaron settled down on the pier, working with the

wreckage of the aircraft that crashed in training. And he began, on July 9, 1943, to become a real sailor.

Taps was at 10:00 P.M. and reveille at 6:00 A.M. At 8:30 he and the other new swabbies reported for mess duty. Soon he was pulling duty as KP, which meant getting up at 4:30 in the morning to start breakfast. By mid-July he was getting ready to go to aviation metal-smith school, which meant learning everything to do with the maintenance of an aircraft except engines and electricity.

Because LeBaron was a Vermonter many of his associates thought he was a real hick. "It's almost the unanimous opinion here that I am a moron, which has plenty of advantages. They also believe everything I tell them because they think I'm too dumb to do anything else. I'm afraid some of them have slightly wrong ideas about Vermont and its people."

Sailor LeBaron did nothing to disabuse his friends of their wrong impressions. He enjoyed the role he was playing.

Sailor LeBaron soon fell in love with Chicago. He liked to go down to the end of the pier and read and write letters. Life was good and he had plenty of liberty. He was also enjoying the shortage of men in the Chicago area, which caused the girl hostesses of the Chicago Service Men's Center to vie for the attentions of the soldiers and sailors.

By midsummer, Sailor LeBaron thought he had it made:

This is my idea of what a city should be. It doesn't seem near so crowded as Boston and there is always a breeze. Besides, everything is free. Jerry Colonna is out at the summer center today but I think I'll stay here and read. It is absolutely astounding to the gang why I spend so much time reading when there are so many women here, and when I went to bed at six that was too much. For two hours they kept waking me up asking if I was sick.

He went to shows, to hear Woody Herman's band play, and to USO performances of Gershwin songs. At the end of July a lieutenant (jg) gave a talk on what the war was about. He told them what they were fighting for was the Four Freedoms. But all LeBaron's pals said they were fighting to get it over with and get home.

So the summer was spent getting ready for school and going to musicals and plays and listening to the big name bands that came to entertain the swabbies.

Everything changed in the middle of August. Then the work began. From 8:00 A.M. until 5:15 P.M.; he had twenty minutes off for lunch. But on the weekends, life seemed to be just right for a boy from Vermont:

> *Just to give you an idea of how to have a good time in this place for practically nothing I'll tell you what I did today. When I got out this morning I went out to the Summer Center and got a bathing suit and went swimming and the water was real nice. Then went in and had some stuff to eat and went out and pitched pennies. They were the center's pennies but it was a lot of fun. Came back and ate again and went to the movies. I don't know the name of it, but it was real good. One with a lot of movie stars, Merle Oberon and some others. That was when I first spent some money because all of the tickets were gone. Then went to the library and read all last week's magazines, drank some milk and came in. I had fifty cents when I went out and twenty when I came in.*

On September 6, Sailor LeBaron saw his first television set and was very much impressed. When television came in, he predicted, motion pictures would go. Over that weekend he stuffed himself with civilian food. "I still can't understand this place. Anything a man in uniform does is okay."

On an early September evening, Sailor LeBaron met a girl who said she came from Milwaukee. He wondered, because she had a Brooklyn accent. He began running down Brooklyn and "then you ought to have seen the fireworks. A sailor may have a line but the stuff some of the females throw beats all that."

He wrote home "they have a saying here that the marines are too slow, the army is just right and the navy is too fast. All of which may be true, but the way the gals flock around a black neckerchief makes you wonder. Something about an open necked jumper makes 'em wild."

Sailor LeBaron kept trading on his Vermont heritage for a little private amusement. The physical education chief gave them a lecture on Chicago, and he asked what it was like in the winter. The PE chief began to wax eloquent about how the lake froze and it got frigid in town, "You will see," he said. And then he asked LeBaron where he was from.

"Vermont," said LeBaron.

"Well. It never gets down below minus twenty there, does it?"

"That's summer weather," said Sailor LeBaron.

Later he wrote home that he was ashamed of himself for pulling the fellow's leg.

I'm afraid he might have believed it. I've got such an honest face everyone believes everything I say, which sometime proves embarrassing. Every once in a while I would say 'I guess I'll go over the hill next liberty.'

In a few hours fellows would begin to come and talk to me saying they didn't think it was a very good idea to go AWOL and Sailor LeBaron would have to let himself be dissuaded.

At the Summer Center every Saturday night they had formal dances with the girls in long dresses. At the last formal of the season, LeBaron and another sailor were talking out on the sand and one of the hostesses came up and began talking about the dances.

"I think the boys really like seeing the girls in long dresses, don't you?"

Sailor LeBaron gave her his Vermont deadpan look. "Oh yes. They must be very long or very short."

The hostess stood there looking at him, and then she gave a strange laugh and walked off.

On September 8, 1943, Sailor LeBaron and his buddies celebrated the fall of Italy and the next day their morale officer gave an inspiring talk on how the Fascists were getting licked.

On October 16, LeBaron's brother Bill came through Chicago, returning from home leave from his ship, the cruiser *Wisconsin*, which was in Seattle. The two spent about an hour together, before Bill had to go off to the railroad station to catch his train west.

For Allan LeBaron Chicago continued to be a sort of paradise. On October 3, he went to a dog show. Then he went to a USO show,

This Is the Army. He preferred the dogs. Then he went with his buddy Lieberman to the Masonic Center for a free breakfast. They met some girls who wanted them to go on a scavenger hunt but they were still hungry. So they peeled off and found a USO where they were serving breakfast "with all the milk you could drink." He decided to go back there the next week.

"Some time," he wrote home to his family, "I am going to the Jewish Center with Lieb because he says they feed real well there."

But then on October 21, Sailor LeBaron's life changed sharply. He washed out of the aviation metalsmith school "lack of aptitude and general immaturity" and was transferred to the Naval Receiving Station at Pier 92, New York City. From there he went to Norfolk and then to San Francisco and ended up in Guam, where there was very little milk and he spent the rest of the war dreaming about Chicago, the perfect liberty town for a boy from Vermont who liked to drink a lot of milk.

TWENTY-TWO

Lieutenant Davenport
and God

Some sailors had their talismans, like a rabbit's foot or a lucky coin or even a tattoo, which they swore would keep them from harm, but one heroic sailor of World War II had a much stronger weapon, which he claimed not only kept him from harm, but all the men in his boat. The sailor was Roy M. Davenport, and the weapon was his faith in Christian Science.

Sailor Davenport graduated from the U.S. Naval Academy in the spring of 1933. He served first on the battleship *Texas* but in 1936 was sent to submarine school and served in the *R-2* until the more modern *Cachalot* came to the East Coast for new engines. Among other equipment she was the first submarine to have the Torpedo Data Computer, and Sailor Davenport operated that instrument. In October 1941 Lieutenant Davenport was assigned to new construction at the Mare Island Navy Yard in California and became executive officer of the *Silversides*, which was being built there. He was at Mare Island, then, on December 7, 1941, when the Japanese attacked. By that time he had joined the Christian Science Church and had developed religious beliefs that sustained him throughout the war. By his own words, during that war he was sustained by his religious belief, an indomitable and resourceful crew, and "the magnificently conceived submarine" of the U.S. Navy.

After the *Silversides* was commissioned in the spring of 1943 she went out into the Pacific on her first war patrol, under Lieutenant Commander Creed Burlingame.

On that first patrol, in the spring of 1942, they sank five Japanese ships. On their second patrol they sank four ships and damaged two. On their third patrol they sank two and now in the last month of the year they were going out on their fourth patrol, and hoped to do as well. Davenport was executive officer on all four patrols. He became notable in the submarine fleet not only for his religious belief but for his trombone, which he insisted on playing inside the boat. The important segment of his war history began on December 17, 1942, in Brisbane, Australia, when the *Silversides* and her crew set out on their fourth war patrol. Skipper Burlingame decided they should give a show for the men of the submarine tender USS *Sperry*, who were the only likely spectators to their departure that afternoon. The officers of the *Silversides* dressed in the uniform of Australian soldiers and stood at attention on the deck of the submarine as it pulled away from the tender. Sailor Davenport played "Waltzing Matilda" on his trombone and then segued into "Auld Lang Syne" and "Aloha." They expected applause from the men on the deck of the *Sperry*, but there was dead silence as they pulled out. When next Sailor Davenport saw the executive officer of the ship he asked him what the reaction of the men of the *Sperry* had been to their performance.

"We figured you would all sober up in two or three days," was the reply.

On this patrol, the pharmacist's mate, Tom Moore, showed how adaptable and resourceful submariners are. One of the sailors complained about a bellyache when they were sailing in enemy waters around Rabaul in the Solomons area, deep in Japanese-held territory. The bellyache persisted and "Doc" Moore diagnosed the illness as appendicitis, but there was no chance that they could deliver the seaman to the hospital in time for an operation. There was every chance that the appendix would burst and that the man would die of peritonitis. So "Doc" Moore and the captain agreed that the pharmacist's mate should try an operation. He was a male nurse and had witnessed scores of such procedures, but of course had never done it himself before. So the "Doc" operated. The operating room was the wardroom and the table was the wardroom dining table. Spoons were used as retractors, and the radioman and another sailor assisted, and Executive Officer Davenport held a searchlight that illuminated the scene. The pharmacist's mate had trouble finding the appendix, but finally did, and snipped it off. They used up two cans of ether during the operation and the exec was afraid the boat would blow up from the fumes catching fire and exploding. But the boat did not blow up, although the operation lasted four hours; the patient recovered and in a week was back at his post.

It was nearly two o'clock in the morning when the operation was completed. At about that time the submarine surfaced, and they saw a ship behind them. They soon identified it as a Japanese patrol craft, and it was coming up fast. The executive officer suggested that they fire two torpedoes from the stern tubes, "down the throat" of the submarine. They fired. But one torpedo broached in their own wake and then exploded. This warned the patrol craft and it was able to avoid the second torpedo. The *Silversides* then went deep to avoid depth charges and, sure enough, the patrol boat came over and dropped many depth bombs on her.

The following morning, still deep in Japanese waters, the *Silversides* was spotted by a Japanese plane while making a periscope sweep near the surface, and the plane came to attack before the submarine could dive. The enemy dropped three bombs right on top of the submarine. Every light went out and the emergency lighting switched on. Men were thrown this way and that. The first bomb exploded over the forward torpedo room, the second over the control room, and the third over the engine room. Some men were hit by flying glass as instruments broke. The skipper took the boat deep to avoid further attacks and the executive officer, who had been asleep, came running into the control room in his bare feet. Luckily he did not cut his feet on the glass from the lightbulbs, which was all around the deck.

When they went deep they found that the bow planes had jammed on the hard dive, and diving officer Lieutenant Bob Worthington found it difficult to manage the submarine and keep it from going farther down. Lieutenant Davenport went into the forward control room, stopped and covered his eyes, and said his prayers in front of the men there. Then he walked forward and found the jammed bow planes. He removed a cotter key, threw a lever 180 degrees, and the bow planes responded. The time he had taken to stop to pray had left him time to consider the possibilities of the situation, and he had gone to the heart of the matter. The shear pins in the rigging shaft outside the hull had broken off and the rigging motor continued to run until they had stopped it in the control room. The motor had stopped in a position with the planes rigged in, and the situation looked desperate. But by turning the level 180 degrees, Lieutenant Davenport had activated the auxiliary power for the bow plane.

The patrol went on. On January 6, they attacked a Japanese submarine on the surface and were sure they had sunk it, but got no credit because no one saw it sink. A week later they attacked a tanker and sank it. Then they were depth-charged by a Japanese escort, and that night when they surfaced they found a leak in the Number 5 fuel tank. They ran on the surface for two days and then came upon four Japanese freighters in a convoy, running toward them. It was a clear day and the sea was smooth as glass, very dangerous for a submarine under water, for the scope would leave a telltale trail and the wakes of torpedoes could be spotted easily. So the skipper decided to stay ahead of the ships until dusk and then submerge and attack.

They fired six torpedoes. The sixth one stuck in the tube. Lieutenant Davenport knew that God was protecting his submarine, and that everything would be all right, but he also knew that he had to convince the crew to keep them from panicking. So he lied like a traveling salesman and swore that the torpedo had ejected. He convinced the crewmen and there was no panic. They ran submerged for two hours and then surfaced and evaded the escorts. When they surfaced they found the torpedo, stuck in the tube, and fired it one more time. It went deep, sank to the bottom, and never exploded.

On this patrol the *Silversides* actually sank three ships but was given credit for none, because no one saw the ships sink. Only later, after the war, did Japanese records prove that the ships were actually sunk.

They returned to Pearl Harbor in February 1943. While aboard the *Silversides*, Sailor Davenport was given a submarine of his own to command, the *Haddock*. Since the *Haddock* was then berthed at Midway, with his new executive officer, Lieutenant E. P. Madley,

Skipper Davenport flew to Midway, and within a week he and the *Haddock* had started out on his fifth war patrol.

They moved on the surface as much as possible to their patrol area, traveling at about three-quarters of the 20-knot surface speed in order to conserve fuel. If they could, they should stay on patrol in their assigned area for thirty days. But if they used up their torpe-does, or had some kind of mechanical trouble, they would head home immediately. The point was to conserve oil so that they would come home with 10 percent of their fuel supply left. That was an order from Admiral Charles Lockwood, the commander of subma-rines of the Pacific fleet, since the *Silversides* on that last patrol had used up so much fuel that they arrived home in Pearl Harbor with only five hours of fuel left for one engine.

By the middle of March the *Haddock* was on station, after having turned back to Midway to transfer an appendicitis case so they would not have to repeat the *Silversides* emergency operation. On the night of March 17, they reached their patrol area off Wake Island. They found the Japanese on the alert, with many searchlights working at night and apparently doing a lot of con-struction work on Wake and Wilkes islands. After a few days they moved toward Truk, to patrol the passes that led through the little islets to the Japanese naval base. They saw several aircraft, and once in a while they took a dive to escape detection. On March 22, they tracked a steamer in a convoy but then lost the whole convoy and could not find it again.

A few hours later they were on the surface when they sighted a destroyer and two cruisers. Davenport gave chase on the surface, over the objections of some of the crew, who felt it was too dangerous to be on the surface in the daytime. He cited the Ninety-first Psalm to them: "He that shall dwell in the secret place of the most high shall abide under the shadow of the almighty."

A few hours later they sighted the destroyer about seven miles away. The officer of the deck wanted to sound the diving alarm but Skipper Davenport restrained him. They were in the secret place, and he was sure they would not be seen by the destroyer. "God was with us," said the captain.

They had no success in the Truk area. There were too many patrol planes, too many destroyers, and not many merchant ships to be seen. They moved to the Palau area, and found a large ship of about 11,000 tons with an escort. They tracked the ship and fired several torpedoes and sank the ship. The escort started their way, so they went down to 350 feet. The escort made several runs and dropped many depth charges, and finally they went down to 442 feet. During the attack their conning tower began to break up, and apparently the Japanese found some of the wreckage, for the next day Radio Tokyo broadcast that an escort vessel had sunk an American submarine in this area. Actually, only part of the radar system of the submarine was destroyed, and this could be and was repaired when they came to the surface. They sank another small merchant ship, but that was all, and so on April 5 they moved off Saipan. But the hunting was not much good there either, and they were bothered by the damage to the conning tower so they turned about and went back to Midway and Pearl Harbor. It had not been a very satisfactory patrol: They were credited with sinking one large and one small transport. But they had familiarized the crew with the boat and the new captain, and they were now going to have the damage to the conning tower repaired and go out again.

The *Haddock's* fifth war patrol lasted from June 30, 1943, until August 10 and they were credited with sinking three ships and damaging three others. The most important matter in the patrol was the expenditure of fifteen torpedoes on one convoy with only two hits. At least part of the reason had to be fault in the torpedoes, which was a common complaint of the submariners in those times.

So they were back at Pearl Harbor, then went out on the sixth war patrol, which began in September. This patrol was more successful, and the *Haddock* sank three ships and damaged another. The big difference with the last patrol was that Skipper Davenport decided his crew needed spiritual guidance, so he conducted a weekly church service on Sunday afternoon, and got an attendance of about a third of the ship's company.

TWENTY-THREE

Aleutian Surprise

At the same time the Japanese launched their assault on Midway, they also occupied the islands of Attu and Kiska in the Aleutians chain. The Aleutians plan had been hitched onto the Midway plan by Admiral Yamamoto partly as a selling device. Many high-ranking Navy officers were opposed to the Midway operation, but everybody favored action that would prevent the Americans from launching bombing raids against Japan, and this is how the Aleutians occupation was presented. But from the beginning, when the Midway invasion failed, the Aleutians garrison was untenable. The cost and difficulty of supplying the Attu and Kiska garrisons was enormous; furthermore, it took valuable transports and destroyers just at the time the Japanese were in sore need for the ships in the South Pacific.

To the Americans the Japanese occupation of the Aleutians created a sore like a boil on the neck that the U.S. high command agreed must be eliminated as quickly as possible. All the available forces were rushed to the Aleutians in the summer and fall of 1942, and by the spring of 1943 resources were made available for the American recapture of the territory in the summer, that being the only season of the year in which the weather made even moderately small military operations feasible.

The occupation of Attu was accomplished in May and the Japanese garrison fought to the last, with only a handful of prisoners taken. Japanese airfields and new airfields were quickly put into use to begin the softening up of Kiska, which was expected to be a much tougher nut to crack than Attu. The preinvasion bombing began in June. That month the Eleventh Air Force dropped 262 tons of bombs on the island and lost only two aircraft.

In June the navy established a destroyer blockade of Kiska and in July a naval task group under Rear Admiral Robert C. Giffen began to bombard the island. This group consisted of Bill LeBaron's cruiser, the *Wichita*, and the cruisers the *Louisville, San Francisco*, and *Santa Fe*, plus the destroyers *Hughes, Lansdowne, Morris*, and *Mustin*. The last two vessels were assigned to anti-submarine patrol, because the Japanese were then bringing in supplies by submarine. The other ships were involved in bombardment and chasing ghosts for the most part, so confusing were the shadows and mists of the northern sea. Bill LeBaron was now a storekeeper second class, a rating he had achieved in spite of an innate dislike of naval officers, which broke out from time to time. But for the most part he followed a folk adage, keeping his bowels open and his mouth shut, and more or less stayed out of trouble.

The first bombardment was on July 6. The ships stood off the island and slammed shells into Little Kiska, North Head, Gertrude Cove, and South Head and the Main Camp area. The Japanese had plenty of artillery on the island but not a shot came in return. After twenty-two minutes there was nothing more to shoot at, and the enemy was giving no signs of life, so the bombardment group quit. Besides, the fog was about to close in, which would have made air-spotting impossible. They had used 100 tons of ammunition.

On July 22, Bill LeBaron's *Wichita* and even more ships, including two battleships, bombarded the island. This time one Japanese battery fired back.

Then in August, the Americans were ready for the landings. Because the garrison of Kiska was much larger than that at Attu, 34,500 American and Canadian troops were involved.

The invasion fleet moved toward the island and on the morning of August 15 minesweepers entered the area and cleared the channels to the invasion beaches. Battleships, cruisers, and destroyers bombarded the beaches and the installations again, and by four o'clock 6,500 troops had been landed. There was no contact with the Japanese, so the Americans thought they had withdrawn to prepared positions on high ground back of the beaches as they had finally done at Attu, and there would make a suicide stand.

The night passed; more landings were made on the morning of August 16 and another 3,000 troops went ashore. The warships again bombarded their targets, and again there was no response. The Americans and Canadians suffered a number of casualties but could never come to grips with the enemy, who apparently fired and then disappeared. It was several days before the Americans circulated all across the island, checking every available bit of cover, and found that they had captured two dogs. The Japanese had evacuated the island ten days before. The American casualties were all from "friendly fire," which meant Americans shooting at one another.

Sailor LeBaron knew nothing at all about all this, because after several months, in which the *Wichita* had participated in the assault on Attu, she had gone off on another assignment.

TWENTY-FOUR

One of the Navy's Goats

Sailor Lawrence Flanagan joined the navy and in the summer of 1943 found himself a radioman aboard the *Thomas Jefferson*, part of an amphibious transport division running between Oran and Sicily.

While in North Africa one member of the crew had picked up a goat to add to the ship's family of stray dogs. With the connivance of the officer of the deck, one night he smuggled the goat aboard ship. And so night after night Sailor Flanagan and some others were awakened by the sound of barking dogs and the *baa, baa* of the goat.

It was not long before everyone in the division knew about the goat. Nobody cared until the *Thomas Jefferson* also took aboard as passengers a cargo of Red Cross girls. Then the ship became the sinecure of all eyes, and the other ships' crews could almost be heard muttering across the water. One of the envious ones was Captain Barnett, the squadron commodore.

One day he could stand the tension no longer and sent a visual message to the captain of the *Thomas Jefferson* asking him to fill a requisition for goat's milk and doughnuts. This was a snide reference to the Red Cross girls, who were known as the Doughnut Girls.

The skipper of the *Thomas Jefferson* was upset at having been made the butt of a visual goat joke, and he collared the young ensign whom he suspected of having a hand in getting the goat aboard the ship and assigned him to walk the goat every evening and be sure the goat was happy.

A couple of nights went by, and then one night Sailor Flanagan heard a long drawn out *baaaaaa*, and then silence. The goat was never seen again.

TWENTY-FIVE

The Forgotten Service

In the annals of the navy in World War II most of the tales are told about the war in the Pacific, for that is where the big actions, the carrier battles and cruiser battles and destroyer battles, were fought. But there was just as much hard work and attention to duty on the Atlantic side of the globe, although the sailors involved did not get the acclaim of their counterparts halfway around the world.

One such story is that of the landings at Salerno.

From the outset, as with North Africa and Sicily, the Italian campaign was a joint effort, and joint efforts are not always conducive to the public relations that bring fame.

The American command at Salerno was the Western Naval Task Force under Vice Admiral Henry K. Hewitt. The British would attack in the north and the Americans in the south, this naval command under Rear Admiral John Hall. The American troops involved were Lieutenant General Mark Clark's U.S. Fifth Army. But while the Fifth Army and Mark Clark are well known, Admiral Hewitt and the Western Naval Task Force have been relegated to the back pages of history. Still they were very much a part of the Sailor's War; one of the unsung characters was a regular-navy officer, Commander Alfred H. Richards, whose command was one of the most dangerous and yet unpublicized in the navy, a group of minesweepers. Before the troops could be landed the landing area had to be examined for enemy weapons, and the mines, if any, had to be swept out of the channels and away from the landing beaches. So Commander Richards' group would go into action early.

It consisted of two units, one commanded by Richards himself in his flagship, the *Pilot*, with the *Sustain*, *Seer*, *Speed*, *Prevail*, *Steady*, *Skill*, and *Symbol*. The second unit, under command of Commander William K. Messmer, consisted of the flagship *Strive* and of smaller craft, the YMS *27, 55, 62, 65, 69, 82, 83, 207, 208, 226,* and *227.* The two units would prepare the way for the American Sixth Corps on four beaches south of the Sele River near Pesto, a village 22 miles south of Salerno.

The navy was going to have some special problems with this landing. In the first place, it was a long way from the Sicilian airfields, and so the land-based air support for the Salerno landings was going to have to be limited. Most of it would come from one carrier and four auxiliary carriers under British command. The second problem was that there was to be no preliminary bombardment by warships, because the army valued the element of surprise more. The navy men, from Admiral Hewitt down, had a tendency to think the generals were out of their minds. The preliminary bombardment of the whole area, the excellent German reconnaissance, the choice of a phase of the moon in which the land would light up, all militated against successful surprise. What the admirals had to conclude was that the generals did not really appreciate the value of a good solid naval bombardment. They had voted against having it, so the navy would have to work without it.

One of Commander Richards' greatest problems was that his sweeper force had not been able to train with the task force since exercises, because they had been needed elsewhere at the time. So they were going to have to "fly blind" when the landings came, and they expected some serious mining by the Germans to be involved.

D-Day for the landings was September 9. On D minus 1 the minesweepers reached the Salerno area and at 10:30 in the evening Commander Richards' flagship *Pilot* picked up the signal from the beacon submarine *Shakespeare* that told him his Unit One was on course. He gave the order to begin the sweep of the approach lane to the southern transport area. In about two hours the sweep had been completed without incident.

The preliminaries of the invasion were already under way. Twenty-four miles west of the Isle of Capri the diversion group of the invasion under Captain Charles Andrews and the picket group under Commander Stanley Barnes had set out to capture the little island of Ventotene. There were sixteen PT boats in the picket group, their major task was to patrol the straits between Capri and Ischia and turn back any small craft that might get in the way of the invasion, innocent though they might be. In the meantime the diversion group, which consisted of American and British small craft, proceeded to Ventotene and demanded by loudspeaker the surrender of that garrison. This happened at just about the time the minesweepers finished their job. The Italian troops on the island surrendered. But, unknown to the Allies, the Germans had a garrison on the island too, and after destroying everything they could they retreated from the coast and took refuge in the hills, setting up a defensive position. The Allied troops tried to locate the German hideout but could not. About fifty American Rangers went ashore and began to search for the Germans, but before H Hour of D-Day they had surrendered and then the naval forces withdrew and left the island to the army.

At this point Commander Richards' sweepers had to get to work to sweep north and south of the Sele River. Only one minefield had been located, parallel to the coast, about 3,000 yards in front of the southern attack area. But this was just by report and the reports were very unreliable. What was known was that the whole Gulf of Salerno could be mined as far as six miles out to sea. There were four major areas that had to be thoroughly swept. So the sweeping began. The problem was that no one knew anything about the minefields, if there were any. They did not know the depth or the possibility of the presence of antisweep devices. So they set the sweep wires at 60 feet.

On the evening of September 8, the sweeping was being conducted, and twelve miles astern of the sweepers was the Oran convoy.

Everything went well until 9:30 that night, when gunfire was heard. By this time the Oran convoy was about ten miles astern of the sweepers. The fright turned out to be nothing important, and at 10:30 the sweep was completed with only one problem. The sweeper *Skill* lost both her starboard and port wires. So the minesweepers slowed from 9 knots to 7.5 and moved into the north channel, taking frequent fixes on the submarine *Shakespeare*, to keep on course and clear the channel.

The minesweeper *Prevail* also lost both wires, leaving six minesweepers to finish the job. The pressure was building, for they could see the first transports of the Oran convoy entering the transport area.

Soon—too soon—the Oran convoy also arrived. And then more sweepers began to lose equipment. Just after midnight the *Speed* related she had lost her starboard gear. At 2:15 the *Steady* lost both wires. Then *Speed* lost her port wire and at 2:20 the *Symbol* crossed over the *Seer*'s wires and both ships dropped out of the formation. This left only the flagship *Pilot* with her port wire and the *Sustain*, with both wires, to finish the operation for which eight ships had been assigned.

This was a real problem, for the channel they could assure the ships was too narrow. Unless the fire-support ships followed immediately and were very careful, they might hit a mine. So Commander Richards decided to wait to finish the job until the repairs could be made to the *Prevail*.

Meanwhile, the second group of smaller sweepers was sweeping the southern channel. They picked up fourteen mines, cutting or exploding them, and set three adrift. Operations were then suspended because of small-boat traffic.

By this time the traffic was getting heavy as several convoys converged on Salerno Bay. From midnight on, frequent flashes of gunfire indicated engagement with the enemy. That evening also the ships were subjected to intermittent air attacks by German planes. A lone low-flying plane was shot down and then another, and around midnight the German planes began dropping flares that illuminated the whole invasion area.

After the beginning of the assault, Commander Richards continued to be very busy. By 5:52 that morning the sweeping of the northern channel was finished to the 39-fathom curve, and ships were moving into the channel under fire from enemy aircraft. At 10:45 the *Pilot* led the cruiser *Philadelphia* through the minefield to the fire-support area. It was 1:30 in the afternoon before the southern channel was completely swept to the 10-fathom curve.

D plus 1 began with a German bombing attack. Then at 10:30 in the morning there was more bombing, which lasted for a while. At three in the afternoon Admiral Hewitt held a conference to see how things were going. The navy decided that from its point of view things were going very well.

By the end of D plus 1 all the areas to be swept had been covered. But on the shore the military situation was not as satisfactory. The Germans were proving very tough.

On September 11, D plus 2, the destroyer *Rowan* was lost, victim of a torpedo from an E-boat. Apparently the torpedo hit her magazine, because she went down in forty seconds.

The landing craft began to pull away from the transports just after midnight and the landings began. Destroyers were supposed to accompany the boats and give them fire support, but Commander Richards announced that the swept channel was not safe for large vessels until daylight (because of the foul ups with lost equipment), and the destroyers backed off.

One of the difficulties that became apparent as the invasion developed was that the problems faced by the minesweepers had prevented them from clearing a channel wide enough for the cruisers to maneuver freely. They were wanted to deliver fire to wipe out a number of 88mm gun positions but found it hard to comply in the restricted waters.

And the Germans had laid land mines from the water's edge in—for a hundred yards or so in several areas. Within four hours it was apparent that the Germans were not at all surprised, that they had improved their defenses in the last few weeks, and that this was going to be a very serious fight. The army, which had vetoed the prelanding bombardment now began calling for fire support. Commander Richards saw that he was going to have to do something to widen the area of operations for the warships, so he resumed sweeping operations, although the great number of landing craft buzzing to and fro got in the way of the sweeping.

At 3:50 the *Prevail* was ready to work again, having rigged her port wire. She joined the *Pilot* and the *Sustain*. They navigated exclusively by radar since mist had begun to obscure the visibility.

By six o'clock Commander Richards reported that a channel 600 yards wide had been swept from seaward to the 20-fathom curve. The destroyers could now move in and deliver fire support. Had it not been for this and the prompt arrival of the destroyers, the whole beachhead might have been in jeopardy. The first three waves landed without serious opposition, but the fourth wave, mostly tanks, ran into serious enemy opposition, particularly by artillery, which knocked out several LSTs. Several battalions of 105mm howitzers got ashore around six o'clock. Luckily they did, because as the chief of staff of the Sixteenth Infantry later said that if they had not gotten through, "it is probable that the beachhead would have been destroyed." The Germans launched a counterattack that morning, supported all along the line by their 88mm guns and by nine 150mm guns north of Battipaglia and half a dozen 105mm anti-aircraft guns at Altavilla, and six more at Roccadspide.

So no matter what the army had said before, it now realized the need for support by the warships, and Commander Richards' re-sweeping of the area under fire was giving it to the navy. Until this point the only fire support given the landing, at the army's insistence, was a salvo of thirty-four rockets fired by a scout boat immediately before the landings. Now the presence of mine-fields and floating mines was impeding the invasion.

At six o'clock the ship *Bristol* asked to be let into the deployment line. The *Pilot* went out to meet the vessel and escort it in and continued to sweep. The *Pilot* exploded two mines, the second of which carried away her only sweep wire. She cut two mines adrift. The *Sustain* exploded one mine and cut one and the *Prevail* cut two mines loose. Altogether they destroyed thirteen mines on this foray, six of them exploding when cut and seven destroyed by gunfire on the surface.

Commander Richards was organizing a formation to sweep ahead of the *Bristol* when he was ordered to send all his sweepers to the southern channel. So most of the sweepers were sent to join the second section, while the *Pilot* took the *Bristol* through the north channel, although she had no operational sweeping gear.

Almost as soon as the *Bristol* was through the channel, a similar request was received from the ship *Woolsey*. This was done too, in spite of floating mines and the difficulties of keeping track of the floating buoys that were drifting south.

By this time the mist had become so heavy that it obscured the view of the mountains, which the sweeper men were using as navigational aids. The *Pilot* very narrowly missed a mine that was only a few feet underwater. A lookout spotted it in time for the quartermaster to make a 60-degree turn to the right and at the same time warn the *Woolsey*.

At 10:45 Admiral Davidson in the *Philadelphia* announced that he was coming in. Commander Richards was upset by the narrow escape of the *Woolsey* in the encounter with the mine and suggested that they give him an hour to stream gear and then he would come out and get the *Philadelphia*. But the army said it now required maximum assistance from the navy ships. The urgency was such that the *Pilot* was ordered to proceed to bring in the *Philadelphia* without any gear, without any protection against mines except for the eyes of the men involved. At this point the haze lifted and Commander Richards was able to get a fix on the land to supplement the radar. So the *Philadelphia* and two destroyers were led through the minefield safely at around noon.

During the afternoon the *Philadelphia* opened fire on a concentration of thirty-five German tanks, and at the end of the firing reported the destruction of 20 percent of them.

So the day passed with one crisis following another for the minesweepers. At eight o'clock that night they were ordered to begin operations in the fire-support area adjoining the transport area to the north. Commander Richards formed up his unit into three groups and set up three lanes parallel to the coast. Twelve of his sweepers were employed and the rest were sent to sea, so they could get out of the way and the crews could get some rest. All the vessels of the sweeper group had been operating at full capacity for thirty hours, and in the American zone alone had swept an area six miles long and five miles wide.

Admiral Hall wanted to move his transports to the line of departure and asked for a report on the sweeping. Commander Richards reported that he had created a swept channel in the southern area 1,000 yards wide, extending from one mile inshore of the transport area to the 10-fathom line, but that every sweep they had made had picked up at least two mines. He did not think the transports should be moved for several hours.

The admiral replied that he now required an anchorage at the land end of the southern channel. None existed. Commander Richards took the *Pilot*, *Skill*, YMS *62*, and YMS *207* and made an exploratory search in the area. They got rid of some mines and by seven o'clock that night could report that the area was free of mines.

In the south there was more trouble from mines and bombs. The tug *Nauset* was hit by several bombs and flames shot up over her boat deck for a distance of fifty feet. The power failed. The ship began to take a list. The order to abandon ship was given, and she was abandoned with heavy casualties. The tug *Intent* tried to take the *Nauset* in tow, but the *Nauset* hit a mine, broke in half, and sank.

Then the LST *386* started down the swept channel and moved as swiftly as possible, under attack from shore batteries. She came across a floating mine, which was avoided by a hard turn of the rudder, but a section of the causeway she was bringing in brushed against the mine and set it off. The starboard engine went out, and she began to flood. She was beached and emergency repairs were made but she could not land her personnel and equipment and she was under fire from a battery of eight 88mm guns on the shore.

Finally the personnel transferred to other ships in the area, and the *386* made it back to Bizerte for repairs.

So at the end of the second day the beachhead was secured and the landings had been successful, although much more difficult than the army had expected. At the moment the Allied troops were hardly more than holding the bridgeheads against very serious German opposition. At the end of D plus 1 the navy forces had accomplished their principal mission. They had established the Allied Fifth Army on the beaches and had suffered very few casualties in doing so. There would be more air attacks, and some ship casualties from the heavy German resistance. The *Philadelphia* was damaged by a glider bomb that exploded just off her beam, blew a man overboard, and caused considerable damage. The *Savannah* was hit on the Number 3 turret by another glider bomb. It killed the entire crew of the turret and exploded in the magazine. It was a 1400-

kilogram bomb, the largest to have hit an American vessel and the first radio-controlled bomb to do so. The *Savannah* was damaged so seriously she had to be withdrawn from the operation.

During all this activity on D plus 1 the minesweepers continued to operate, on the principle that German planes might have dropped mines in the water during the night.

Every day the situation of the Allies improved, and by September 18 they were well ashore and moving. Naples surrendered on October 1, and the Allied troops continued to move. The Salerno invasion had been successful, in spite of some rough spots, some misunderstandings between army and navy commands, and some very heavy German resistance. One of the basic reasons for the success of the operation was the unsung hard work of the men of the minesweepers.

TWENTY-SIX

One for the Trombone

On his sixth war patrol, Lieutenant Commander Roy Davenport became a sort of unofficial chaplain as well as submarine commander. He wrote a note to the crew telling them what wonderful peace of mind he had gotten from his daily study of the Bible. Since the submarine was too small to have a chaplain, he offered to conduct a regular religious service on Sundays. Twelve men of the crew of some 70 signed up, and so he began. Soon it grew to an average attendance of 25 men, who said prayers and sang; the commander accompanied them on his trombone.

While the *Haddock* was at Midway undergoing a refit, Skipper Davenport set up shop in a building on Sundays and held services. Soon there were more than 100 men coming to his informal church. He also had a chance to show the power of his particular belief, Christian Science. The ship's cook was hit on the head by the hatch of the icebox, and a deep gash was cut in his forehead. Others called it an accident, but Skipper Davenport's religion said there are no accidents, that he was spiritual and perfect. The skipper held the cook's hand as the pharmacist took stitches in his head. Ten days later the cook came to the skipper's cabin and they took off the bandage. The sutures were lying in the bandage. The wound was perfectly healed and there were no scars.

Such wonders occupied the minds of the men of the *Haddock* while they waited to go to sea again. One day Captain Styer, the squadron commander of submarines, asked Davenport how he squared his strong religious feelings with his competence in killing Japanese.

"Captain," said the skipper of the *Haddock*, "it is because I am religious that I am able to do this. I know it is definitely right with God for us to win against these Japanese who are trying to destroy our principles of life and liberty. If it is right and just to win, then we will know what to do and how to do it. I take my promise of safety from the Ninety-first Psalm."

It was a wonder unknown to Skipper Davenport that another religious naval officer, Vice Admiral Matome Ugaki of the imperial Japanese navy had almost similar views then, but as the war turned more and more against the Japanese, the admiral became less and less sure that God was on his side, while Skipper Davenport became more and more sure.

Fortified by his belief, the skipper took the boat out again on October 20, 1943, on the submarine's seventh war patrol. Their assigned area was again the Truk–Saipan sea routes. On November 1, they sank two ships, and leaving the survivors in the water unmolested, they headed off to find other game. They found big game, and on November 2 sank a destroyer and were then hunted by two other destroyers of what was obviously a hunter-killer group of antisubmarine-warfare specialists. But they got clean away. Two days later they sank two more ships.

Skipper Davenport's church service became ever more popular as they sank ever more ships. He and the crew agreed that when they got back to base they would ask for an enlarged dinette, where they could hold church services for more people. Davenport sensed that the interest in religion was healthy for the crew, and that there was an almost total lack of fear on the *Haddock*. "To dwell in Truth and Love is to dwell in the calmness, poise and fearlessness of righteous thoughts. The men were gaining new confidence and had almost complete lack of fear."

So the happy patrol continued until its end. Then Commander Davenport asked for transfer to a new construction and to go on a lecture tour. Both recommendations were passed along by Admiral Charles P. Lockwood, the commander of the Pacific Fleet submarine force, and at the end the year Commander Davenport was ordered to Mare Island Navy Yard to fit out the new submarine *Trepang* and take her to sea.

TWENTY-SEVEN

Mr. Kaiser's Coffins

This is the story of the USS *Natoma Bay*—Escort Carrier 62 as she was known to the navy—one of the "Kaiser Coffins," as she was called by the knowledgable among her crew who took a look at her compartmentalization and began to wonder what would happen if she were ever hit by a torpedo. The answer was discovered in the invasion of the Gilbert Islands in November 1943, when the *Liscombe Bay* was torpedoed and went down with the loss of more than 600 lives, two-thirds of the crew, the heavy loss being primarily caused by the construction of the ship—without adequate transverse bulkheads to slow flooding.

When the Pacific war began, Japanese naval air power was twice that of the United States, and although at the battle of Midway the odds were shortened when the Japanese lost four major carriers, they still had more airpower than the Americans. The answer, beginning on December 7, 1941, was a crash program and a major carrier-building program in the United States. The first effort was to convert the hulls of a number cruisers to become light carriers. But almost immediately a greater need was seen, primarily in the Atlantic, where the German U-boats were chewing up British and American convoys. The British invented the escort carrier and began using these in 1941, first on the Mediterraanean run. When the Americans entered the war they improved on the concept, and Henry Kaiser, in particular, found methods of welding steel plates and thus cutting the time enormously in the building of seaworthy hulls.

The escort carriers that began to come off the ways in a matter of weeks were not the most battleworthy of ships, but they did the job they were supposed to do, manned by brave men who were willing to accept the odds. As the story of the *Natoma Bay* and its sailors shows, these little carriers did much to win the war for the Allies.

The hull of the *Natoma Bay* ship was laid down in January 1943, at the Kaiser shipyard in Vancouver, Washington. By the time Alan LeBaron joined the navy and started aircraft metalsmith school at Chicago, this little carrier was about half-built. She was launched in July and commissioned on October 14, 1943.

She was 512 feet long, 65 feet in the beam, displaced 7,800 tons, could make 22 knots, and carried a crew of 860 officers and men. She had one five-inch gun and 36 antiaircraft guns, but her reason for being was to carry twenty-eight aircraft and be useful with many tasks, from convoy escort duty to air support of land forces fighting in the Pacific islands, and delivery of aircraft and ammunition to the big carriers of the fleet. Her first skipper was Captain Harold L. Meadow.

Late in November the ship was in San Diego, and VC-63, the squadron that would be assigned to the carrier, came aboard as a part of its training program for a short stint, and then the carrier took on her first useful job, which was to ferry aircraft from the West Coast to Hawaii. Then in January 1944 she took aboard VC-63, which had been practicing its techniques and training steadily since May 1943. The pilots had improved their skills since the short cruise on the *Natoma Bay* and now trained for duty on escort carriers, which were too small to have the usual three squadrons of fighters, dive bombers, and torpedo bombers, and instead had one composite squadron under one commander, Lieutenant Commander S. S. Searcy, Jr.

There was a bit of embarrassment in the training program, with a number of crashes on the qualification and shakedown cruise in November. Commander Searcy went into the drink off the bow of the ship during a takeoff. He was rescued by a destroyer escort, unhurt except for his reputation. Many of the less experienced pilots also had expensive baths in the Pacific, and the number of blown tires, barrier crashes, and plunges into the island was impressive. But the difference between the American and Japanese naval air forces was that the Americans were willing to take the risks and pay the price to build an air force quickly, while the Japanese stuck with their safe-and-sure training program that produced far fewer accidents but also far fewer pilots and aircrewmen.

The *Natoma Bay* and her air squadron left San Diego on January 4, 1944, for Pearl Harbor. There were a few weeks of passage and training and then at the end of the month the ship left for the war in the Pacific. They were part of the task force assembled for the attack on the Marshall Islands and their assignment was Majuro. The traveling group joined by the *Natoma Bay* consisted of the *Natoma Bay*, the escort carrier *Nassau*, the cruiser *Portland*, ten troop ships and freighters, two minesweepers, and many destroyers. Before the invasion her planes were flying combat air patrol and antisubmarine patrol.

On January 30 and 31, the planes of the *Natoma Bay* attacked the Marshalls. Several planes were damaged in operational accidents, including one fighter that stood on its nose at the end of the flight deck, and two torpedo bombers were shot up when they bombed an airfield at Taroa. Both of them landed safely. Operations continued on February 1 and 2, and on the latter night the carrier entered Majuro Lagoon and anchored—the first American carrier to anchor in a captured harbor.

On February 3, the crew had some excitement when they saw the battleships *Washington* and *Indiana* come into harbor after colliding. The Washington had lost 60 feet of her bow. The carrier fueled from the oiler *Pecos*, and the men of the *Natoma Bay* had a swimming party over the side.

But on February 4, it was back to the war, and the ship sailed for antisubmarine patrol and combat air patrol around the atoll. For several days they alternated with the *Nassau* in and out of port, flying combat air patrol and antisubmarine patrol one day and relaxing the next.

On February 7, the squadron of the *Natoma Bay* suffered its first combat loss. A TBM piloted by Ensign R. I. Goranson with AOM3 c E. R. Bailey and ARM 3/c E. B. Barron aboard was lost while on antisubmarine patrol around Majuro. No one knew what had happened. Had they encountered bad weather and gone down? Had they been shot down by the Japanese? The answer was not found, and after a search they were officially declared missing in action.

On February 8 the planes of the *Natoma Bay* were patrolling around Wotje and Taroa islands and coming under heavy antiaircraft fire as they did so but on February 11 they returned to Majuro.

On February 12, four officers and one enlisted man went aboard the fleet carrier *Intrepid* to pick up some spare parts. Before they could get off the ship, it sailed, and they went on a mission to Truk. In the course of the action the *Intrepid* caught a torpedo and had to return to Pearl Harbor. The four men from the *Natoma Bay* then were flown to Espiritu Santo, where they stopped and waited for their ship to appear. They had spent a month and had traveled 8,000 miles and did not have the spare parts.

For several days, the planes of the *Natoma Bay* were busy attacking the Japanese on Taroa and nearby islands. The pilots flew combat air patrol and antisubmarine patrol and made some raids on the Japanese-held islands and did some spotting for the warships that shelled the islands. Aerial photographers also kept track of the Japanese repairs of the airfields on these islands. Wotje, which was a major Japanese air base, got much of attention. They found two Japanese boats using palm leaves to camouflage themselves and sank them by strafing. Three Japanese jumped off one of the sinking boats. Seven planes were hit by antiaircraft fire of Wotje on February 18. The runways were put out of commission by bombing and strafing, but the next day the Japanese had them repaired and working again. For several days the Seabees had been hard at work at Majuro putting the air strip there into shape for American use, and had lengthened the runway to 6,000 feet. Planes from the *Natoma Bay* landed there on February 19.

The *Nassau* broke a turbine and had to head back for Pearl Harbor and repairs, so the *Natoma Bay* took on her spare parts and planes and got rid of her wreckage.

On February 24, there was a boxing and wrestling show aboard the *Natoma Bay*, followed by a short beer party and a movie. On

March 2, there was a similar party aboard the new carrier *Enterprise*. The big carriers were in the harbor, preparing for further operations and there was a good deal of camaraderie, somewhat marred by the habit of the big carriers to requisition the best aircraft from the escort carriers and give them their older models in return.

On March 7, the *Natoma Bay* and the *Manila Bay* with three destroyers were heading for Espiritu Santo. They arrived on March 12, at the same time that the *Enterprise* task force arrived, but the small carriers anchored in North Bay and the large force in South Bay.

On March 15, the *Natoma Bay* joined Task Force 37 for air strikes against Kavieng on New Ireland and was involved with support of Southwest Pacific operations and South Pacific operations in the isolation of Rabaul and the building of an airfield at Emirau Island.

March 20 was D-day for the Kavieng operation. Four battleships and twelve destroyers shelled Kavieng, while the planes of the *Natoma Bay* spotted for them. Lieutenant J. H. Dinneen became the first in the task force to shoot down a Japanese fighter plane. That day the ship had submarine contacts all day long and at least one torpedo was fired at the *Natoma Bay*, but an emergency turn ordered by the bridge made the torpedo go astern of the ship. That day the marines also landed on Emirau Island as a part of putting the ring around Rabaul.

On March 22, and 23, the antisubmarine patrol was having some results. One plane spotted a submarine, but it crash-dived before the plane could get in range. The next day a torpedo bomber dropped depth charges on another submarine and the crew thought they had scored a kill.

On March 25, a submarine was found 500 yards from the *Natoma Bay* and a destroyer dropped a dozen depth charges. There were several other submarine contacts during the day but no confirmed sinkings.

On March 27, the *Natoma Bay* picked up a convoy at Buka Passage, headed for Emirau, where the Seabees were to build another air base. They ran rings around the slow convoy, delivered it on March 30, and headed back for Guadalcanal escorting an LST and LCI. They delivered these vessels on April 1 and rejoined the

Manila Bay, and went in to Tulagi, where there was mail for them. The pilots got off the ship for eight days. Even if the entertainment facilities of the base left a great deal to be desired, it was good for the sailors to have their feet on dry land for a change.

For the next two weeks the *Natoma Bay* and the *Manila Bay* escorted convoys back and forth to Emirau Island.

The air squadron had some losses. Ensign E. H. Lange was lost in a storm, in which every pilot had to do what he could to save himself. Lieutenant J. H. Dinneen landed at Emirau and flipped his plane on its back. He was injured. Ensign L. D. Venable landed in the water alongside a crash boat in Emirau harbor. Only Ensign H. V. Jamieson landed safely aboard.

It was hard duty. The planes were aloft every hour of every day flying escort for convoys from Guadalcanal.

By April 19 the carrier force had swelled, with the joining up of the *Corregidor, Coral Sea, Sangamon, Chenango, Swannee,* and *Santee* and fourteen destroyers. It was now a formidable fighting force, eight escort carriers and fourteen destroyers. They were going to join up with the Seventh Amphibious Force, which included the LST *458*, to land those troops at Aitape and Hollandia.

On April 22, the pilots and air crews were up at 4:00 A.M. and fifteen minutes later were eating breakfast. At 4:45 they were called to flight quarters and half an hour later the launching of the air strike began. It involved twelve fighters from the *Natoma Bay* and ten torpedo bombers which took off at dawn and hit the airfields and beaches at Tadje, New Guinea, along with the planes of the *Manila Bay* and the *Coral Sea*. The *Coral Sea* lost two fighters and the *Manila Bay* one torpedo bomber, but the *Natoma Bay* planes all returned—one of them spectacularly. Lieutenant (jg) H. L. Coster made a perfect night landing on the carrier in 15 knots of wind, in a blinding rainstorm with all the ship's lights out.

Next day a dozen fighters and the torpedo bombers again sallied at dawn and hit the same targets.

For a week they stayed in the area, patrolling and fighting. On April 26, the big carriers ran into trouble in the north and the

Natoma Bay sent fighters to help; they found ten Japanese torpedo planes attacking and helped drive them off.

But the ship was having engine trouble and needed some work in a dockyard, so on April 27 they headed for Seeadler Harbor. A sailor fell overboard, and they stopped and picked him up. On April 29 theirs was the only carrier left in Seeadler Harbor. No shore leave was permitted because there were still 1,800 Japanese on the island and the fighting was still going on. It was dangerous just being in the harbor, they discovered. One officer on another ship was killed by a sniper from the shore.

By this time it was decided that the job on the engines was too big for local authority to handle and that the services of specialists and a big facility were needed. The *Natoma Bay* should go back to Pearl Harbor for repair. On May 7, it left with the *Manila Bay* and three destroyers. They headed east through heavy weather. On May 15, when they were flying antisubmarine patrol and the ship was taking water over the flight deck, the wind was so strong it pulled the tailhook out of a landing torpedo bomber, and the plane went through the barrier, wrecking two planes. But by May 18, when they reached Pearl Harbor the weather was again fine, and they flew off the squadron to the naval air station at Kaneohe on the north shore of Oahu.

TWENTY-EIGHT

Waiting for an Airfield

After the *Natoma Bay* had her engines repaired at Pearl Harbor in the spring of 1944 she was scheduled to take part in the operations against the Marianas. The escort carriers would be used to protect the troops landed on the island of Saipan, which would leave the big carriers free to go out and fight the Japanese fleet. But not only would the *Natoma Bay* fight the battles of the air off Saipan, she was also elected to carry thirty-seven P-47s of the army air force Nineteenth Fighter Squadron. They would be landed in the Marianas just as soon as possible so that the troops ashore would have land-based air support.

The *Natoma Bay* found smooth sailing on her way to battle. The big news of the week she sailed was the report of the invasion of Europe, which began on June 6 on Normandy beachheads.

They arrived at Eniwetok. There was still plenty evidence of the fighting that had taken place here, but the Marshalls were now part of the American base system. The carrier left Eniwetok on June 16, bound for Saipan, and was ordered to retire westward and wait until the battle of the Philippine Sea, between the American and Japanese major carrier fleets, was decided. But on June 18, the Japanese recaptured the airfields on which the *Natoma Bay*'s P-47 fighters were supposed to land, and that afternoon ships off the beachhead came under heavy attack. The *Fanshaw Bay* shot down five Japanese planes, but was hit by a bomb that afternoon. The next day, the *Natoma Bay* was thirty miles off Saipan. That morning the Japanese had air superiority in the area, because the big carriers had gone to fight the Japanese main fleet, and the freighters of the invasion force were coming under attack from the air once again. On the twentieth and twenty-first the *Natoma Bay* was still confounded by the disruption of the American plan. There was no place for the P-47 army fighters to land and so they had to stay aboard the carrier. It was June 22 before the marines captured Aslito airfield and the Seabees got it in shape in a hurry to take some of the army fighter planes. At 7:30 that morning the *Natoma Bay* catapulted off twenty-five fighters, which left a dozen to be catapulted off the next day.

On June 23, the *Natoma Bay* got rid of the rest of the army fighters but came under attack from Japanese Zero fighter planes rigged up to carry bombs. The little carrier was the center of the bombing raid, and there were many near misses although not hits. She headed back to Eniwetok that afternoon and arrived on June 29. That night many Japanese planes attacked Eniwetok, but a number of them were shot down by the new P-61 night fighters.

July 4 the *Natoma Bay* picked up a load of wounded from Saipan and one Japanese prisoner of war—Seaman Ogashi, who had been the rear gunner in a Betty bomber and the only survivor of a plane shot down off Saipan. He spent seventeen days in the water before being picked up by an American destroyer.

Ogashi told the air intelligence officers his story and that he did not intend to return to Japan, because he had been disgraced by being taken prisoner, and if he went home his family would give him a knife with which to commit suicide.

The *Natoma Bay* was taking him to Pearl Harbor, and soon she headed out with the *Manila Bay*. On July 8, they were in Pearl Harbor unloading the wounded and taking on passengers for the American mainland. They were going home for a "blow!"

But it was not destined to be a long one. They unloaded wounded and passengers, and fifteen-day leaves began. Then early in August, they unloaded Captain Meadows, who had not been a popular skipper, and took on Captain Albert K. Morehouse. About 30 percent of the crew was transferred out; they got a new air officer and a new engineering officer and a new air squadron, VC-81.

This meant the ship had to take a bit of time for breaking in the new crew, so on August 22 she went out of San Diego for a trial run and operations and gunnery practice.

On August 24, the *Natoma Bay* left for Pearl Harbor, carrying sixteen B–25s and a new addition. She was now the flagship of Carrier Division 24, and Rear Admiral Felix Stump and his staff were living in admiral country, with their own bridge and their own ways. There was no squadron aboard; the carrier would pick up the new squadron at Pearl Harbor.

The weather got heavy, and most of the passengers and most of the crew got seasick, but by August 31 they had recovered enough for gunnery practice, and on September 5 the new squadron flew aboard. There was only one barrier crash that day. But on September 7, when they were out practicing, they held qualification landings and there were three barrier crashes. Next day, they were giving some practice to Air Group 100 when an F6F went into the catwalk, making the men of VC-81 feel a bit better when they saw the "big boys" doing it too.

The *Natoma Bay* now had a new responsibility as flagship, and this meant she must be a ship in fighting trim. On September 10, they were at Ford Island, getting ready for the admiral's inspection, and on the thirteenth it came off very successfully. Everybody was pleased, and two days later a happy ship shoved off for the wars again. The scuttlebutt said it would be Yap. They would be traveling with the *Manila Bay*, forty transports and landing craft, and a flock of destroyers.

But by September 28, after they had come to Eniwetok and gone again, the scuttlebutt changed and said they would be going to the Philippines for a really big operation. The ship sailed for Seeadler Harbor in the Admiralty Islands, and VC-81 conducted training exercises en route. It was an exciting trip. A destroyer rammed a hole in the side of the carrier while transferring mail, and a fighter spun in while trying a landing and the pilot was lost.

On October 12, the *Natoma Bay* left Seeadler Harbor as part of an escort carrier force of twelve ships, sailing with eight battleships, four cruisers, and forty destroyers of the Seventh Fleet. General

MacArthur was aboard the *Nashville*. They were taking him back to the Philippines.

The task force sailed through bad weather. Flight operations were scheduled for October 17 but were canceled when the force ran into a typhoon with wind up to 70 knots. That day the task force sent landing troops to two small islands that controlled the entrance to Leyte Gulf and they captured the islands, also alerting the Japanese to the invasion. Chief Photographer's Mate Robert Johnson flew with the planes to take photos. One of the group's destroyers was sunk in the action.

On October 18, the eighteen escort carriers of the Seventh Fleet split into three divisions. Admiral Stump's division had six carriers and six destroyers. The planes of the *Natoma Bay* attacked the Leyte airfields and took photographs.

The next day air operations continued and one fighter was lost. Lieutenant Hunter's plane suddenly went into a spin from an altitude of 500 feet and crashed and burst into flames in the water. A TBM had its flaps shot out and so could not use them for landing aboard the carrier. It lost its tailhook. That morning the carrier's Combat Air Patrol (CAP) intercepted eleven Betty bombers and twelve fighters and engaged them, shooting down several and driving the others off.

On October 20, the high level of air action continued. The *Santee* had two near misses from bombs and shot down one of six attacking planes. The *Natoma Bay* fighters shot down a two-engined bomber forty miles out, and the *Sangamon* was hit by a 250-pound bomb. All the carriers were supporting the Leyte landings that day, in which 125,000 troops were put ashore and the bridgeheads were established in the northern and southern sectors of Leyte Island. For the next four days the escort carriers flew constant missions, as ordered, against antiaircraft batteries, bridges, artillery batteries, armored vehicles, and dugouts. A mission was flown to attack Japanese airfields on Cebu, and six fighters from the *Sangamon* were shot down in this action.

The men of the *Natoma Bay* were very excited because they learned that most of the Japanese fleet was headed out to fight, and that while they were coming a cruiser was sunk, a battleship had been badly damaged, and a carrier was hit. The fact was that the battleship *Musashi* was sunk, and so were two cruisers and another was badly damaged, but no carriers were found and none were hit that day.

The morning of October 25, 1944 was supposed to be another day of busy air operations of the same sort. The instructions were to load for a direct support operation. Then suddenly in came a directive that ordered four torpedo planes to be loaded with torpedoes and to stand by. This was something different.

TWENTY-NINE

MacArthur's Seabees

Oh, 35 days at Camp Peary,
Five weeks of a peace wrecking hell.
I can't say I'm sorry we left there.
I'm ready to cruise for a spell.

We lived like hogs in a mudhole,
In a two-by-four hut made of tin.
They said 'twas the rain made it muddy,
But 'twas only the tide coming in.

I'm packing my bags for to travel,
I'm washing the mud from my face.
I don't give a damn where they send me.
As long as it's some other place.

Send me to the front in the morning,
Where the Axis may turn on the heat.
If the only way back is through Peary,
Don't worry, I'll never retreat.
        —Song of Camp Peary

William T. Casey was a patriotic young man, but because he was color-blind he had been rejected for military service in 1942. It seemed that while other young men went bravely forth to do heroic deeds for their country, he was going to have to sit the war out on the sidelines. But then along came the Seabees, because the navy's need for men who could build roads and runways under fire was very great, and so William Casey left New England and one hot morning in July 1943 got off a train at Williamsburg, Virginia, to join the 119th Naval Construction Battalion. Sailor Casey was seventeen years old and weighed 142 pounds, and from his father, who had served in World War I, he had learned the rules of survival in military life.

As the military took over at Williamsburg and he headed for boot camp at Camp Peary he tried to remember that.

In their weeks at Camp Peary, the young men destined to become Seabees learned to march. Their instructor was a recycled marine from World War I, a Mr. Bailey. He was really a good teacher and a thoughtful man, unlike the drill instructors at Parris Island and the Hollywood version of a marine. He wanted his boys to learn, so he taught himself to do the manual of arms in reverse so he could demonstrate and watch his students at the same time.

But it was march, march, march for the boys of boot camp. After a day of hard work and learning Mr. Bailey would assemble his platoon in the evening for more practice. There was a competition coming up, with the victorious platoon winning the prize of a swim in the camp swimming pool. After many a practice session, Mr. Bailey's platoon won.

So Sailor Casey and his friends learned. They learned to wash clothes in a tin pail, with a box of Rinso and most of a bottle of Clorox per load. They learned to stand inspection; they learned to do and to avoid KP and volunteering. They learned military courtesy, which meant salute everything that moved, and how to make a military bed.

They learned mosquito control, which consisted of digging in a swampy section of the camp. They learned to use construction equipment, if they did not know already. And then one day in August, they were pronounced Seabees and a battalion, named the 119th Naval Construction Battalion, and shuffled off in dress whites for a journey to Camp Endicott, Rhode Island. The first reaction of the young men was relief at having escaped the heat of Virginia tidewater country. Then they were plunged into a routine of rifle ranges, GI movies, and lectures, an obstacle course, a judo mat, and other exercises designed to make fighting men of them. They had liberty in Providence, and they got home leave, which Sailor Casey took on his eighteenth birthday.

After that it was Eastport, Maine, and then a train ride across the country to California at the end of 1943, heading vaguely toward the war. They lit at Port Huenemel on the outskirts of Los Angeles, where they learned to fire the Springfield rifle. Then came a train ride to San Pedro, where 1,200 men with seabags, field packs, rifles, and helmets were put aboard the transport USS *West Point* and shipped out on a ten-thousand-mile voyage across the Pacific. The ship was once the luxury liner *America*, but now she was a troop carrier and every man had a narrow canvas bunk for a bed. Sailor Casey's memory of the voyage was of one long, continuous line, waiting for something, two meals a day, an occasional glimpse of the sea and the sky, lifeboat drills, calls to General Quarters, zigzagging, and the final landing at New Guinea's Milne Bay.

New Guinea, Casey soon learned, was hot, humid, and wet. It rained all the time, everyone had dysentery, and they had to work as stevedores. The job Sailor Casey rather enjoyed was a team effort to clean out the bowels of a Liberty ship in short order. But it was not always pleasant, as the day that they unloaded a ship full of cement bags and returned to camp choked and covered with cement dust, to find that the water had been turned off.

It did not seem long from their March 1944 arrival at Milne Bay until they were split, and most of the battalion was sent to Hollandia and the remainder to Tanah Mereh Bay. Sailor Casey was in the latter contingent. The voyage aboard the cargo ship *Morgan Robinson* was notable for the captain's excursions to find souvenirs. He liked to stop at spots where the Japanese had recently retreated and take a party ashore to hunt for samurai swords, flags, and the like, with very little attention paid to warnings that the Japanese had left booby traps behind them. The vessel was a contract merchant vessel with a civilian crew. Captain and crew were at constant war, and the atmosphere reminded Sailor Casey later of the movie *Mr. Roberts*, about a similar situation in the South Pacific aboard a ship. One day, a piece of cheese disappeared from the Seabee stores. The captain's reaction was to order an armed sentry to patrol the refrigerator with a fixed bayonet.

The first mate was a religious fanatic with an unkept beard and long hair that reminded Sailor Casey of an Old Testament prophet. The mate roamed the ship in shorts, with a Bible tucked under his arm.

Sailor Casey managed to make friends with the steward, who needed a mess attendant and he got the job temporarily, which removed him from the navy mess and into the upper reaches of society, which was the kitchen of the officers' dining room. He had just about anything he wanted to eat. It seemed a very short voyage to Tanah Mereh Bay, where he returned to navy life with Company A of the 119th Seabee Battalion.

It was a long time before Sailor Casey learned what he was doing in Tanah Mereh Bay. The reason for the Seabees being there was to establish a refueling point for ships moving up from Australia and New Guinea to take part in the coming invasion of the Philippines. His company built a "tank farm" in a cleared space near the harbor from steel sections bolted together. First they had to get the raw materials, which were steel parts delivered by ships and which they had to unload. On one of these unloading missions, Sailor Casey was standing by the rail of the ship being unloaded when the heavy crate that had just been lifted from the hold by crane began to swing toward him. He was threatened with being knocked overboard, not into the water, but onto the deck of a pontoon barge below. He leaped up and landed on the crate, grabbed the cable, and held on for dear life until it was put down on the deck.

It was onerous work, with the worst of it being after the tanks had taken shape and had to be sealed. The Seabees who did this job were lowered from the top with safety lines and hauled up and out if they became sick or passed out from the fumes.

After four months the job was done. A company packed up its seabags and rejoined the rest of the battalion at Hollandia, where the others had been building Admiral Thomas Kinkaid's headquarters for the Seventh Fleet. Here Sailor Casey did stevedoring again and sometimes pulled guard duty. One night he was on duty at the morgue after a heavy day of work. He went to sleep with his rifle on his knees. Suddenly he sensed the approach of the enemy and leaped to his feet, put his rifle at the ready and sang out "Who goes there?" in best approved fashion. The enemy replied, "That's all right, it's the Officer of the Day." The crisis was resolved without bloodshed or court-martial.

There were other adventures, as on the day they were unloading cases of five-inch shells for transshipment to a warship, when the eyes in the cases broke loose from the cable of the hoist and sent five-inch shells cascading to the deck of the ship. They were perfectly safe, the shells had not been fused, but the Seabees didn't know that and they watched the fall with so much trepidation that several men of the company leapt overboard and had to swim for their lives. Many jobs like this came, and the scuttlebutt had it that the men of the Seabee battalion were at last going off to war. The Philippines had been invaded in October 1944. The war was moving westward.

THIRTY

Navy Revenge

David Wheeler Mangum joined the navy and was sent to flying school as an enlisted man. He graduated and began flying combat aircraft, and in 1944 as an Aviation Pilot First Class, he was flying a torpedo bomber from the new carrier *Hornet*. When Mangum began flying combat, he was nineteen years old, and his Gunner was a chief mechanic who outranked him.

In the summer of 1944 the *Hornet* was part of Vice Admiral Marc Mitscher's carrier striking force that accompanied the invasion forces heading for Saipan and looking out for the Japanese fleet under Admiral Ozawa. In June they found that fleet and broke it up at the Battle of the Philippine Sea. After that there were no more fleet engagements until the Battles of Leyte Gulf, but in the interim the carriers ranged around the Philippines looking for targets. Pilot Mangum found one. It was a Japanese destroyer, and he made an attack on the ship. He came in low and direct, looking down the four 5-inch gun turrets and expecting to be disintegrated in midair. But the Japanese did not fire at him, and he got to release distance and tried to send off his "fish." The torpedo release failed. Finally Mangum flew up and over the bow of the destroyer, only fifty feet off the water, at 140 knots. And still the Japanese did not fire at him. He got back to his carrier a very quiet young man. After he landed his handlers reported that the gas tanks held only six gallons of gas.

Not long after this affair, Pilot Mangum made a low-level bombing run on three Japanese ships and dropped three 500-pound bombs on them. The first hit the water line of the first ship. The second bomb was a direct hit on the second ship, which turned out to be an ammunition carrier and blew sky-high. The second ship blew up with a roar and very nearly tore the wings off the TBF. Pilot Mangum blacked out. When he came to he was in a vertical dive at 60 knots, and his radioman was dead, killed by antiaircraft fire from the ships. Mangum managed to get the plane out of the dive and back to the carrier.

There he was recommended for a Navy Cross, but the recommendation was conditional. He would have to accept a commission as ensign to get it. Pilot Mangum refused. He did not want to be an officer. He was happy with his life as it was. So the recommendation was changed, and instead of a Navy Cross he was awarded an air medal.

"Talk about going from top to bottom," he said. "Navy revenge!"

Mangum served throughout the rest of the war and was discharged as a Chief Aviation Pilot. But when he decided to enlist in the navy reserve, he was told that he was not welcome, and an officer had the brass to demand that he remove his wings, because enlisted men were not granted pilot status any more.

THIRTY-ONE

The Navy's Infantry

A French magazine called them *Les Phantom Divisions, Les Beach Battalions de l'US Navy*. So little is known about their operations that this magazine, *Armes Militaire*, suggested their role in World War II was purposefully concealed for security reasons. They were akin to the army combat engineers, with whom they worked, but they were 100 percent navy. Sometimes they referred to themselves as "The Navy's Infantry" or "The Navy's Elite." They did not serve on ships, and none of the battalions survived the war as a unit. There were twelve of them altogether, all serving in the European theater of operations. Their job was to get the troops ashore on enemy beaches, and then to keep the men and equipment and supplies moving.

The Americans learned in the first North Africa landings and the landings in the Aleutians and at Guadalcanal that they needed a high degree of coordination between the army and navy, more than their normal units provided. For example, the army and navy used different communications systems. Several of the beach battalions were employed in the Normandy landings. One of them was the Sixth Beach Battalion, which was organized at Fort Pierce, Florida under Commander Eugene Carusi on October 9, 1943. The men took their initial training in their specialties at Little Creek, Virginia, which was also the training ground for the underwater demolition teams and later became the eastern center for the navy Seals.

On January 20, 1944, the Sixth Naval Beach Battalion arrived at Salcombe in southwest England. It was assigned to the Fifth Special Engineer Brigade, along with three battalions of combat engineers, while the Seventh Beach Battalion was assigned the Sixth Second Engineer Brigade.

Altogether twelve beach battalions were formed by the navy as the need was perceived for highly trained forces that could clear obstacles from the beaches and then maintain communications with the ships at sea, repair boats, and keep the invasion going. In some ways their job was very similiar to that of the underwater demolition teams formed at the same time. In fact, both Beach Battalions and UDTs participated in the Normandy landings.

Naval Beach Battalions were:

1st Naval Beach Battalion. Formed February 1943. Employed in the invasion of Sicily, Salerno, and Anzio.

2nd Naval Beach Battalion. Formed February 1943. Employed at Sicily, Salerno Anzio, and Normandy.

3rd Naval Beach Battalion. Used in the loading of troops and supplies on transports.

4th Naval Beach Battalion. Salerno and Anzio.

5th Naval Beach Battalion. Formed August 1, 1943. Trained in England. Employed at Normandy.

6th Naval Beach Battalion. Formed October 15, 1943, Normandy.

7th Naval Beach Battalion. Normandy.

8th Naval Beach Battalion. Formed October 1943. Used in landings in South of France.

9th Naval Beach Battalion. Formed April 4, 1943. Used in the loading of troops and supplies on transports.

10th Naval Beach Battalion. Formed April 30, 1944. Used in loading of troops and supplies on transports.

11th Naval Beach Battalion. Formed June 1944. Used in loading of troops and supplies on transports.

12th Naval Beach Battalion. Formed in December 1944. Used in loading supplies and troops in transports.

THIRTY-TWO

The Normandy Invasion

On January 1, 1944, a New Jersey boy named William Weedon was approaching his eighteenth birthday and wanted to get into the war. He took a trip to Newark, where he tried to enlist in the army air corps but failed by one point to pass the examination. Then he tried to join the merchant marine but slipped up and told the examining doctor that he walked in his sleep sometimes. They would not take him.

So William Weedon went next to the navy and they found out about the statement he had made about sleepwalking. He had to get his mother to make an affidavit and have it notorized, saying she had never seen him walk in his sleep, to get by the medical examiners. On February 5, he took his affidavit to 383 Madison Avenue in New York and passed the physical. He was in the navy!

He and forty other young men were sworn in, given a sandwich and an apple for lunch, and then a taste of the old service game: hurry up and wait. It was nine o'clock that night before they were put on the train at Pennsylvania Station for boot camp at Sampson, New York, and six o'clock in the morning before they arrived, hungry young men who had nothing but candy to eat for the long night's ride. They had breakfast and then a lecture and then they collected their gear. The method was simple: Each man held a mattress cover open and walked along the supply line and the supply clerks threw everything they needed into the mattress cover. William Weedon was surprised to find that although the clothing and equipment were thrown at him as he moved along, everything fit except the hat. He never did find a hat to fit him while he was in the service.

They were then assigned to quarters on the third deck of the barracks and told that they were one hundred men strong, and would now be known as Company 320. They had a little time to put their gear in shape, navy fashion. They changed into dungarees and fatigue shirts and then took off their civilian clothes, which they would not see the like of again for many a moon.

They went to lunch and were surprised that the food was good. They went to the dispensary and got a shot in each arm. The shots kept coming for several days until they had each collected two typhoid, two typhus, two tetanus, a yellow fever shot, and a diphtheria shot. In the next few days they had radio tests, swimming tests, boxing tests, rifle practice, lots of gymnastics and workouts, and a great amount of guard duty. Seaman William Weedon became an expert at pulling the dog watch (12–4). Since it was winter, they had a lot of snow to shovel, but since it was winter they were spared the obstacle course as part of their training. They got up at 5:30 and had to have their bunks made and gear stowed by 6:00. At 6:15 they were in the messhall. Usually it was snowing as they walked the two blocks to the messhall.

One week the company served as air raid wardens. The next they were on kitchen police, and Weedon cut his thumb with a knife while peeling potatoes. It became infected and he got out of peeling potatoes.

Their company learned fast, and they won the pennant for best company of the week twice.

William Weedon spent six weeks in boot camp and at the end of it he was granted a fourteen-day leave. He went home and when he came back to Sampson, he was put in the Outgoing Unit and soon arrived at Pier 92 in New York. He spent twelve days there waiting, for what he did not know. But it was good duty, working in the ship's service, making milkshakes, and dipping ice cream. He made a trip home during Easter Week, expecting to have Easter off as an extra, but then learned that all liberty was canceled. On Easter Sunday, instead of going to church with his family, he boarded the *Queen Mary*, the great Cunard liner that had been commandeered by the Royal Navy as a transport. After a few hours there were 2,400 American sailors aboard and 25,000 American soldiers.

They sailed on Monday, and a few hours out Seaman Weedon got seasick. He was sick for two days and not much better for the rest of the crossing. "The Limeys fed us hash almost all the way across."

The *Queen Mary* followed a tortuous route to avoid German U-boats. One day they were up near Iceland and a few days later they were down near Bermuda, and so many men were sick that they had to stand in line to throw up in the heads. Usually they did not get there in time, so the steel helmets came into use.

The passage was worrisome to the landlubbers but nothing happened. One night they heard an explosion. One of the people on watch had spotted a floating mine and exploded it with rifle fire.

The *Queen Mary* landed them in Scotland, near Glasgow, and they were put up on a base there. Seaman Weedon thought the grass looked awfully green and later he found out why. It rained there 360 days of the year.

Seaman Weedon stayed a week there, and had liberty in Glasgow. He found many red-haired girls there, chubby and healthy-looking, and found that they all walked very fast.

Soon the sailors learned the reason they had come to Britain. They were sent in a draft to Cardiff, and there they became the crew of LST *391*. They were assigned to duty and to action stations. Weedon was operator on the Number 1 20mm gun. The ship soon left Wales and arrived in Portland. There Seaman Weedon saw his first air raid. It was not very spectacular—a single German plane came over; the British antiaircraft gunners on the seashore shot it down with a 90mm gun.

They learned to chip paint from the steel decks of their LST and fill the holes with red lead and paint the deck gray again. They went on working parties to an underground ammunition dump and there loaded rockets that they carried to LCTs. They went to Plymouth and had lessons in tying rhinos up to the two door, rhinos being flat barges used to carry cargo to the beaches. Nobody said anything, but they knew that they were going to be involved in the invasion of Western Europe that everyone knew was coming.

The first official word arrived on June 1, 1944, when the skipper of the LST read to them a letter from General Eisenhower's headquarters announcing that they were to be involved in the invasion of France. After that they were restricted to the ship.

On June 4, the LST loaded up with troops, a headquarters unit of the U.S. First Army. A brigadier general was the top-ranking officer. He came up and joked with the sailors as they stood watch and loaded up five tanks, many command cars and jeeps, and several ammunition trucks, each carrying 30,000 pounds of explosives.

It was eight o'clock on a night in June that *LST 391* sailed from Plymouth into the teeth of a storm. The storm grew worse and so they sailed up and down along the English coast, waiting for orders. Hundreds of vessels were doing the same. Then they received a message saying the invasion of Normandy had been postponed for twenty-four hours because of the weather. So they continued to sail up and down the coast until six o'clock in the morning on June 6.

When they first sighted the French shore, Seaman Weedon said a little prayer. They were standing off Omaha Beach and preparing for the landing of the troops.

They saw the battleships *Arkansas, Texas*, and *Nevada*, which were shooting at what were said to be 88mm gun positions. About every two minutes one of the battleships would let fly a salvo from its big guns. Their LST was just ahead of the *Texas*.

Seaman Weedon saw his first dead man that morning, an American sailor. The body came floating by their ship, and Weedon saw that the body had the helmet buckled around the neck and guessed the sailor was a crewman on a landing craft and he had died of concussion from a gunfire.

Weedon had been taught never to buckle his helmet, because men got their necks broken that way. He also saw an airplane pilot's body floating by and many small boats that had been sunk just off the beach. He saw the remains of an LST, Number 499, which had been sunk.

From the LST *399* they heard machine guns on the beaches to the left. From his watch point on the bow, Weedon could see troops running and trying to get over the hill. He saw tanks leaving the beach, then saw them blown up before they got halfway up the hill.

On the port bow lay a French village, which kept changing hands. One time the swastika flag would go back up, and then they saw the American flag raised, and then the swastika again. At about four o'clock in the afternoon a squadron of Spitfires came over and dropped bombs, used rockets, and soon the Americans captured the town. Seaman Weedon saw a Spitfire shot down by antiaircraft fire.

On the beach they saw an LCI (landing craft infantry) blown sky-high by an 88mm shell.

All this while the battleship *Texas* was firing over their heads and the captain feared the battleship would blow their mast off.

At about six o'clock that night the Luftwaffe arrived at the beach and moved up and down strafing, and dropped a few bombs. And as darkness fell the battleships and the German 88s on the beaches began a duel that lasted all night long, filling the air over Normandy with fireworks.

The next day the beach was very quiet, and only a few air raids disturbed the peace. The troops had moved inland, so the battle was not so apparent on D plus 1. But for the next five days the men of LST *391* stood four-hour watches, which meant four hours on and four hours off. No one got any sleep, because the Germans sent a plane every two hours or so, just often enough to keep everyone off balance.

LST *391*'s passengers were scheduled to leave on D plus 2, but when they learned that the Germans were only six miles away still, they decided to wait another day.

That night the captain of the ship had word from the force headquarters that he was not to fire at anything in the air, because the Allies were sending a 5000-plane force to hit the Germans. But the Germans sneaked a plane into the formation somehow and it dropped a bomb that fell near one ship. This ended the quiet and every ship, it seemed, started to fire—except LST *391*, which followed orders.

Seaman Weedon and his buddies watched as several American planes were shot down by "friendly fire." Three barrage balloons were also shot down. The men could see the boats outside trying to get in. A number of ships were sunk in those days, some of them by the Allies to complete their artificial harbor but some by the Germans boats.

After five days LST *391* transferred its passengers ashore and its cargo to an LCT (landing craft tank), because the LST was called to Utah Beach to pick up a cargo of wounded and take them back to England.

As Seaman Weedon recalled:

> *We hit the beach at about 2 o'clock in the afternoon on June 11, and then a German 88 opened up on us. I didn't see how he could have missed us. We could see the flashes from his guns. Three destroyers were firing on this battery, but they were a mile off. Luckily for us, seven B–26 bombers came over and someone got in touch with the leader and asked him to hit the position. One bomber dropped his whole stock right on the target. I never saw such an explosion before or since.*

The LST decided to pull off the beach rather than take the chance of more hits coming closer. So they started off. They had a difficult time getting loose from the suction of the sand, but they made it and stood offshore waiting for the casualties to be brought out on landing craft. It was dark by the time the landing craft pulled alongside, and they had a lot of trouble getting the wounded off. A German Me-109 found them and came in to bomb. He dropped one bomb about a hundred yards off the stern but a second one fifty yards off the port quarter.

Seaman Weedon thought that the sky was full of planes that night, but the fact is that the German air action during the whole period was minimal. But he was not sorry when they pulled off the beach that night and headed for Southampton.

On the way to Southampton at nine knots, they collided with another LST and smashed in the bow and bow gun. So when the ship got to Southampton it had to go into drydock for two weeks, and the men had liberty.

At Normandy the Second Navy Beach Battalion went in before the Fourth Division; the Sixth went in before the First Division; and the Seventh went in preceding the Twenty-ninth Division. The Sixth, on Omaha, was commanded by Commander Eugene Carusi. The unit had been formed at Fort Pearce, Florida, in 1943, and then trained at Little Creek, Virginia. On January 20, 1944, the unit arrived at Salcombe in southwest England. There they trained some more.

The battalion was made up of three companies, and each company of three platoons. For operations each company was to be attached to a unit of army combat engineers. Each section of the beach where the infantry would land had its own beach battalion group made up of a company of combat engineers and a beach battalion platoon.

Each of these platoons was divided into four sections, communications, medical, small-boat repair, and hydrographic. The hydrographic section's job was to mark the channels of approach, to blow up the obstacles, and to direct the landing craft in to shore through the channels they made. The small-boat repair section was to work quickly to repair damaged landing craft and get them to sea again. The communications section was responsible for contact between the beach and the ships at sea. Each medical section was commanded by a doctor who treated the wounded before their evacuation from the beach.

When they landed on Omaha Beach, their mission was to break through the beach obstacles and make sure that the breaks were wide enough for the landing craft to come in to shore with the landing troops. The idea was to attach explosives to all the obstacles in a given area, then blow them with a single explosion. They would use Hagenson charges, which looked like a musette bag, and plastic explosives to blow up the Belgian gates, and the other obstacles.

But planning and doing were two separate things. When they came ashore to blow the obstacles, they were under heavy fire from German machine guns and field pieces, and the gap assault teams did not to manage to keep precisely to their plans. They wanted to blow holes 50 meters wide and 270 meters deep in the defenses to let the troops move easily, but they could not do it. They did manage to blow five of the twelve areas they had ticketed by the morning of June 6.

It was rough work. The battalion suffered 52 percent casualties of the men who came in on D-day. Typical of the beach battalion men was the story of Joe Geary.

He started in to shore very early on the morning of June 6 with the hydrographic section of Company A of the Sixth Battalion. He reached the beach and took shelter behind an overturned landing craft. Then a mortar shell burst on the landing craft, and he was wounded by several shell fragments. He was wounded in the neck. He made it to the beach, spent the night in a slit trench, and was evacuated the next morning.

Bob Giguere, a sailor of the Ninth Platoon of Company C, jumped off his landing craft when it was riddled by machine-gun fire. When he got to the beach he found himself alone, the only one of his unit to make it. A small group of the soldiers of the First Division came rushing through and shouted at him: "Don't stay on the beach!" He thought they knew what they were doing, so he joined them. They rushed along the land above the beach, stopping at pillboxes to throw in grenades and fire their weapons. They were headed toward Colleville-sur-Mer. They passed several civilians and then took refuge in the church in the village. There Giguere was wounded by a shell fragment and evacuated the next day. He received the Silver Star medal for his accomplishments.

For the first two days of the Normandy assault the beach battalions worked night and day, without sleep, and many of the men were wounded. They had to handle the problems of getting the troops and the supplies into the beach and then unloaded in an orderly fashion. At first everything was brought in by DUKW amphibious craft. It was many hours before the beaches were clear enough to let LSTs come up and discharge their cargo directly onto the beach.

But every hour the beach battalions were moving obstacles aside or blowing them up. By June 12, the beachmasters had achieved a delivery of 9,500 tons of supply per day, which superseded their most fervent expectations.

It seemed to get easier each day until June 19, when a terrible storm hit the Normandy beaches and the artificial harbor (Mulberry) brought in by the Allies was destroyed. That put the beach battalions back to the same feverish work, getting the stores ashore and head where they ought to go. It was again a question of blowing up obstacles, many of them sunken or damaged landing craft and ships. The beach battalions did it.

Of the forty-two officers and 368 men of the Sixteenth Battalion who came in to shore on June 6, four officers and eighteen men were killed, twelve officers and fifty-five men were wounded, including Commander Carusi, wounded by an antiaircraft shell on Omaha. The beach battalion stayed on Omaha until June 28 and was then transferred back to the States to be a training unit. They went to Oceanside, California, where most of them got into units scheduled for the Pacific.

Seaman Larry Flanagan had moved up from the Mediterranean command to the British Isles too, and his ship was involved in the Normandy landings as a troop transport. After a few days the ship returned to Scotland. But then came a call for rated radiomen from the transports to be detached and shipped back to the Normandy beachhead, where they were desperately needed to man naval radio communications on Omaha Beach.

Flanagan traveled from Rosneath, Scotland, to Plymouth by train. His seabag was lost on the rail trip, so he got to the beach with no naval uniform. He was put up by the British at Raglan Barracks at Devonport and the British supplied him with British uniform, shaving gear, and a backpack, including a short-handled spade. Then he went by ship to Omaha Beach, where he found himself deep in confusion and almost as deep in mud. He reported to the naval officer in charge, Omaha Beach and was issued a puptent, some clothing from the beach battalion's stores, and assigned to stand communications watches.

It was tough duty for a sailor. He was used to hot showers and hot food, and he had a mess kit, cold chlorinated water to drink, K rations to eat, and no showers. Food was served outdoors and if it rained, the food was served in the rain. On the good side, they weren't being shot at any more as they had been when they first landed the troops on the Normandy shore.

After a few weeks on the beach, Sailor Flanagan decided one day to take a stroll down to Vierville, the village nearby, and so he and a buddy started walking. They walked to a POW camp, where the Red Cross girls were serving coffee and doughnuts. They got in line wearing their helmets, army field jackets, marine pants, and ranger boots. The German POWs were around, washing up the mess gear and doing other tasks. It seemed to take a long time in the line but finally they got near that little window where the Red Cross ladies were dishing out the goodies.

One of the Red Cross ladies looked them over.

"This is for the fighting men," she said.

Sailor Flanagan just looked at her. All he could think of were the Willie and Joe cartoons from *Yank*, Bill Mauldin's drawings of those two dirty, unshaven soldiers who were always just coming back from the front and always being put down by someone in the rear echelon.

"Fighting men! What the hell were we doing here?"

After a few weeks for repairs, Sailor Weedon's ship was put right again and began shuttling cargo across the Channel and wounded and prisoners back to England. On their eighth trip they moved through a British minefield and two Liberty ships had their sterns blown off by mines. They did not dare stop to pick up survivors. On their tenth trip they had another collision with an LST outside Southampton and turned back to port. Again they had to wait for repairs, and while they did they had some new excitement. The first of the German V-1s began to arrive in England then, and they could see them passing overhead and hear them whistle.

On their twelfth trip they got lost from the convoy and went across the Channel alone, afraid of attacks all the way. On the fourteenth crossing they saw an American destroyer sink a German U-boat.

By the time they made their fifteenth trip the port of Cherbourg had been opened and they went there on August 16, 1944. They anchored in Cherbourg harbor that night. At about 3:00 A.M. Seaman Weedon was awakened by an explosion that threw him out of his bunk and onto the deck.

The first thought was to get my shoes as I knew there would be a lot of glass on the deck. I had put my shoes on the ledge above my sack. When I found them they were on my sack. I could smell fuel oil but none of us were very scared although some fellows alerted us to keep calm. I decided to put on my clothes, but because I couldn't see a thing I didn't know quite what to do. My clothes were not on the hook on the door where I had left them but on the floor there was a whole pile so I grabbed some and got dressed. One guy wanted to light a match but when we changed his mind, I started heading for the end that I thought was the bow but it turned out to be the stern. I passed the first compartment and looked down into the hatch to the auxiliary engine room and saw the fellow who had been on watch coming up the ladder with the water pushing at his heels. I found out that when he got to the top he fainted. The fellows were beginning to come around with flashlights but the fumes were getting awfully thick. I passed out. When I woke up I was on my hands and knees crawling along in the dark. Then I fainted again and somebody carried me topside. As soon as I hit the fresh air I woke up. I had a cut on my head and a headache. They took seven of us ashore to the hospital, and when we were running through the streets of Cherbourg I expected somebody to throw a hand grenade at the ambulance, but nobody did. The hospital was an old French school. I stayed for four days. On the second day we went back to the ship to see what we could find of our belongings, but the salvage crews had stolen everything. We were without food or clothing. All we had was what we wore. We were taken off the LST and put aboard a seagoing ferry. We had some boxes of K ration so that was what we ate.

After a few days their LST was salvaged and a seagoing tug took her in tow and back to Plymouth. The crew was sent to the base at Saltash across the river from Plymouth and stayed there for a month. That was when Seaman Weedon began to drink beer, because they had liberty whenever they were not on a work party. "We were almost like civilians. Boy, it felt good!"

Five days before they were to leave that base, he went to a navy dance and met a girl named Lee. It was love at first sight. He met her aunt and her uncle and the last day before he shipped out he met her mother and father.

They left for Portland by truck and almost got wrecked on the road when the trucks slipped on wet leaves. But all was well and they arrived safely, to be broken up as a crew and apportioned to several other LSTs in Flotilla 12. He and two others were sent to LST *337*, but they did not sail out of port. Instead they spent every day chipping paint and filling cracks in the decks.

Seaman Weedon then became a cook. About November 15, 1944 they were ordered to Dartmouth College to rejoin the old crew, and while they were there he was awarded a Purple Heart for the incident in Cherbourg harbor.

Early in December they left Dartmouth by train and went to Wales, where they boarded the USS *Lakehurst*, an army transport, and started back to the US. The diet was mostly powdered eggs and dehydrated potatoes. It took fourteen days to cross the Atlantic, and they hit two hurricanes on the way. They landed at Brooklyn on December 22 and were met by the Red Cross with coffee and doughnuts and milk. They then were put into a cattle train on the Long Island Rail Road and went to Long Island. They were there overnight and then Seaman Weedon had a twenty-one-day leave. After that he reported to Norfolk, where he stayed for two weeks. They were then shipped to Fort Pearce, Florida, where Seaman Weedon went through amphibious training as a signalman. He did a lot of drinking and one night in Stuart he broke a window and was put in the civilian jail for twenty-one days. He had a pancake and two strips of bacon for breakfast and a pancake and beans for dinner; that was all. No soap to wash with. After he got out of the civil jail he was thrown in the brig, where he spent eighteen days of what he called "just confinement." He was then given a summary court-martial and fined $130 and given thirty days on bread and water with full rations every third day. His head was shaved.

After Seaman Weedon got out of the brig he was sent to Tampa, where he was made a guard. He did not stay long there, but after two weeks the navy decided to send him to the Jacksonville Hospital as a battle fatigue case. He stayed there for a month and then was given a medical discharge.

So, well before the war ended, Seaman Weedon's naval career was over.

THIRTY-THREE

Southern France

The Eighth Beach Battalion was organized by the navy at Camp Bradford, Little Creek, Virginia, in October 1943. It trained and sweated and made its way to North Africa and then to Italy. It was scheduled for the beach operations in the Allied invasion of southern France in the summer of 1944. Here, based on a diary by Sailor Clifford Legerton, is an account of the invasion.

On August 11, 1944, elements of the Eighth Beach Battalion boarded the British LCI *258* at Naples and moved with the invasion fleet to Salerno, where the fleet spent the night. Sailor Legerton had taken a nap that afternoon and so missed supper, but since it was only bread, jam, and coffee, he did not feel that he had missed much. He decided to go for a swim in the Mediterranean. He blew up two life belts and threw them over the side of the LCI and then went down the ladder. The water was warm and he enjoyed the swim. After coming out he washed his face and head in freshwater and stayed up until 9:00 P.M., going to bed with the half moon coming up over the harbor of Salerno. It took him back to his home days in Charleston.

Sailor Legerton woke up for breakfast on the morning of August 12, had breakfast—bread, jam, and coffee again—and then went back to sleep until 9:30. He wrote letters in the morning, but in the afternoon the first lieutenant brought out the maps of the invasion area, and the men of the beach battalion began to go over them. The maps marked the beach on which they would land. Legerton was very pleased with the beach they would hit; he thought it was the best of the lot. He only hoped that afternoon that they would be easier to take than they expected.

Legerton took another long nap that afternoon. He went on deck for a while but then went back to his bunk. He slept until suppertime and then ate a K ration. He was still hungry and opened a C-ration can but could only eat half the contents.

D minus 2. August 13.

Sailor Legerton got up at 6:00 A.M. and went on deck until 10:00 and then back to bed. Later in the morning the army served breakfast. Bread, jam, and coffee. He decided on a K-ration breakfast.

Land came into sight that morning; it was Sardinia, Legerton thought. Two army combat-engineer sergeants were playing cards and he talked to them for a while. He was much comforted by their conversation. They were old hands at amphibious operations:

> *One thing that gives me a good deal of hope is the fact that so many of these boys have been in three or four invasions and have come through. So why can't the eighth Beach Battalion come through its first invasion?*
>
> *There is not the slightest bit of nervousness or excitement aboard this ship. There are no loud noises, and no yelling as is sometimes the case aboard ship. Everyone who talks, talks in a low voice. Morale is very high in this group.*

He noticed that the supply of K rations was getting down, because they were so much more palatable than C rations. He was feeling very well off. He knew where the K rations were kept and he had lucked into a size 34 field jacket just before leaving. Before that he had been wearing a 36, which was too big for him.

That day the officers gathered their men into small groups and talked about the coming invasion. Army and navy groups mingled; he listened to army officers tell them what to do and how to do it, and something about their objectives. Later his lieutenant called the navy group together and told them what their special part of the job would be and to expect the worst, although he really believed it was going to be a pushover.

At bedtime Sailor Legerton opened his Bible and began to read the ninth chapter of Luke. He came to the nineteenth verse and stopped: " 'Behold, I give unto you power to tread on serpents and scorpions, and all the power of the enemy and nothing shall by any means hurt you.' Only time and prayers will tell if this will be true."

He went to sleep vaguely comforted by his reading. Next morning, D minus 1, Legerton was still waiting, still vaguely apprehensive. He woke up and ate the ham and eggs from a breakfast K ration and then went on deck. The ship was at rest, docked in Corsica. He was making lemonade in his canteen cup and listening to the BBC. The radio was talking about the Americans, who were pushing the Germans back in northern France.

The LCI was docked next to the LCI *303*, which was carrying the headquarters of B Company of the Eighth Beach Battalion.

"We hear that today, August 14, is D-day minus one. One day and tomorrow we will go on THE REAL THING. May God be with each and every one of us on this landing. I have complete faith."

In the afternoon the ship pulled out of the harbor and away from the beautiful view of mountains rising sheer above the water. They soon crossed the path of another convoy, which included many of the big ships of the invasion.

Sailor Legerton wrote some more letters home, for lack of anything else to do, and then took a nap; he doubted that he would get much sleep the next night.

Then it was night, and the next morning it was D-day.

Sailor Legerton was a busy man the next morning, but by nightfall he found an old paper bag and wrote an account of the day.

D-Day.
Well, today is the day we are to hit the beach on the real thing. I could see from the rail of this LCI the battleships belching fire at the shores of southern France. I wondered how the boys on those ships could stand the shock and noise. We have passed APAs and many other ships, we now know that H-hour is at 8 o'clock on August 15, and that we will go in at 9 o'clock. We were told that the Paratroopers landed at 4 o'clock. From Corsica to Green Beach this LCI did not stop at all. It went straight for Green Beach and we landed at 9:05. Some timing!

On hitting the beach the first thing we did was try to take cover, which we did not need, for the enemy had pulled out. I landed first from my group and Lt. (jg) H. R. Taylor landed just after me. When we were on the water's edge, I said "Mr. Taylor, nothing has happened yet." He said "Keep your fingers crossed.

Well, we did not find much opposition so we began to walk around freely. For most of the day my carbine was left on the beach. I did not carry it because we did not need them. We were lucky. Other landing parties at other beaches did not fare so well.

Not long after we landed the 143rd Regiment, a part of the 46th Division, came in. The 141st and the 142nd had landed before I did. In the 142nd were Captain Johnson and Captain McSwain, both of Winnsboro, whom I had met earlier in Italy.

I soon found the Command Post and already hundreds of the Supermen [German prisoners] were coming in. I left and went back to Mr. Dillon. It was while I was sitting with him on the water edge of Green Beach that we got our first taste of the enemy. He was on the other side of St. Raphael and he began lobbing his famed 88mm shells on our beach.

Those shells did not miss me far. They really came too close. One burst about a yard in front of me. At least that is what I felt like. I fell to the ground when I heard them coming and made for the other side of the beach between shells. My helmet fell off one time, but all the way across the only thing I felt was a little rock that hit my back. When I got to the other side of the beach I could hardly walk. My knees ached because I had fallen on them so often trying to dodge those 88s. Just after the shelling and while I was trying to stop shaking, an A-3 boy got up and walked over to a bush and came back with a tiny mockingbird. He must have lost his mother. And he could not fly well. The boy let him go later.

During the first shelling and while dodging them I had my kodak in my hand all the time. I am glad I did not lose or damage it. After the shelling stopped we all started to work. I was sent to the CP and while on the way I saw a sight I will not forget. I met about eight French civilians. All were crying for joy, they were so happy we had come.

Later I saw a Frenchman who had been wounded. He was being carried on a litter. His face was bloody but not too bad. I smiled and waved at him and he smiled back. Well, ships came in all day with supplies and during a good part of the night. About 3:30 the Germans sent some more 88s over. I was expecting them so I was ready. I heard one and went back to the hill. I figured out one thing that made me feel better during the shelling. The shells all seemed to be falling on the lefthand side of the beaches [as] I faced the sea. They were coming from St. Raphael. Between St. Raphael and the beach where they were landing was a hill. That the shells had to clear, so I thought they would not fall very close to me if I got up close to the side of the hill and away from St. Raphael. Afterwards I was over where those guns were located and figured that I have figured the thing out right.

One British LCT was hit and the flag is at half mast. Somebody must have been killed by that shell. An American LCT caught fire, and a fireship pulled up and toward her well off the beach. Then about 6:30 US LST 202 was hit by a radio-controlled flying bomb. I saw the German plane that dropped it, but no one recognized it was a German plane until it dropped its bomb. The ship did not have a chance even to get its doors open. Seventy percent of the crew and army men aboard were killed. The army had put up barge balloons in the afternoon; our officers frankly found that the Germans had the range of those balloons and I knew that much earlier I saw a shell hit one. After they were pulled down we did not have a single shell on the beach.

Company B of our battalion was to land on Red Beach at 2 o'clock, which was H-hour for that beach. They found it too well defended so had to come through our beach.

B Company relieved us on the beach at 6 o'clock and I went to Regimental Command Post where I found some of my army friends. One sergeant asked me if I would like to sleep in the room with him. I told him I would be grateful as to do so. I went out, took some life belts to make a bed. About that time the German plane came over. I dashed back to the CP with four life belts. The attack was pretty bad, very thick. So I stayed under cover. What goes up is bound to come down, you know. I blew up the life belts and found that two were no good so I had only two to sleep on. I had my pack so I used that as a pillow. I slept in my clothes for about three nights . . . one never knows what and when something might happen.

That German plane was a Messerschmitt 109. The plane came from our left flank, let out one radio-controlled bomb. The boys who were closer to the bomb said they saw it wig-wagging. It got an incoming LCT, 282, as I have already explained. Night came and Sergeant Crianer said that this morning Green Beach was the hottest beach he had been on. And he had been on four invasions. This makes his fifth. I found later that he said this was the hottest because in his other invasions he had never gone in so early before. He is in the 504th Combat Engineers Battalion.

D + 1. *I woke up twice during the night. It was not because of the gunfire, it was just that I was unable to sleep. I got up at 7 o'clock but did not come down to the beach until about 8:30. I went out to an LST and got my canteen filled and came back to the CP where I am just waiting to be called for a message. A boy in Platoon A-1 has just put up a radio and we are for the first time finding out where our 7th Army is and how it is doing. We cannot get news on the beach, have to get it from the States. That seems odd, but it is true. New York City is sending us the news at this time.*

Well, time went on and we operated the beach until 3 o'clock in the afternoon and then Company C of the 8th Beach Battalion took over. I came back to the CP and spent the night but before going to bed I went out to take a look around. In the very next yard I saw hundreds of POWs. Some were Germans, some were Poles and some were even Russians. And some, who later helped us, were from Indochina, and Siam. They looked too happy for me to believe they were POWs.

I then went out further on the beach, but I learned a lesson—never go out without your helmet. About the same time as last night the Germans sent a plane over. Attack went up and I dashed for the closest wall and hugged it for about fifteen minutes. After that time I always went out with my helmet.

Dillon and Mr. Taylor could not find room in the CP so went with Platoon A-1 somewhere near by. I asked Mr. Dillon if I could stay and he said yes, and I was glad for the army boys gave me coffee, water and rations. They have been very nice to me. A funny thing happened before I went to bed. I was in the next yard and walked up to an MP and asked him about the prisoners he was guarding. He looked at me and I realized he did not know my uniform so I said, "You don't know me but this is the uniform of the US Navy Beach Party. At first I think he took me to be a spy of some sort. He then told me about the prisoners and said that he would go with them all the way back to Italy.

D + 2. *This is written on the back of an old V Mail envelope, the only paper I could find.*

Ever since D-Day night I have been spending the nights in regimental Command Post Building. The room has an iron bed, a table, easy chair, wash basin, dresser, clothes closet and a small window. It is the first room I have spent the night in since Norfolk. It is a big change from the

GI way I have been living. One of the boys has a little pet hawk and another has a little puppy. The civilians have some chickens and goats just outside our window. They do not live here, but come every day to take care of the chickens and goats.

I have not slept so well for the past two nights, but as time goes on I hope to get over my scared spells and sleep better. German prisoners have been coming in by the hundreds ever since D-Day. On D-day plus 1, two hundred and seventy came in one lot. I asked Mr. Dillon if I could again spend the night in the CP and he said I could but wanted to know if I had a comfortable place to sleep. Later in the evening at about 4 A.M. that German plane came over again. I do not know but I heard that it dropped one bomb that landed at the water's edge. I went to bed and at about 4 o'clock the army boys moved out and I took over the civilian bed where I slept well until 9 o'clock. Mr. Taylor came for me about 2 o'clock that afternoon and we went to Red Beach. We put up at a house here and I had another sleep, in a civilian bed. Every night until D-Day plus 6 the Germans sent planes over Red Beach in air raids. I could see the planes very clearly. There was a lot of attack sent up but as far as I know none of the planes were shot down. The only ship that I saw blown up was LST 282. I am glad that I did not see more.

We remained on Red Beach until we returned to North Africa after August 21. We had a quiet time with the Germans, were well billeted, and we enjoyed our stay.

THIRTY-FOUR

Paving the Way

Sailor John Liuzzi qualified as a salvage diver in 1943 and was sent to North Africa and then to Italy as part of a team of divers whose job was to open up the harbors for Allied ships. This meant cleaning up the debris of battle and bombing on the ocean floor. They went first to Anzio, then to Ciritavecchia, Piombino, and Leghorn.

It was quite a job, because the Germans had been very efficient in their campaign of destruction as they left Italy, fighting and holding mile by mile. They had taken to the breakwaters of the harbors many ships they could not use and sunk them one on top of another. Thus the harbors were very effectively closed to the Allies, and that meant that men, gasoline, weapons, ammunition, and other supplies could not come in. The divers used thousands of tons of dynamite to blast all this debris away and reopen the ports.

After the invasion of southern France in August 1944 the Allies desperately needed a harbor in southern France to carry their fighting to the north and east into the Vosges Mountains. Toulon was completely blocked with sunken naval vessels and merchant ships. So Admiral Sullivan, who was in command of naval forces, chose Marseilles as the port he would use.

A convoy of 120 ships bearing badly needed supplies was brought to Marseilles, but the harbor was blocked by ships sunk by the Germans.

Sailor Liuzzi and his crew were sent to open the harbor. They first went to the breakwater from land to estimate the number of ships blocking the harbor. They reported their findings to Lieutenant Commander Potts, who was commander of their unit activities.

He reported to Admiral Sullivan: The major problem was that one oceangoing ship had been sunk just inside the breakwater, then another just as large had been sunk to lie crosswise over her.

The divers evolved a plan for the attack and Commander Potts approved. They would load the overhanging stern of the top ship with dynamite and run a snake charge around the shell. Hopefully, when the blast came, the ship would break up and the sections would drop to the bottom, thus giving clearance for the Allied ships to pass through into the inner harbor. Liuzzi was ordered to dive and start the job, which began at seven in the morning. He went down and the crew began to send down the explosives. They loaded all they could on the hulk. Sailor Liuzzi then attached it to primacord, their fusing device, and came up at about noon after a five-hour dive. They backed away from the area and blew the charge. As soon as the debris had settled a man went down again and found that they had been successful. The hulk had sunk to the bottom and no longer proved an impediment to navigation. Commander Potts signaled to Admiral Sullivan that the port was now open and Marseilles was ready for business.

That day the ships began moving into Marseilles, and in a matter of hours supplies were on their way to General Patton—who as usual was moving so fast that he had outrun his supply train and was in a very vulnerable position. Sailor Liuzzi got the Bronze Star for his five-hour dive. The whole affair received scant notice from the Allied reporters because the liberation of Paris had captured the headlines, but Patton had just had a narrow escape. And it is possible that the course of the war had just been changed by the efforts of a team of navy divers hundreds of miles away from the fighting.

THIRTY-FIVE

At Leyte Gulf

On the morning of October 25, 1944, the *Natoma Bay* was cruising off the eastern entrance to Leyte Gulf with the rest of the group of small carriers when the force was electrified by the appearance of a strong body of Japanese battleships, cruisers, and destroyers coming down on them from the north, where they had moved unnoticed through San Bernardino Strait after a long run from Borneo. Two forces of Japanese ships attempting to fight their way through Surigao Strait had been defeated during the night and the larger force of Admiral Shoji Nishimura almost completely wiped out. But this threat, which utilized the major remaining strength of the Japanese fleet, could mean the decimation of the ships standing off Leyte Island and the isolation of the American troops fighting on Leyte.

At 6:58 that morning the escort carrier force under Rear Admiral Clifton Sprague, which was farthest north, was attacked. At that time the *Natoma Bay* was loading planes for air-support strikes during the day, but the plan was changed abruptly and four torpedo bombers were ordered to take on torpedoes and go attack the Japanese who were threatening the Sprague group.

Lieutenant William V. Morton of Squadron 81 led the four torpedo bombers out to rendezvous with other bombers and launch a combined attack. But the rendezvous did not occur, so Lieutenant Morton led the *Natoma Bay* bombers in their own attack against three cruisers. A cruiser turned in to meet the attack, which put Lieutenant Morton's plane in a bow-on position. He strafed the cruiser as he crossed the bow and then dropped his torpedo against another cruiser just beyond the first one. The torpedo hit on the starboard beam, aft. The other three *Natoma Bay* bombers dropped on the first cruiser. Lieutenant Wilbur F. Hiser's torpedo hit admidships. The other two torpedoes were not seen to hit.

As Lieutenant Morton's plane passed over the cruiser a 25mm shell exploded behind the instrument panel and a fragment hit the lieutenant in the right thigh. The explosion also wrecked the hydraulic controls, propeller control, and all the engine instruments. ARM 2/c Merrton G. Cole was taking pictures and observing the attack when a 40mm shell came through the bomb-bay window and exploded inside the tunnel. Cole was injured severely and the gunner, AOM 2/c Joseph Bosze, came to his assistance and gave first aid. The lieutenant turned back toward the fleet and made a successful water landing without flaps even though the bomb-bay doors were open. All three crew members survived and were picked up by a destroyer escort.

The last two torpedoes aboard the *Natoma Bay* were loaded on bombers and the planes were catapulted downwind because the wind was coming from the north. They were ordered to attack the nearest battleship. As they flew in they could see enemy shells falling all around the screening destroyers and escort. Ensign George W. Gaienne and Ensign Robert F. Voltz joined torpedo planes from other carriers and attacked a *Nagato*-class battleship. The *Nagato* turned into the attack and combed the torpedoes, all of them missing. But the two ensigns saw the torpedoes hit on an *Atago*-class cruiser on the starboard beam of the *Nagato*; this cruiser then sank. In retiring Ensign Voltz's plane was hit by a 40mm shell outboard of the starboard wheel well. The hydraulic system was damaged, but Voltz managed a safe landing aboard the carrier.

Four of the fighters of the carrier, on combat air patrol, found a Japanese torpedo bomber about fifteen miles from the task force and attacked. Ensign Ralph L. Walker pursued the enemy plane into and out of a cloud and shot the Japanese plane down.

Since all the ship's torpedoes had been expended, the next flight of four torpedo planes from the *Natoma Bay* was loaded with 500-pound bombs. Ensign John T. Goodwin made three gliding runs on a battleship before his bomb would release. On his third run he put a stick of four bombs into the water, near-missing the battleship, running from the stern to amidships. One bomb probably did considerable damage.

Lieutenant Wesley M. Skill made a diving attack on the same ship. One of his bombs hung up and the other fell short.

Ensign Kenneth E. Wavell dropped three bombs on the last battleship in the line. The second bomb hit the turret just forward of the bridge. Lieutenant (jg) Leon S. Conner made a run on that same ship; one of his bombs hit the edge of the deck on the starboard quarter.

Lieutenant Skill and Lieutenant Connor each had two bombs left, and they joined up to attack a cruiser. Conner's bombs dropped short but Skill's were a near miss and one hit amidships.

Although the attacks of the various elements of the escort carrier force were not coordinated that day, the pilots made a good job of working together in the air over the target. When Lieutenant Conner was about to return to the carrier, having dropped his bombs, he spotted a lone torpedo bomber circling a cruiser that was dead in the water. The pilot had a torpedo and wanted someone to strafe for him while he made his run. Lieutenant Conner obliged, and the TBM scored a hit amidships but was shot down by the enemy antiaircraft guns as he pulled out of his torpedo run.

Back on the *Natoma Bay*, more torpedo bombers were loaded with 500-pound armor-piercing bombs. Lieutenant John B. Augur took off, as did Ensign Robert Praetsch and Ensign Charles L. H. Boldt. Lieutenant Augur scored a near miss on a cruiser. Ensign Praetsch dropped a near miss on a battleship, and Ensign Boldt disappeared. He returned when the carrier put in at Manus. His plane had been hit by antiaircraft fire, forcing him to make a water landing. All three crew members floated around for two days before they were picked up by a destroyer.

Three more TBMs attacked the Japanese force, dropping general-purpose bombs—all that were left. Lieutenant Roy S. Reeves attacked a cruiser and scored a hit on the bow that started fires. Ensign Gordon Kesterke scored a hit behind the bridge.

The last strike of the day from the *Natoma Bay* was made by four torpedo planes and twelve fighters, with planes from the other carriers. By the time they attacked, the Japanese had decided to leave the scene as too hot for comfort and were moving north again and had reached the tip of Samar Island on their way back to San Bernardino Strait. It was 5:15 in the afternoon.

Gaiennie put two bombs into a cruiser; Lieutenant (jg) Joseph Cady and Lieutenant Conner made near misses on the same ship. Altogether their attack was useful; the ship made a great deal of smoke and began to lose way. Conner then went back to make a pass with his rockets and never came back.

The twelve *Natoma Bay* fighters made repeated strafing runs over the Japanese ships. In their action reports later the Japanese gave much more credit to the airmen of the small carriers than the American navy ever did for this action off Samar. The whole affair became so involved in a controversy between Admiral William F. Halsey, the Third Fleet commander, and Admiral Thomas Kinkaid, the Seventh Fleet commander, that the role of the escort carriers was ignored. The fact is that the Japanese thought these were fleet carriers, and the pilots behaved with such skill and perseverance that the men of the big carriers could not have done any better. The complaint against Halsey was that he should not have gone chasing the Japanese carrier forces to the north but should have stood guard on San Bernardino Strait. Had he done so, there would have been no action off Samar, and the small carriers would never have been able to prove that they were perfectly capable of doing on a small scale anything the fleet carriers could do. It was because of the battle off Samar that, as the Philppine campaign continued, the Seventh Fleet stopped complaining about not having enough support from the fleet carriers. They did not really need them; their triple handful of escort carriers was quite capable of doing the job.

It was true that in the battle off Samar the Americans lost one carrier, the *Gambier Bay*, to shellfire from the Japanese ships. They lost another that day, the *St. Lo*, to a kamikaze, and three of the destroyer screen sacrificed themselves to help save the small carrier force. But those ships were put at risk as they ought to have been, doing their job, just as Halsey was doing his job in chasing and destroying the remnants of the Japanese carrier fleet in the north. The result of the three battles of Leyte Gulf, at Surigao Strait, off Samar, and off Cape Engano, was a tremendous American naval victory that effectively ended the Japanese fleet of World War II. The little carrier *Natoma Bay* played a vital role in that operation.

THIRTY-SIX

God and the Wolfpack

There is an old saying, "I can fight my enemies well enough, but Lord, protect me from my friends." This certainly applied to the submarine *Trepang*, which Commander Roy Davenport commissioned in the summer of 1944, for first she was hit by a ferryboat in San Francisco Bay, a ferry with no one at the controls, just as she was getting ready to take Commander Davenport back to war. And she was frightened by a whale (or, rather, her crew was) when the captain was on deck, and he and two other men were left hanging as the boat submerged. It all ended without tragedy and a good laugh, but there seemed to be a certain safety in being in the bosom of the enemy.

In September 1944, as the *Natoma Bay* and other ships prepared for the invasion of the Philippines, the *Trepang* was on her way out for her first war patrol, which would take her to the Nanpo Shoto, the fringe islands of Japan itself. On October 1, they hit a tanker with a torpedo, and it sank later. They also sank an escort vessel of 1,900 tons, although they did not know it at the time.

Later that day Skipper Davenport held religious services for his crew. They hit a patch of rough weather for a week and changed patrol areas in a typhoon.

Off Tokyo Bay they sank two more ships, on October 11. The next day they came across two battleships screened by two destroyers. They attacked, sank one destroyer, and hit the first battleship with a torpedo that sent flames mast-high. With their stern tubes they attacked the second battleship. In this encounter they came to within 350 yards of one of the destroyers, and most of the men on the bridge thought they were sure to die that night. Skipper Davenport, buoyed by his faith, had no doubt that they would come through safely.

That was about the end of the excitement on that patrol, but it had been enough. Their results were quite spectacular: a tanker, a transport, an escort, a full-size destroyer all sunk, and a battleship badly damaged. God certainly did seem to be on Commander Davenport's side!

Proudly they brought the new boat home. Commander Davenport and a "Makey-learn" new skipper named Commander W. B. Thomas, who was along on the patrol to gain experience, conducted church services. Commander Thomas was now a convert to the church-services-on-submarine groups. They brought the submarine into the forward base at Majuro proudly flying a broom, which meant a clean sweep. They had gotten rid of all their torpedoes and they had made them count.

By this time Commander Davenport had evolved his theory of Christian warfare, which he explained to his friend Commander Richard Peterson, commander of the *Icefish*, a contemporary of the *Trepang*. They had gone out at the same time and Davenport had a distinguished patrol while Peterson had scored a zero.

Here is their conversation as reported by Davenport in his book *Clean Sweep*:

DICK: *Roy, I can't understand one thing. I think I'm just as good a Christian as you are, but when I go on patrol I don't know whether we're going to be successful or whether we are going to return. People don't know whether we will be successful or whether we will return, but when you go out on patrol everyone knows that you will be successful and you will return. I don't understand why so many of your attacks take place at night.*

ROY: *Dick, of course you are just as good a Christian as I am. The good thoughts people have for us are also helpful, for I, too, know we are going to be successful. It is right with God that we win the war. We'll be in the right place at the right time. My men will know what to do and how to do it regardless of their degree of training, and whatever they have to do they can do without harm to themselves.*

That so many of our attacks take place at night on the surface is God's way of working this out. We can make recurrent attacks, can see what we accomplish and we have greater speed on the surface. The only difference between the two of us is that when you feel that your patrol may not be successful and that you may not return, you open the avenue for these things to occur.

Whatever the reasoning, the Davenport system seemed to work. A higher-ranking officer told him that there had been considerable discussion of putting him up for the Medal of Honor for his attack on the Japanese battleships, but that ultimately it was not done because the element of risk did not seem to be great enough. In any event, the patrols were successful, time after time, as Commander Davenport continued to talk to God and sink enemy ships.

THIRTY-SEVEN

Sailor Adrift

After Sailor C. W. Lynch's experiences aboard the *Lexington* in the Battle of the Coral Sea he wandered about in America, AWOL, for nearly two years before he was picked up by the Shore Patrol and ultimately shipped back to Boston and put in the brig awaiting disposition of what everyone told him was a case of desertion. What the brig lawyers indicated was that the decision was going to be whether they shot him for desertion or just sent him to prison forever.

Ultimately his case came up before a Captain's Mast and he was haled to the Fargo Building, where a captain in all his gold braid sat in judgment. The captain looked at the record.

"Don't you remember me from the old *Lexington*?" the captain asked.

Lynch was too scared to remember anything, but he lied manfully.

"Yes, sir. I sure do, sir."

The captain smiled and looked at the record again.

"Seven days' restriction and forty-six dollars fine," he said. "You will be reassigned to the carrier *Hancock*."

So Sailor Lynch was slated to be a member of the crew of the new carrier. If there was anything he did not want, it was to go back to sea, and if he was going to sea, if there was any sort of ship he did not want, it was another carrier. He put in for a transfer; it was refused. He went to see the chaplain. He got a lot of sympathy and advice to bear with his lot. He was a pretty lucky young man, the chaplain told him.

Sailor Lynch went to sea with the *Hancock*, and the first chance he got he jumped ship. After a few months he was picked up again, shipped to Honolulu and then to Ulithi, to rejoin his ship. He served in Task Force 38.2 until the end of the war.

THIRTY-EIGHT

Noumea *Interlude*

The Sixth Naval Construction Battalion left Guadalcanal aboard the SS *Hunter Liggett* on January 5, 1943, headed for New Zealand and a respite from a very hard war. For two months the sailors reveled in the fleshpots of Auckland. Lieutenant Commander Blundon was promoted to full commander in recognition of the unit's performance on Guadalcanal, which had set the standard for the Seabees everywhere and earned them the reputation of the "can do" outfit.

In March 1943, the Sixth Seabees was sent to Noumea, which was the hub of Admiral Halsey's South Pacific Command. They would be there for a year and a half. They built mobile hospitals Number 5 and Number 7 and a supply depot on Ducos Peninsula, which included a large number of fuel tanks. They built a net depot and many roads, camps, pipelines, and power plants.

It was all carried out in an atmosphere quite unlike that of Guadalcanal, luxurious by comparison, with movies, beer, and liberty in whites. No more sixteen-hour days with two meals a day and a diet that consisted of Spam for weeks at a time, alternated sometimes with corned beef. There were no Pistol Petes and no Japanese battleship guns to boom at them, no Washing Machine Charlies to drop bombs on them when they least expected it.

The big excitement was on November 1, when Admiral Halsey's fleet was loading up for the invasion of Empress Augusta Bay on Bougainville and 1,500 tons of ammunition went up in a giant explosion that nearly wrecked the Nickel Works at Noumea and the

Nickel Dock. For the men of the Sixth Seabees it was a challenge reminiscent of Guadalcanal days. They worked all that first night and the next morning had the pier in shape to take ships and load on schedule.

Seabee Alfred G. Don and his companions of the 25th Naval Construction Battalion were split, some of the Seabees going to Bougainville with the Third Marine Division to attack Empress Augusta Bay and then build airfields which would help to isolate Rabaul while others, including Don, remained in New Caledonia, maintaining the division camp.

> *Once the officers and men of the 25th NCB had returned from Bougainville, we started making preparations for our next adventure— that of returning to recapture the Island of Guam along with the 3rd Marine Division.*
>
> *Once on-board the US Vessel President Adams, we started up the slot to the Marshalls for joining the 7th Fleet that was massing for the forthcoming push on the Marianas. Up and back from the Marshalls in a short space of time, due to the rescheduling of "D" Day. Finally, after a couple of weeks later—on 21 July 1944 we joined the 3rd Marine Division in landing for the recapture of Guam. The fighting lasted until 10 August 1944, when the Island was declared secured of enemy action. As a member of the transportation section, I and many others were working 12–13 hours a day to supply roads and supplies to the Marines as they advanced in their fight with the Japanese. Once this fighting was over, we got down to building our own permanent camp site, as well as rebuilding the torn-up roads and airstrips. One of our first civic action projects was to rebuild the water reservoir and its water lines to have water distributed throughout Agana and surrounding areas. We built new bridges, camp sites for the Marines, worked on a field hospital, quarry, fuel farms, ammunition dumps, the famous B-29 field known as "Northwest Field" along with other Naval Construction Battalions and Army Engineer Battalions. The list goes on and on. I believe one of our best construction feats was the blasting out of a mountainside, the road that finally reached its top and had the Fleet Headquarters of CINPAC, Admiral Chester W. NIMITZ built for him and his staff from which they could continue operating the plans of war to move onto the forward areas in the Pacific and bring about the final surrender of the Japanese.*

It can be said, that the 25th Naval Construction Battalion along with the cooperating efforts of other SEABEE Battalions, Army Engineers, and the Second Marine Engineering Battalion under the operational control of the Fifth Naval Construction Brigade, were responsible for approximately 75 percent of the total construction on Guam to develop it into a major Advance Base from the beginning to the end of the 25thNCB's service on Guam.

The invasion of Bougainville completed the ring of air bases around Rabaul that imprisoned the Japanese in the South Pacific and soon the war moved up to the Philippines and beyond, and Noumea settled down again to become a backwater as it had been before. On September 4, 1944, the Sixth Seabees left for America and home after twenty-six months of war duty.

On September 18, the transport *General Hugh L. Scott* reached the Golden Gate and home leave. After that the Sixth Seabees was reorganized, and many of the original members were transferred out to other units.

In May 1945, the Sixth Seabees sailed for Okinawa and went to work on that island, preparing for the coming assault on Japan. But in August it all ended, and the Seabees of this unit were almost all such high-point men that the decision was made in the fall of 1945 to decommission the whole organization.

Seabee Alfred G. Don and the 25th NCB stayed on Guam.

In November 1945, after the dropping of the two atom bombs on Japan, our job was coming to an end. I had, by this time, earned enough "points" to allow me to head for home. The Navy had put a program called the "Magic Carpet Run" into effect by then. This consisted of many ships designed to pick up hundreds and thousands of the troops in the Pacific area and get them back to the good old USA. I was one of 10,000 who boarded the USS Yorktown, an aircraft carrier that had its hanger deck fitted with 6-tier high bunks to hold this many men. On the Port side was saltwater showers. On the Starboard side was saltwater heads. Because there were so many on-board, they could only feed us two meals a day from Guam to San Francisco.

I am sure you all have heard the SEABEE motto to be "CAN DO." This SEABEE "DID" while on-board the carrier. I volunteered to work in the fireroom in exchange for being able to eat the noon meal with "ships company" as well as taking "Fresh water" showers in the back of the steam boilers in the fireroom. I also had to beg, borrow, but not steal (pay for) a complete Navy uniform since all we had was Marine uniforms. When the ship finally docked in Oakland, California I was ready to dress out as a proud Navy SEABEE. We took a ferry over to Treasure Island, which was the processing center. You couldn't believe the number of Navy personnel trying to get processed. We headed for the Base galley and our first fresh *fruit, vegetables, and milk in over two years. It was so crowded for processing, they gave some of us a three day pass until they could catch up with all the backlog. Wow! San Francisco and now having a good beer to drink, food to eat, and plenty of sightseeing, the days passed quickly and finally underway by air to New York for processing and discharge. My wife met me there and we spent a couple of days visiting and sightseeing before heading home. After 30 days, I decided the SEABEES was the place for me and my family. I shipped over and headed back to Port Hueneme, California to start my lifetime career in earnest with the SEABEES.*

THIRTY-NINE

Typhoon!

Norman Ostrom joined the navy in 1942, and after boot camp he sought service with submarines. He was assigned to the USS *Skate* and made four war patrols in her. Of all his experiences the one he would not forget was the day the *Skate* blundered into the path of a typhoon.

Skate was on her sixth war patrol in early October 1944 and was cruising in her patrol zone, not far from Okinawa. The weather had been foul for several days, but on October 7 it suddenly turned much worse. The submarine began to heave and plunge and roll. Belowdeck the crew of the submarine could feel the motion and hear the thunder of the sea crashing down on the deck and tank tops. Sailor Ostrom was sitting on a bench in the crew's mess:

> *The ship rolls to port and the table I have at my back pressed painfully on my back for what seems to be a very long time. Then the ship rolls to starboard and I am forced to stand and lean towards what was very shortly ago the high side. It is impossible to relax. Our muscles are constantly at work trying to keep us upright. As we are tossed about we attempt to hold onto whatever is near. To move from one compartment to another is extremely difficult. You must time the ship's roll to be at a place where there is a smooth surface when the ship rolls for it is impossible to hold yourself off the many pipes and valves that line the passageways when the ship takes these terrible rolls.*

Ostrom grabbed a pipe in the overhead to steady himself as the ship suddenly took a violent roll. The submarine moved over farther; his feet left the deck and he was hanging from the pipe. He looked down. If he fell, he would go smack into a menacing-looking cluster of valves and pipes. His grip was hurting his arms and he felt like letting go. The ship began to recover, and he felt like turning loose, but then it hit another wave, and he hung for agonizing moments. Finally the ship righted itself and his feet came back into contact with the deck.

He went to his bunk. "Lying in a bunk is difficult, for you must constantly hold on to keep from being thrown out." He dozed off and then awoke to find himself airborne. He grabbed with his right hand and caught the bunk rail as he was flying over the side. He went down onto the deck on his left hand and both knees.

When the watch was called he looked for his shoes; they were gone from under the bunk, where he kept them. Someone turned on the lights, and there all the shoes were in a large pile in the after port corner. They were black issue navy shoes and they all looked alike, so every man sat down on the deck and found two shoes that were comfortable and then went about his duties.

In the engine room the sea poured through the engine air induction, and the engine-room bilges had to be pumped almost constantly. In the control room the conning-tower hatch was latched down, but water still poured in so constantly the deck was wet and slippery. Rubber sheets were hung over the electrical switches on the starboard side to protect them from the water, but water got into them nevertheless and the open switches arced from contact to contact so that the board resembled a neon sign.

On the bridge, the skipper has had to make concessions to the storm. The port and starboard lookouts are allowed to leave their exposed normal positions high on the periscope shears and to stand behind the conning-tower, but this is not very much protection from the raging seas that are constantly breaking over the deck. The after lookout is allowed to leave his exposed position on the after part of the cigarette deck and come forward to stand behind the periscope shears.

Sailor Ostrom went on lookout watch. He climbed to the bridge through the conning-tower hatch in dry foul weather gear. In five minutes he was drenched to the skin, and stayed that way.

The submarine runs mostly in the trough, not by choice but blown by wind and wave.

The waves rise up on each side of us like cliffs. We watch as the boat sinks lower and lower into the water, and then the water starts to flood the cigarette deck. It is necessary to run the turbo blower to blow the water from the ballast tanks and lighten us. But then the ship rolls again and we sink lower and lower. Looking at the sea washing over the decks I say to myself, if that wave breaks I will surely be washed overboard. And even if I am not washed overboard I surely will not be able to hold my breath until the ship comes to the surface.

Eventually the submarine came to the crest of the wave, and on top of the waves there are smaller waves. As they rode the crest, the sea howled and the wind shrieked and Ostrom could not hear the shouts from the bridge watch only a few feet away.

The wind cuts the tops off the waves like a knife, and they came hurtling at the boat like a wall of water. At first he turned his back and crouched low. When the water hit it was like being hit with a baseball bat. It drove him across the deck, still in a crouched position. Then he tried to stand and face the wall of water, it hit full in his chest and filled his hood with cold seawater that ran down his back. He was completely drenched and totally miserable. The rain and wind-driven spray has reduced visibility so much that a ship could pass two hundred yards away and they would not see it.

Sailor Ostrom went on wheel watch. He put the wheel on full right rudder and waited for the ship to swing to the ordered heading, and then put the wheel full to the opposite direction. It did not make much difference; the sea was in control. The skipper ordered them not to use more than twenty degrees of rudder. They would go for fifteen or twenty minutes before the ship would swing back to its ordered course. They were at the sea's mercy.

It grew so rough up on top that the skipper ordered the boat submerged for safety. They went down to a hundred feet but still the violent motion of the sea on top of them could be felt. The depth gauge swung wildly.

Ostrom had always enjoyed rough weather at sea, seeing the water being forced through the bullnose as the bow of the boat was driven onto an oncoming wave, the sea thundering along the deck to run into the conning tower fairing sending spray and foam in all directions. He enjoyed the shuddering of the hull as the seas threw themselves at the ship. Sometimes the stern would rise clear of the water and then the propellers would come out and race and the ship would shudder. He never had any fear for the ship, so stoutly was she built. But this typhoon was different, something else.

After the war, Sailor Ostrom met a sailor from the submarine *Tang*, which also suffered through this same typhoon and they compared experiences. The sailor from the *Tang*, who was then a rear admiral, said that the waves were so high they completely covered the extended periscope for periods of fifteen seconds. He estimated the wave heights to be a hundred feet and the wind velocity 150 knots and the maximum roll of the ship at seventy degrees.

Typhoon! It was an experience that anyone who lived through one would never forget.

FORTY

The Escort Carriers Carry the Ball

The fact seems to have eluded most historians of the Pacific war that the role of the escort carriers, particularly in the Philippines campaign, beginning with Leyte gulf, became increasingly important as the major carrier force was otherwise occupied. The escort carriers took over the duties of softening up for invasion and troop support under the most difficult conditions, with the addition of the new enemy, the suicide pilot who would do anything to score a hit on a ship.

After the harrowing adventure of the battle off Samar, the carrier *Natoma Bay* headed for Manus and resupply. The ship recovered one of its torpedo bomber crews that had been shot down while fighting the Japanese ships off Samar.

Early in November the planes of the *Natoma Bay* were flown off near Manus Island and landed at the Pityliu Island Naval Airfield. The pilots lived ashore during this stop at Manus and continued operations from the field. On November 14, a TBM conked out on a mission and the pilot made a water landing. Apparently someone had not been taking very good care of the life rafts aboard the aircraft: The big one could not be removed from the plane and the small one leaked. The crew inflated their life jackets and swam ashore to a small island. They were picked up the next day by a Grumman Duck.

On November 17, Ensign Billie Peeler and Lieutenant Lloyd Holton were on a routine flight in a dive bomber when it spun into the water and crashed, killing both officers.

The respite on land lasted until November 27, when the squadron was ordered back aboard the carrier. The seven escort carriers of the fleet that had been damaged in the Leyte operations headed back to the United States for repairs, but the *Natoma Bay* was unhurt, so she stayed. Soon she was back at Leyte and then heading for Palau. All around her ships of the American fleet were falling victim to kamikaze attacks.

On December 10, the *Natoma Bay* joined the invasion fleet covering the movement into Mindoro Island as a preliminary to the assault on Luzon Island. Just beforehand, four bombers were sent off to Peleliu and replaced by extra fighter planes. This change represented the navy's reaction to the kamikaze operations. On December 13, the Mindoro invasion force was attacked heavily by suicide planes and Japanese bombers. In their convoy a cruiser was hit, and a destroyer. The *Natoma Bay* was under attack on the afternoon of December 13, but received no hits. The cruiser *Nashville* lost 170 men and the destroyer lost fifty. Meanwhile *Natoma Bay* fighters shot down four Zeros and a few hours later another three, while the ship's antiaircraft guns got another.

While on antisubmarine patrol Lieutenant Mac Roebuck jumped two fighters; one ran for home and the other was shot down. He then was jumped by two other Oscars but managed to get away with a single bullet in the radio gear. That same afternoon Ensign Robert Mount shot down another Japanese plane.

The next day Lieutenant Stewart Gingrich and a division of fighters jumped four Zeros and shot all four down in short order. The other pilots were Ensigns Houston, Therrell, and Miller, on detached duty to beef up the fighter strength of the carrier. Lieutenant Commander Robert Barnes led a fighter sweep on Japanese ground bases at Mindoro and Negros and on the latter island destroyed four planes on the ground at Dos Hermanos airfield.

On December 15, the Japanese came again to the fleet, and this time suicide planes very nearly hit the *Marcus Island*, the carrier next to the *Natoma Bay*. The two suicide bombers came down straight from 22,000 feet, hit the water just off the bow of the ship, and killed four men with near misses. On December 16, while flying over Mindoro Ensign Miller got on the tail of a Japanese plane and scored a damaging burst. Then his guns jammed and Ensign Lewis

Tomkins finished the plane off. That afternoon Ensign John Clifford shot down another Japanese plane.

As the historian of VC-81 put it, the success of the squadron and the whole air operation was measured not by the number of aircraft shot down but by the complete mastery of the air over the convoys and the carrier forces, keeping damage to the fleet at a minimum in spite of the suicide planes.

The *Natoma Bay* then returned to Manus, arriving on December 23. At that point some of the hysteria about the kamikazes had evaporated and the squadron was turned back more or less to its original strength of twelve torpedo bombers and two dozen fighter pilots with twenty fighter planes.

At the end of the year the *Natoma Bay* joined the assault group heading for Lingayen Gulf. All the way the ships were under air attack, from the kamikazes primarily, and the *Ommaney Bay* was sunk. Here, as seen from the deck of the *Natoma Bay*, is Chief Robert Johnson's diary account:

> *4 January. General Quarters at 3:45. Our AA display changed the minds of the Jap pilots. An Australian cruiser got one.*
> *9:00. Secured from General Quarters.*
> *5:15 P.M. Under air attack. General Quarters.*
> *5:25 P.M.* Ommaney Bay *hit by suicide dive bomber making run out of the sun. After knocking the top of the island off, it hit the middle of her deck, setting everything on fire.*
> *5:35.* Ommaney Bay *abandoning ship with destroyers standing by. Ammunition is exploding all over the ship.*
> *6:00 P.M. Her torpedoes exploded, shaking everything within miles.*
> *7:30 P.M. Secured from GQ. The* Ommaney Bay *is still burning. One of our destroyers is getting ready to sink her with a fish.*
> *8 P.M. The destroyer put two torpedoes into the* Ommaney Bay, *sinking her with a very large explosion. About 800 men were picked up leaving about 100 dead. About 100 were burned and injured.*

The battle continued the next day as the invasion convoy was off Mindoro. The *Manila Bay* was hit on January 5.

Here is Chief Photographer's Mate Johnson's account:

5:30, General Quarters beginning a series of all day affairs. We are now nearing the China Sea. Bogeys are all around us. Some are shot down by our planes.

1,035 miles off Manila Bay. Bataan is visible.

4 P.M. Under heavy air attack. Our CAP shot down one plane very close to our formation. Three planes shot down by AA while making low-level attack, one diving on a destroyer, but missing. The Louisville *hit on bridge by suicide bomber. Admiral and captain killed. She is burning. A number of planes (5) making low-level attack from port side of formation. Everyone is throwing up much AA but they are clever pilots and seem to get through. The* Manila Bay *hit by two suicide planes in middle of flight deck. All communications, radar and lights out. Using emergency steering. They are controlling the fires. DD hit by suicide bomber; fire rooms and engine rooms flooded; she is abandoning ship. Suicide planes dove on* Savo Island, *overshooting her, clipped her island while missing the ship. Suicide attack on this ship, strafing while coming in plane exploded thirty feet from fan tail. No one killed. AA shot down two more planes. We landed* Manila Bay's *planes. They say she will be in operation again in two days.*

The *Manila Bay* was able to carry on operations two days later.

On January 6, the *Natoma Bay* was running flight operations in support of the landings. The air patrol shot down four Japanese planes, Lieutenant Commander Barnes shot down two, and Lieutenant Walker and Lieutenant Sargent each got another. Sargent then went after a second Japanese plane low on the water and, making a sharp turn, miscalculated and his wing struck the water and the plane cartwheeled and crashed. He was killed.

On January 7, a *Natoma Bay* fighter collided with a Japanese plane and both went down. The torpedo bombers that day sent off seven planes to bomb an ammunition dump, and they were jumped by four Japanese fighters. The turret gunners shot down one Zero and drove off two others. One Zero made a head-on pass at the bomber piloted by Lieutenant Voltz. The bomber went into a spin, but the lieutenant succeeded in fighting it, and he headed out to sea toward the carriers. No one seemed to notice that a Japanese fighter was after him and made six passes before the pilot ran out of ammunition. This was a very effective pilot. He killed the gunner and wounded radio operator Michael Sweeney, who then tried to operate the turret but found the mechanism wrecked.

At that point the plane was almost inoperable, riddled by 400 bullet holes. Most of the instruments in the cockpit had been shot up and did not work. When Lieutenant Voltz got back to the carrier, he could not lower the hook because it too was shot up. There was no way to land on the carrier, so he made a water landing under very rough conditions. Even the flaps could not be lowered. In the landing radio operator Sweeney was knocked out and his shoulder broken, to add to his other injuries. Lieutenant Voltz got him out of the plane and held onto him while he inflated the life raft. A little later a destroyer picked them up.

That day Chief Photographer's Mate Johnson flew over Lingayen Gulf and took mapping photos of the area where the troops would land. He also took pictures of about fifty Japanese transports, tankers, and landing craft under attack at San Fernando. He flew in a TBM with two fighters for escort. He watched as the fighters shot down three Japanese planes, and he photographed ground activity, with Japanese trucks and tanks being strafed and rocketed by American planes.

That day the *New Mexico, West Virginia, California, Columbia, Louisville, Australia,* and two destroyers were hit by suicide planes while in Lingayen Gulf shelling the shore. The antiaircraft gunners shot down eighty-five Japanese planes.

On the afternoon of January 9, twelve fighters were launched by the carrier for combat air patrol. The kamikazes were active again against the fleet. One group was jumped by six Zeros from high altitude, and after a hard time the pilots shot down two Zeros. The *Kadashan Bay* was hit by a suicide plane at the water line and had to be taken under tow. The *Kitkun Bay* was hit by another and all hands but the salvage crew abandoned ship.

One division also shot down two Japanese army fighters. That day the landings began at Lingayen and San Fabian. The next day the *Steamer Bay* joined the carrier division, replacing the *Ommaney Bay.* The *Kadashan Bay,* under tow, was hit by another suicide pilot.

On January 13, Ensign McFarland, flying a fighter plane, had to land at Lingayen airstrip with mechanical problems; coming in, he hit a bomb crater and damaged a propeller blade. Parts were dropped off the next day and the plane was repaired.

The *Salamaua Bay* was hit in the middle of the flight deck; the plane went through the hangar deck and the bomb continued down into the engine room. That day Chief Johnson saw another destroyer hit and burning.

All week the seas were running heavy and it seemed that green water was coming over the flight deck half the time. But flight operations continued. On January 15, Ensign McFarland started back to the ship, but other pilots told him his plane was on fire and he bailed out sufferering a compound fracture of the left thigh. One more pilot was out of action.

Operations continued day after day until January 28, when the *Natoma Bay* moved into position to support landings in the Subic Bay area. The activity continued to be exciting. Here is the account from the war diary of VC-81:

> On January 30 our local CAP was vectored out to a bogey which turned out to be a lost army transport which was low on fuel. Two of the CAP were detailed to lead him to the Lingayen airstrip. While returning, the two pilots, Lieutenants Gingrich and Juston, spotted a Japanese submarine running surfaced about 60 miles from the base. The task group remained in this area another day while the USS Tulagi (CVE 72) conducted hunter-killer operations without any success.
>
> On the night of January 31 Mindoro Strait was transited after contact had been made with another Japanese submarine. This one was surfaced and its course was directly towards the ships when it was contacted by the USS Boise's radar. Four destroyers were left behind and the USS Moore (DE 442) made short work of the raider.
>
> Surigao Strait was transited on 2 February, no contact having been made with enemy aircraft in the Sulu and Mindanao seas. On February 5 the ship dropped anchor at Ulithi.

So the excitement was over for a while. The big news was that there was fresh fruit and fresh meat waiting for them at Ulithi. As Chief Johnson observed happily, "fresh fruit and U.S. meat, not that darn Australian 'goat.' "

FORTY-ONE

LST 246

Sailor William D. Askin was a plank owner on LST *246*. He enlisted in the navy in 1942 and came out in 1946 after working on the mothballing of ships at the end of the war. In the winter of 1944 to 1945 he and LST *246* headed across the Pacific for Lingayen Gulf. Largely from the pages of his diary, here is the story of that expedition:

January 1, 1945. Aboard LST 246 some 5,000 miles from Frisco out of Manus Island and on way to attack Luzon Island in the Philippines on the 9th. Rate Y 2c.

Skipper had talk at 10 o'clock and told crew dope on invasion. Looks fairly tough. But air superiority is expected all the way. Chow was usual lousy but this being New Year's the cook broke out a steak. I had a bottle of beer saved from Espiritu Santo and it was really good. Folkers, Parkhurst, and Hallack all shoveling it in.

Listened to Tokyo Rose in afternoon. Heard broadcast from Tokyo and a Japanese lieutenant is claimed to have downed 12 B–29s. Big laugh all around. Quite interesting to hear, though. Very good English spoken.

Worked a little and had cokes. Day very hot. Evening broke out MacDonald's sign rummy gift and now at it. Douched. Racked.

January 2. Heard Tokyo Rose again. Comes in loud and clear. Tokyo Rose played a symphony. POWs sent home messages and others did a skit. Newscast was good. Claimed to have ruined 500 B–29s. I don't think we have that many. Typed up log and did very little else. Rose Bowl result: U of Southern California beat Tennessee 25–0. Sat around and discussed college. Had last two bottles of beer from Espiritu Santo.

January 3. Had tetanus shot. Damned near fainted and heard about that all day. Had a flash red in the morning and everybody damned near fainted. General Quarters. All we sighted was a C–47 and two Hellcats all afternoon.

January 4. We are in sight of Japanese-held land now. The Philippines. Saw first land at 12:35, small mountain rising up. Rained like hell in the afternoon and yours truly was cool for a change. Sold shoes to Vernon for 300 percent profit. Moving through the straits now and may be bombed tomorrow.

January 5. General Quarters. Secured to Condition 1 easy, with all men at stations but we could relax. On the bridge all day until dark. Traded off phones one hour out of four.

They heard over the radio that a Japanese midget submarine had attacked a cruiser twice and was under attack, but nothing more.

On January 6, life began to become more exciting. The crew of LST *246* was called to General Quarters at 1:00 A.M. but the alert did not last. Another call to General Quarters came at 5:00 A.M. and lasted two hours.

From the radio they learned that the destroyer *Reid* had been sunk and the cruiser *Columbia* hit by shellfire in Lingayen Gulf. That was their destination, although at the moment they were in the Sulu Sea in sight of Panay Island.

On January 7, General Quarters was called in the afternoon and Askin rushed to his duty station on the bridge. He had some unkind comments about the officers of the LST: *Jellyfish* was his word. One Japanese plane was shot down by a destroyer before the alert ended.

On January 8, there were several calls to General Quarters, and a nearby destroyer shot down a Japanese plane during one of them. They heard about a destroyer action between three American destroyers and one Japanese, and the sinking of the enemy.

D-day for the Lingayen operation was January 9, and the men were up at 4:00 A.M. and at General Quarters almost continually from that point until nine o'clock that night. The Japanese planes began to arrive at dawn and the men of LST *246* counted nine separate air raids. They claimed hits on one Zero fighter. Smoke was seen to emerge from the plane. They were about two hundred yards off the battleship *Pennsylvania*, and when the battleship fired its 16-inch guns, Askin thought the LST was going to fall apart.

H-hour for the landing was 9:30 and the landings were unopposed except for sniper fire. The LST beached on Orange 2 at 3:30 in the afternoon. They began unloading successfully but lost their stern anchor and cable.

The night was fairly quiet. But morning brought an enormous amount of smoke from the screening destroyers. They got under way to the *Pennsylvania* to take off empty shell casings. They picked up survivors of APD 10, the SS *Brooks*, which had been hit by a kamikaze while alongside the *Pennsylvania*. The destroyer *Leutze* tied up alongside and unloaded more empties. They left the vicinity at about three o'clock and took some more empties from the *Leutze*. They saw LST *1028* and LST *925* hit by suicide boats, a new weapon the Japanese had been saving for this invasion. They were motor boats to which an explosive charge had been wired. The idea was for the coxswains to steer them into an enemy ship and jump overboard, but by this time the plan had been refined so that the coxswains stuck with the ships and became human torpedoes just like the kamikaze pilots.

During the hours of darkness the American P-61 night fighters caught hell from the invasion fleet. All the ships seemed to be firing on these American planes, and it also seemed a wonder that any of them survived. Sailor Folkers got hit by a splinter of friendly anti-aircraft fire and became the current hero of LST *246*.

Altogether ten men were hurt and transferred to other vessels, bound for hospital ships. They got under way that day and out of the immediate area, forcing their way out through the smoke from the destroyer screen.

On January 11, it appeared that the LST was bound for Leyte to pick up another load of supplies for Luzon. They joined a large convoy with several destroyers and one escort carrier, the *Kitkun Bay*.

A notice was posted on the bulletin board to warn the sailors that the Japanese suicide boats were more dangerous than they thought. Not only did they have explosive warheads, but swimmers went out from them with limpet mines to stick to the sides of the ships. Whoever posted the notice suggested that was what had happened to the two LSTs hit the previous night.

On January 12, they were moving through the straits again and then toward Leyte, which they reached on January 15. The Filipinos came alongside in small boats and they traded with the sailors, canned goods and chocolate for fiber hats, purses, and Japanese occupation money. They also traded off much of the ship's supply of saltwater soap for guerrilla currency and for coins. Several of the ships in the anchorage were hit by kamikazes that night, but the LST was not even close.

Every day the bumboats came alongside and the sailors traded. Sailor Askin went over the side into one of the boats and brought back a fistful of Japanese occupation currency. What he was going to do with it he hadn't an inkling. He talked to a girl named Rosalyn who told him how terrible the Japanese were. "Sure," he said, "she probably was telling the Japanese just the opposite."

The Filipinos announced a dance at the local high school that weekend and invited all the sailors. Several of those in the boats had instruments, a violin and a guitar that looked like it was a thousand years old. They played for the sailors, "Pistol Packin' Mama," for example. The girl named Rosalyn knew the words to "Stardust." In the scuttlebutt exchanged between ships, they learned that day that the command ship of their group, the destroyer *Calloway*, had taken a kamikaze at Lingayen and many of the men, many of whom Askin knew, had been killed.

On January 18 they had shore leave. Askin went into town and got "the dope" about what was happening. The Americans were winning the war. There was a long line in front of the local brothel, and the price was ten pesos. One of Sailor Askin's buddies gave him a drink out of a bottle of Filipino "whiskey." "My God," said Askin, "it would take the varnish off a chair."

That day the sailors of LST *246* discovered that when they had come up on the beach, they had really come up, and the tides since had not been so high. They spent the whole afternoon trying to retract off the beach, with no results. They brought two tugs up and these could not pull the ship off. They pumped out fuel and took everything they could off the ship to lighten it, but still the ship could not move. That night at eleven, when most of the sailors were asleep, the LST finally floated off in the high tide.

On January 19, the sailors loaded the LST with troops, 365 enlisted men and twenty-one officers of the First Cavalry Division, for another trip to Lingayen. Once again the LST got stuck and had to wait for the high tide to float off. Then they anchored and waited for the convoy to form up. It was January 22 before they got under way for Lingayen once more. Their convoy was 69 LSTs and eight merchant ships, screened by destroyers.

Generally speaking, when they were not at sea, life was pretty dull aboard the ship for Sailor Askin and he spent most of his free time reading books from the ship's library. As a yeoman, he had fitness reports and other paperwork to do, but most of this was periodic and did not take much time.

One of the crew had picked up a monkey, and after they got him defleaed and cleaned up, he seemed to have the makings of a pet. But two days out the monkey decided he had had enough of seagoing life and jumped overboard, never to be seen again.

That day came an air raid alert and the crew went to General Quarters, and the antiaircraft guns of the convoy began firing. They very nearly shot down a P-61 night fighter.

The convoy arrived at Lingayen on January 27 and found everything quiet except for several air raids by Japanese bombers. These had become almost routine. In the last few hours of the voyage their port propeller had begun to act up. Several members of the crew went diving to have a look at it. They moved on one engine to the San Fabian area and beached the ship. The troops were still aboard, waiting for orders to get off. On January 20, they disembarked and took their vehicles off the ship. Askin went ashore that day and saw a great number of ambulances bringing wounded men for shipment back to Leyte. The front line was then 60 miles from the beach he was told. He bought a Japanese pistol from a soldier for a hundred dollars. He wandered up and down the beach between air raid alerts.

They waited for another convoy to form up and take them back to Leyte. The captain and the convoy commander decided that LST

246 should be towed back because of her faulty propeller, and she was hitched to LST 276. But about an hour out the tow line parted, and then LST 246 was on her own with her single engine.

When they got back to Leyte most of the LSTs moved out, but 246 was stuck, with her bad propeller. Finally they salvaged a fly-wheel from LST 925, which had been blown up by the Japanese and was wrecked on the beach, and this seemed to solve their problem. But still they waited and did nothing. Sailor Askin went swimming, played cribbage, drank a lot of Coca-Cola, and read. He was very bored and wanted to get transferred off that ship.

On February 7, they tied up to the cruiser *Portland* and took on 25,000 gallons of fresh water. Next day they loaded and joined another convoy. When they got to Lingayen this time, one of Sailor Askin's buddies had a letter from home telling him that his brother had been killed at Lingayen. He couldn't believe it: so near and yet so far. It was the talk of the ship for the rest of the day. On February 14, Sailor Askin got a Valentine's Day present from the navy, news that he would be transferred the next day to the transport *Leonard Wood* and would be going back to the United States for leave. His last day aboard was spent doing paperwork so that the crew would get campaign bars for the Philippine campaign.

February 15 was the day of departure: "Up at reveille and went like mad through chow and last-minute work. Finally shoved off at 0900 after goodbyes to all the boys. Don't shake any officers' hands. Came along to *Leonard Wood* and they directed us to the *Warren*, where we came aboard and were put in the forward troop compart-ment. It was 'hotter than hell'."

It was all new and not very pleasant. He had to have his life jacket on to get in the chow line. They were in a convoy of fourteen ships and were supposed to arrive in the United States in one month.

So Sailor Askin began his voyage home. There was nothing to do but loaf and eat and read. Or so it seemed. But then on February 17, the captain learned that Askin was a yeoman, and sent a chief to bring him to the bridge and get to work on paperwork. But after three days he ran out of paperwork and then it was back to loafing and bull sessions where the sailors bitched about having nothing to do.

They arrived at Ulithi in the Carolines on February 18. There they were transferred (after several days of false starts) from the *Warren* to the *Sea Fiddler*, because the *Warren* was scheduled to take marine reinforcements to the Bonin Islands, where they learned from the scuttlebutt, the invasion was costing an inordinate number of casualties.

On February 25, they were under way again, this time headed for Eniwetok with a single destroyer escort. They arrived at Eniwetok on March 2, stayed two days, and then upped anchor and headed for home territory, Pearl Harbor. March 13: "Arrived in Pearl and, Dear Diary, Today I saw a WOMAN! Looks nice, doesn't it those words!!

> *Well, anyway we pulled in about 10 and tied up at Able 31 just below the section Base. Liberty in dungarees was granted to all so we took off at 1400. Went to the SubBase and the women in the canteen were really the nuts. God, man, they were gorgeous. Then we saw the shift break and all women leave. Geez! Saw a dame marine and a WAVE and they looked all right from where I sat. We bought a lot of gedunk and stuff and back to the ship. The base has really changed a lot since May. Back aboard, read, showered and racked.*

The next day Sailor Askin was determined to go into Honolulu but he did not have a pass. So he put his dungarees on over his whites, got a yard pass, and shoved off:

> *Changed in rec. station and left dungarees with the chaplain. Bus broke down just inside town and hoofed. All the whorehouses are closed. All amusement centers are closed. Ciro's was empty. Got a ticket from Shore Parole for not squaring hat and no rate. Sadie was very glad to see me and had a few drinks. Met a buddy there at Broadway. Got a pair of shoes, magazines, book by T. Thayer, candy, calendar, and left to return to ship. Got picture taken with Hula gal and back to yard. Got dungarees and changed over. Ate at repair dock cafeteria and then caught bus back. Women all over the town, Waves, Wacs, Marines. Not bad, not good. Hit rack early but thirsty after all that rum . . . !*

The next day the ship pulled out for the American mainland, escorted by a single patrol craft.

The lights of San Francisco were clearly visible at sea as they approached the Golden Gate on the night of March 21.

The homecoming sailor passengers were up at 2:00 on the morning of March 22 and at breakfast at 2:30. It was raining. Sailor Askin and his gear got off at Army Pier No. 7 in the rain and onto an army ferry, and then to Treasure Island. There he walked, lugging his seabag for about a mile, found the chow line, filled out his leave chit, got a liberty pass, and took his gear to be checked. He went into town carrying two small bags. He called a girl he knew, but she was not at home. He walked "all over hell and gone" and then finally rented a room at the Spaulding Hotel. He dressed in a tailor-made uniform and a new raincoat and went to the girl's house in a taxi. He had a rye and Coke and felt very drunk.

The next day Sailor Askin went to the base for a screening test given by the navy. Then he returned to San Francisco and had a few drinks and went shopping. He bought the insignia for his new uniform and got it sewed on, including the Amphibious insignia, of which he was very proud. He met the girl and then went bar-hopping: the Gotham Bar, the Club Savoy, where Billie Holiday, the blues singer, was star of the floor show. They drank until midnight, then had waffles, and the girl dropped him at the hotel and took the taxi home.

On March 24, 1945, Sailor Askin was up early and went to the base for formalities. He had thirty-five days' leave, ninety-two dollars in back pay, several hundred dollars of saved pay, and a brown traveler's bag. He left the base, went to San Francisco and engaged a bed for the night at the Pepsi-Cola Serviceman's Center, and went out to Mills College, where he knew some girls. They were having a dance. He and one other sailor were in the dining hall with eight tables full of women for dinner. They went to the dance and he danced with his date, a girl named Carol. He stayed at Mills until about 1 A.M. and then went back to the center by trolley and to bed.

March 25 was Sunday. He drove out into the suburbs and had dinner with friends. Then he picked up his luggage and took the ferry to Oakland and then the train east. He met a sailor and they shared a seat and talk.

"Train shoved off at 4:40 and we were on our way." Snow came soon in Nevada and at one station he got off and bought a quart of whiskey but didn't get a chance to drink any of it right away.

On Monday, the train sped on. Sailor Askin woke up late and watched the land go by. He left his new friend Bill and wandered around the train. He met a soldier named Tommy and shared his bottle with him. "Met a doll, not pretty but built, named Mary, a gunner's wife. We sat around hitting the quart now and then."

Later he went back to his own door and ran into a WAC, "a red head, and after chow we began a friendship. She was very loving and I didn't hate it at all. Pulled into Salt Lake about 7:30, got off and back on. Back on train settled in for a night of love but had a little trouble for a while. We went into another car and began a very good love job. No strain and I was going great but too many people passing through. She finally fell asleep in my arms. . . ."

The next day they reached Denver, which was home for Sailor Askin. He said goodbye to his traveling friends and got off the train, met by old Denver friends, and the partying began. He had thirty days for drinking and chasing girls and there was much drinking and many girls, but finally it ended and he had to go back to the war and LST *246*.

FORTY-TWO

Going to Manila

In the winter of 1945 Sailor William Casey's Seabee battalion was ordered to move from New Guinea to the Philippines. They packed their seabags and their packs and climbed aboard a group of LSTs for the trip from Hollandia to Manila.

"The images retained," said Casey many years later,

are a strange mixture of sights and smells due in part to a nauseating combination of bilge water and diesel fumes rising from the tank deck where our heavy equipment was chained, like some huge ungainly beasts of burden. It was this lethal combination of fumes when combined with the motion of the ship that tempted me to consider mutiny when I was ordered to stand watch on the tank deck. Fortunately the order was rescinded.

The company spent most of the trip on the main deck. It was a pleasant trip. The weather was good and Sailor Casey had plenty of time to read. He read *A Tree Grows in Brooklyn* on that voyage as the LST made its ponderous way north to Manila.

Sailor Casey's first view of Manila was of the skyline of modern high-rise buildings and it looked civilized and wonderful. He did not see in the setting sun that lighted his picture the dreadful results of the last-ditch stand of the 20,000 Japanese naval defenders who had chosen to disobey General Yamashita's orders to make Manila an open city and had fought for every foot of it, leaving the old town devastated.

After the usual snafus, the LSTs moved up on the beach to unload the 119th Seabee Battalion's "men and mules." And it was here in the rubble of the beach that Sailor Casey had his first encounter with the Japanese. He met a part of a Japanese soldier, the remnant of a bony leg in a canvas jungle boot pointing up to heaven. The image stuck with him.

When Sailor Casey got to Manila he circumvented censorship to tell his parents where he was by referring to "dewey mornings" in his letter home. He thought his father would make the inference, since the elder Casey was fond of a bit of doggerel about the Spanish-American war:

Dewy was the morning upon the first of May.
Dewey was the Admiral of old Manila Bay. . . .

How successfully the attempt to fool the censors turned out was never firmly established, but Sailor Casey did not have the feeling that any great revelation had been made.

The 119th set up camp in a village on the outskirts of Manila. They were not far from the Clark Air Field and one day, through an acquaintance, Sailor Casey had a chance to go for a ride in General George Kenney's personal B–17 bomber. He got a glimpse of the life of the generals:

The stark interior of the B–17 had been drastically altered in appearance so that it now resembled a well-appointed cabin cruiser. The curtain that shielded the windows were neatly pinned back with the stars of the general's high office. Even the once-lethal bomb bay had been dramatically altered and now functioned as a refrigerator for the general's beer supply. From my Dad and from reading I was prepared for that gulf which separated the enlisted man from the officer class. I was never surprised to discover that generals and admirals lived in a world far removed from the world of lance corporals and seamen.

Casey's village was haunted by small boys who prowled through the garbage the Americans threw away and took it off to make meals for Filipinos, a matter that caused Casey a good deal of emotional stress. It was also regularly visited, on paydays, by a number of old crones who brought their chuck-a-luck games to the camp to fleece the unwary. The younger women of the village washed clothes, ironed, did a little light sewing, and sometimes rendered other services to the sailors.

From time to time the demands made by the brass on the Seabees strained their "can do" ability. One day they were assigned to move a heavy piece of equipment to the upper floor of a tall building in Manila. The move involved hoisting the equipment from the street level, many ropes, and much skill. But one of their members, Johnny Walko, was an experienced rigger, so the job got done. There were many more like it.

With the capture of Manila and the routing out of those few Japanese who had holed up in the town, life settled down in the Manila area and the Seabees soon found their most onerous task was fighting boredom. But the rebirth of Manila kept them going. The city came alive with parades, street music, carnivals, and religious festivals, all of which provided amusement for the sailors. So Sailor Casey sweated out the last months of the war.

FORTY-THREE

Sailors' Mother on the Home Front

Mrs. W. R. LeBaron was really a navy woman. Her husband, four sons, and son-in-law were all serving in the United States Navy in World War II. She was living in Woodstock, Vermont, and keeping all the family in touch by acting as a sort of private post office, receiving letters from the farflung family and sending portions of one member's letters to the others.

On December 7, 1941, she pecked at her typewriter:

> *Enough time may sometime pass so that the above date can be written and it will be just another date. It hasn't yet. It still brings back to vivid and miserable memory the heartsickness we all felt concerning Ted on this day in 1941. [Ted LeBaron was in the heart of the action at Pearl Harbor on that day; see Chapter 2.] I cannot forget Jack's efforts that night when he followed me upstairs to assure me that he KNEW Ted was all right. [Jack LeBaron was serving aboard the net tender* Holly.] *Nor the fact that Bill was in the yard half an hour after we arrived back from Boston, dependable solid Bill. [Bill LeBaron was serving aboard the cruiser* Wichita.] *Nor Allan's awkward attempts, and they were very awkward, to lessen my anxiety when I knew his was just as great as mine. [Allan was now serving at Guam.] Nor the nightmare quality of the next eight days until the cable arrived "Ted okay." The most welcome word that was ever heard. Nor the strain that I put upon Dad and Marilyn and Allan by just having to live in the same house with me. I hope I've grown some since then. There has been a hundred years worth of experience in which to do it.*

Because of the censorship the letters were mostly about packages received and sent, sunsets, and life in America. From Guam,

Allan LeBaron was writing about chocolate, cheese spread, and peanut butter he had just received from her. He had just been gigged by higher authority for failure to pass daily inspection of his tent. ("We mustn't let the boys forget that this is a military organization.") The men of Allan's tent had been caught in flagrant delicto, and he got four hours' extra duty.

The LeBaron family had a great surprise at Christmas 1944. Two of the sons, Ted the airman and Bill from the *Wichita* got home for Christmas. The mother was worried about Bill. He had been aboard the *Wichita*, from February 1942 and steadily from March 22, 1944, until December, when he got leave in San Pedro. In that time, the *Wichita* had been involved in the defense of Guadalcanal, the action at Rennell Island, the Battle of the Komandorskis, the occupation of Attu, the New Guinea operation, the Marshall Islands campaign, the occupation of Kwajalein and Majuro, the occupation of Eniwetok, attacks on Jaluit, the Truk raid, the Marianas campaign, Palau, Yap, Ulithi, Woleai, Sabang, Ponape, Surabaya, and (in the European theater) the Algeria and Morocco landings, fighting off Casablanca, the Tunisian operations, and escort work in the North Atlantic. He had gone for months without mail and had come to the point where he felt that no one in the world, including his family, gave a damn what happened to him. They had just gotten Bill calmed down when he had to go back to San Pedro to join the *Wichita* again.

FORTY-FOUR

The Triumph of Skipper Davenport

By 1944 the American submariners had reached the organizational stage the Germans had achieved in 1941, and they were prepared to undertake wolfpack operations. But they were unable to achieve the same tight control of their farflung submarine operations that Admiral Dönitz had managed with his unique system of dictatorial control. Commander Davenport became the leader of a "coordinated attack group" called Roy's Rangers, an attempt to utilize the wolfpack system to the American conditions. On November 16, 1944, Davenport set sail again in the *Trepang*, but this time as group commander. The submarine was now commanded by Commander Thomas. The other submarines in the group were the *Segundo* and the *Razorback*.

The problem at this stage of the war was that there were so many American forces operating in the Pacific that they tended to get in one another's way. The task group was assigned a safety zone in which they were supposed to be able to operate without interference from surface ships or aircraft. But the plan did not work out very well. For example, on November 23 the three submarines were assigned the task of searching for the survivors of a B–25 bomber that had been shot down in the Saipan area. They did not find any, although they spent two days trying, and then they lost contact with the surface escort that was supposed to be in their area and spent another day trying to reestablish contact.

Two days later they arrived at Saipan without being bombed or being attacked by American surface ships, which seemed something of a wonder. The three ships of the three-submarine pack then refueled and moored. They had accomplished nothing so far. Here they picked up the *Spearfish*, making a four-ship work force.

By December 1, the submarine pack was in its assigned area and patrolling. But what they discovered was a vastly improved Japanese aerial surveillance system that kept the *Trepang* down most of the daylight hours and interfered seriously with "wolfpack" communications.

It was December 6 before they made contact with a convoy of seven ships. In the next few hours the American submarines sank all of them, and on December 8 the wolfpack was dissolved and the *Trepang* set sail for Pearl Harbor. December 10, was Sunday, and Commander Davenport changed hats and became a minister again, conducting divine services for the crew, along with Lieutenant Robert W. Stecher.

And, after all this, the *Trepang* got back to Pearl Harbor on December 22, 1944, in time for an American Christmas.

All of this, said Commander Davenport, was the work of God. In citation he mentioned the *Haddock*. After he gave up command of that submarine, the new skipper had stopped having divine services. And, said Commander Davenport, the *Haddock* became "just another submarine." She no longer had the success she had enjoyed under his leadership, apparently because she lost God.

Now with the *Trepang*, her commander after Davenport conducted church services, and "the *Trepang* experienced even greater protection than we had had and was equally successful."

At the end of 1944, after the second cruise of the *Trepang*, Commander Davenport gave up his skipper's job and went on to other duties to give another officer a chance at command. In it all, Commander Davenport won five Navy Crosses, to become one of the most highly decorated officers of the United States Navy, a fact he put down to the intervention of God.

When the war was won, he had only one regret. He felt that he was slighted by some other officers in the service, who found his intense religiosity out of place, and he felt particularly injured by writer Clay Blair, Jr., who in the book *Silent Victory* mentioned several incidents and names of nay-sayers in connection with the Davenport adventures. And so Commander Davenport, who retired as a rear admiral from the service, wrote his own book to set down his philosophy and his own story of his military life.

FORTY-FIVE

Fighting the Kamikazes

The war in the Pacific went on. Sailor Askin returned to duty aboard his LST. MacArthur's Seabees continued to work in the Philippines. The LeBaron boys continued in their farflung duty, Ted to Quonset Point, Rhode Island; Bill still aboard the *Wichita* running up battle stars; Jack now on shore patrol in Manila; and Allan at the Naval Supply Center in Guam.

The *Natoma Bay* and the other carriers of the escort fleet moved from invasion to invasion. On February 8, Admiral Stump left the flagship and Admiral Sprague came aboard. It seemed that the whole American fleet was sitting in Ulithi harbor that day—the fleet carriers, battleships, cruisers, all the support ships of invasion. They were preparing for the next move, which would be against Iwo Jima.

In the second week of February 1945 the *Natoma Bay* moved out to Saipan, and then with other elements moved toward Iwo Jima. They would stand offshore three days before February 19, which was D-day for the marine landing. The escort carriers would have the job of defending the fleet, because the fleet carriers were going to Japan to draw out what was left of the Japanese fleet, if anything, and to strike the Japanese at home. Just before leaving Ulithi the ship received seven new rocket-equipped fighter FM-2s and two new BM-3 torpedo bombers.

On February 16, the invasion fleet was 150 miles off Iwo. It was cold, and the weather was very rough. The flight schedule was heavy. The *Natoma Bay* lost a fighter that day. Visibility was very bad. Ensign Valpey was launched ninety minutes before sunrise as part of an eight-plane combat air patrol. Because of the overcast, which rose to 7,500 feet, he was unable to find his division. He encountered strong westerly winds and followed the lost-plane procedure until he ran low on fuel and made a power water landing seven hours after launching. He inflated his raft and got clear of the survival gear. He spent the next two and a half days in the water, until he was found by a search plane from the *Anzio*, which dropped a larger raft, food, and water. His position was 135 miles east of Iwo Jima. He was picked up later in the day and returned to his ship by destroyer.

The work of hitting the Iwo Jima defenses started on January 17. The pilots found plenty of flack opposition in spite of the fact that Iwo had been hit hard by bombers for a long time before the invasion.

On the bomber runs, the pilots encountered heavy antiaircraft fire and four of the eight bombers were damaged. Lieutenant Commander Morton's plane was so badly hit that it had to be jettisoned on return to the carrier. Lieutenant Reeves had a third of the starboard elevator shot away. Lieutenant Wavell was hit in the port wing, the bomb bay, and the starboard stub wing. He had to pump the bomb bays open in order to bomb. On that run he was hit twice in the starboard wing and in the elevators. Ensign McMahon's plane was hit in the tunnel and through the bomb bay. The radioman's clothing was set afire by a smoke bomb set off by shrapnel. The hydraulic system was knocked out and with five bombs still aboard Ensign McMahon had to make a water landing. The plane stayed afloat for only ninety-seven seconds, but all the men were evacuated and picked up by a destroyer.

On February 17, a fighter sweep of Chichi Jima included four fighters from the *Natoma Bay*. They found Japanese aircraft on the field and strafed them and attacked shipping in Futami Harbor.

On the afternoon of February 21, Ensign Kesterke ferried a passenger to the carrier *Bismarck Sea*. Just after they landed the carrier was hit by a suicide bomber and Kesterke and his radio man abandoned ship and went into the water just before the *Bismarck Sea* capsized. They were picked up by a destroyer.

FORTY-SIX

The UDTs in Action

The first Navy Underwater Demolition Team went into action at Casablanca in 1942. From that time onward the UDTs increased in number and improved in skill, much of it derived from testing and exercises evolved at the school at Camp Perry, Virginia, run by Lieutenant Commander Draper L. Kauffman. He sent units to the Pacific that were involved in the Marshalls, Marianas, Palau, and Philippine invasions.

Commander Kauffman kept asking for transfer from training to action, and eventually he got it. The high point of his action career came at Iwo Jima.

When the army air force high command said it needed an air base between the Marianas and Japan to fly protective fighters on the B–29 missions, the navy knew that the capture of one of those islands so close to Japan was going to be difficult. All of them were heavily fortified, and their defenses were increased as the war drew closer to Japan. So the navy assigned three marine divisions, the Fourth, Fifth, and Third to the operation, although the commanders hoped they would not have to use the Third Marine Division men, saving them for the next big battle.

For four months the Americans conducted a heavy aerial-bombardment campaign against Iwo Jima, and when they prepared to invade they got ready for the heaviest ship bombardment of the war. They also prepared to meet heavy Japanese underwater obstructions and assigned Commander Kauffman four Underwater Demolition Teams, Numbers 11, 12, 13, and 14, to make sure the island shores were secure before the marines landed.

The island is not very large—four and a half miles long and one half mile wide. The Underwater Demolition teams were to clear two miles of beach on the southeast side of the island, from Mount Suribachi on the south to what the marines called the East Boat Basin.

Each Underwater Demolition Team had its own headquarters and support ship, one of the old destroyers that had been converted to destroyer transports. These were the *Barr, Bull Bates*, and *Blessman*.

The action began for the UDT men on D-2. The weather, which had been terrible, improved somewhat, and the fighter planes of the carriers made several sweeps across the island. There was also to be bombing by heavy bombers from shore bases and heavy shore bombardment from the navy fleet off the Iwo Jima shore. The bombardment began at 7:00 o'clock, and minesweepers also went into action. The *Pensacola* noticed that the Japanese were firing on the minesweepers and put her guns on the spot on shore and silenced the Japanese fire within five minutes. But the Japanese had revenge: They opened fire on the *Pensacola*, hit her half a dozen times with six-inch shells and wrecked her combat information center, set fire to one of her observation planes, killed seventeen men and wounded ninety-eight. The damage was great enough that she had to retire from the action temporarily to take care of her wounded and fight fires.

By 9:00 o'clock the battleships *Idaho, Nevada*, and *Tennessee* were all firing on the shore from points about two miles offshore, but at 10:15 they were ordered to stop so that the UDT men could do their work. By that time the minesweepers finished with their efforts, having swept the water 750 yards offshore.

On the morning of February 17 the UDTs went into the water. The four teams all left their APDs and went into the small boats to carry out their tasks. They headed in to the 500-yard line, where the swimmers then plunged into the water to carry out their missions. They were followed by seven landing craft made into gunboats which fired 20mm and 40mm guns, at the beaches and launched 4.5-inch rockets. The boats came under heavy fire as they supported the UDT men. LCIs *471, 438, 441* were all hit by Japanese gunfire and LCI *474* was struck repeatedly and had to be abandoned and sank. LCI *409* suffered 60 percent casualties in two trips to the shore and back. Altogether twelve of the craft took part in the action and they took the beating.

LCI *466* was observed by novelist John P. Marquand, who was aboard the *Tennessee* as a correspondent. Marquand wrote about the sight:

> *There was blood on the main deck, making widening pools as she rolled in the sluggish sea. A dead man on the gun platform was covered by a blanket. The decks were littered with the wounded. They were being strapped onto wire stretchers and passed up to us over the side. The commanding officer was tall, bareheaded and blond and he looked very young. They passed up seventeen wounded men and five dead.*

In all on the gunboats that supported the UDT operations forty-four men were killed and 152 were wounded.

The Navy answer to the heavy Japanese fire was to increase the tempo of the bombardment and seek special targets. They asked for an extra air strike and got it. But the destroyer *Leutze* was hit by Japanese fire, which killed seven men and wounded thirty-three others, including the commanding officer.

By noon all the swimmers had been recovered. What they had found was surprising and pleasing to them. There were very few underwater obstacles, and most of these were mines. There were a few sunken rocks off a point called Futatsu Rock. The UDT men planted a light on Futatsu Rock and removed the mines and the dangerous sunken rocks. But the real obstacle to the landings, they discovered in their charting of the beach, was going to be the heavy surf just offshore.

When the Japanese saw the UDT men leaving their *APD*s in landing craft and saw the heavy concentration of ships and landing craft along the south shore of the island, they got the idea that the landings had begun and the shore guns, which had been silent during several days of bombardment began to fire on the UDT men worming along the beach. Commander Kauffman was using a landing craft outfitted as a gunboat as a communications boat to direct his teams. During the operations the boat was struck by an eight-inch shell from a Japanese shore gun and the radio operator who was standing next to Kauffman was killed, but the commander was unhurt.

The men moved into the cold water and made careful reconnaissance of the island shore, although the cold water caused some of them severe cramps. Some of the swimmers got onto the shore itself and brought back examples of the beach floor. The navy was upset to learn that what they were going to land the marines on was volcanic sand, light and fluffy but completely unstable. A man could walk in the volcanic sand with effort but he could not run, and vehicles were going to bog down.

While the swimmers were gathering the sand, they put up a sign on the beach for the marines who would land in a few hours:

WELCOME TO IWO JIMA

Then they slipped back into the water and swam back to their landing craft, their jobs apparently ended.

But the commanders wanted more information about the western beaches. They could not get it that afternoon, because too many of the gunships had been put out of action. They had to wait several hours, while the destroyers and other ships moved in and delivered covering fire. Then the UDT men could go to the west side and repeat there what they had done in the morning on the main landing beaches. By six o'clock in the evening the job was all done. Their casualties had been very low. One man was wounded on Futatsu Rock and one man was missing. He was last seen swimming toward Suribachi Mountain beach, bracketed by enemy shellfire. He was Carpenter's Mate First Class Edward M. Anderson.

Commander Kauffman had a right to feel that his job had been well done, but Iwo Jima presented some new problems. On the evening of February 18, the night before the scheduled marine landings, the men of the APD *Blessman*, which included the sailors of UDT 15, were relaxing, playing cards, and writing letters home in the messroom below deck at around ten o'clock at night when a kamikaze plane approached the invasion fleet and dropped two

200-pound bombs. One hit the *Blessman* and penetrated into the messroom before exploding. The blast killed eighteen UDT men and wounded twenty-three others, plus eleven of the ship's crew. The *Blessman* caught fire and the fires began to spread because the firefighting equipment had been damaged in the blast.

Commander Kauffman was aboard the APD *Gilmer*. He and the captain of the *Gilmer* knew that the *Blessman*'s magazines were full of the explosive the UDT men used to blow up obstacles, but they moved up to the damaged ship. The *Gilmer* turned her hoses on the *Blessman*, and Commander Kauffman led a boarding party to help the wounded and put out the fires. They were successful and saved the ship and the crew. But 40 percent of the men of UDT Team 15 were casualties that night, the highest casualty rate of any UDT team in the war.

When the marines landed, there were problems with the reef. Kauffman's UDT men guided the marines through paths to the shore, a job made dangerous by the shelling of the Japanese shore guns. They continued to function as guides and did special jobs such as blasting out boat landings during the course of the Iwo Jima invasion.

The second-guessing of the Iwo Jima operation in America did not wait until it was all over. In the United States the Hearst newspapers led a campaign to force the United States government to replace Admiral Nimitz's leadership of the Pacific Ocean areas and put General Douglas MacArthur in charge of the whole war in the Pacific. The complaint about Nimitz's leadership was enormous and began to have effects. The losses of the marines on Iwo Jima were the most serious of the war. The critics said it should never have been invaded, that the bombardment was too little, that not enough troops were used. None of this was true. The reality was that the Japanese defenses of Iwo Jima were the most perfect that the Americans had yet found, and they gave a good indication of what was to come. That the possession of Iwo Jima was important was indicated by the fact that American B–29s, crippled over the Japanese homeland, began to land on the airfield even before it was safely in American hands.

The complaints became so loud that they began to affect the national feelings about the war, and Secretary of the Navy James V. Forrestal received many telephone calls and letters of complaint from anxious mothers and other family members about their sons on Iwo Jima. He had to remind Americans that when the Japanese attacked Pearl Harbor they threw down a gauntlet that the Americans picked up. There was no way to end the war without fighting it to a finish, he said.

For the marines it was tough going all the way. Iwo Jima was declared secured on March 16, 1945, but it really was not secured. The marines continued to fight and to take casualties. They suffered almost 3,000 casualties between the time the island was "secured" and the time the fighting actually stopped. General Howland Smith had hoped to employ only two marine divisions on Iwo Jima, but part of the Third Division had to be used as well, and the marines ashore wanted more help but it was denied to them.

Before the action ended it had cost the marines more than 25,000 casualties and the navy almost 3,000. Those casualties were heavier than the Japanese, although nearly all the Japanese on the island fought to the death. The count of Japanese dead was not quite 21,000, plus 216 prisoners. When the fighting was over the marines estimated that there were still one or two hundred Japanese left on the island who would have to be dealt with by the army garrison that was going to take over. All that for an island that one marine remarked "wasn't worth fifty cents on the real estate market."

One reason that General Smith and Admiral Richmond Kelly Turner denied the marine command on Iwo Jima more troops of the Third Marine Division was their concern over the next operation, at Okinawa. The Japanese had proved a very tough opponent with his back to the wall at Iwo Jima. Now, heading for Okinawa, the marines and the army commanders and the navy expected that it might be much worse.

The reason: Okinawa was considered one of the original parts of Japan, not quite the homeland but a possession so ancient that it had been thoroughly Japanized, although the people retained their language and their culture. If the Japanese had fought this hard for a lonely rock that had no other reason for being than defense, how then would they fight for a part of their integral homeland? The question worried the high command, but it was not long in being answered.

FORTY-SEVEN

Okinawa

The escort carriers continued to support the marine operation on Iwo Jima in March. On March 3, Chichi Jima was hit again and eight *Natoma Bay* fighters went along, with rockets to fire on Japanese shipping. One fighter was shot down, and two were damaged by antiaircraft fire when they attacked shipping in Futami Harbor. They made three attacks, on the first firing rockets at the shipping and on the second and third attacking antiaircraft positions to protect the torpedo bombers that followed them. They were retiring toward the entrance to the harbor when Lieutenant (jg) Huston's FM-2 was hit by flack and went into a 45-degree dive and struck the water, exploding on impact. That same day when Lieutenant Tate was launched, the plane veered to the left because of the heavy roll of the ship, and in spite of his corrective measures the plane went over the after stack and into the water. He was picked up five minutes later by a destroyer. Later in the day the *Natoma Bay* combat air patrol shot down a Japanese bomber headed toward the fleet.

On the night of March 7, the escort carriers had expended all their bombs and most of the ammunition available and they were ordered back to Ulithi. They had scarcely anchored there when Japanese suicide planes attacked the anchorage. One plane flew over the *Natoma Bay* at 100 feet and into the new fleet carrier *Franklin*, which was anchored nearby. The fires started by the suicide plane did extensive damage. The other kamikaze hit the beach, killing a few men, but doing little damage.

On March 13, Squadron VC 81 was relieved by Squadron VC 9. Six Navy Crosses were awarded for heroism in the Leyte campaign.

The squadron headed back to America and leave, but not the *Natoma Bay*. She was scheduled for the Okinawa invasion and set sail on March 21.

What the men knew about Okinawa was that it held 60,000 Japanese soldiers, 450,000 civilians, and 4,000 prostitutes in Naha. It seemed unlikely that the last statistic would be useful.

On March 22, the CAP shot down a Betty bomber and that night an F6F night fighter flew into the ship's island while making a night landing. The pilot was never seen again.

From March 25 on, the planes of the *Natoma Bay* were busy with the invasion buildup and then the invasion, flying one mission after another all day long. The CAP shot down five suicide planes just after dawn on that first day. The fliers discovered that their unit was a part of one group of seven escort carriers, and a similar group was operating not far away.

On March 27, one TBM was shot down and most of the ship's planes returned with significant antiaircraft fire damage. In the three days ending March 29, the ship had been called to General Quarters sixteen times. Almost all of these were kamikaze attacks or scares.

More than 500,000 American troops were to be landed on Okinawa. Their way was to be cleared by a thousand men from ten underwater demolition teams in the biggest UDT operation in history. This was to be the biggest amphibious operation in the Pacific.

The UDT teams were organized into two groups, Group Able and Group Baker. The first assignment of Group Able was the capture of Kerama Retto, a small group of islands fifteen miles west of Okinawa. This operation was scheduled before the landings on Okinawa because the navy command anticipated very strong kamikaze opposition and wanted a refuge for its ships. On March 25, three UDT teams started their operations in the Kerama Retto. The waters were very cold, so the swimmers coated their bodies with axle grease, a coating that also helped protect them from Japanese snipers.

In the landings one platoon from UDT 19 landed on what was thought to be an uninhabited island. The swimmers were basically unarmed. They had their knives, which were intended for the cutting of ropes and other obstacles, and one man had a pistol. They soon found that the island was very much inhabited by Japanese soldiers. The Japanese opened fire as the UDT sailors came out of the water, and one man was wounded. The wounded man was carried back to the team's boat and Ensign Bob Killough held off the Japanese with his pistol while the rescue was made. Then Killough followed the rest of the platoon, firing the last shot from his pistol before he went into the water. The platoon made it safely back to their mother ship.

On March 26, the beaches of Kerama Retto were all clear and the landings began on six islands. On the next day five more landings finished off the capture of Kerama Retto. In these islands the Americans found many nests of suicide boats, 300 in all, hidden in little inlets among the islands. They had been prepared to attack the invasion fleet and would have caused serious damage if they had gotten among the cargo ships of the main Okinawa landings.

For this operation a whole new command organization had been established, with a planning organization. The majority of the staff officers knew nothing about UDT; they were coordinators and strategists. Thus UDT at Okinawa passed from the ranks of the experimental organizations of the navy to a brass-loaded command, but the organization was necessary to carry out so large a UDT effort, to clear twenty-one landing beaches of thousands of obstacles.

At Okinawa the Japanese had installed thousands of obstacles, particularly on beaches Red 1, Blue 1, and Blue 2, north of the town of Hagushi. Nearly 3,000 obstacles were found and destroyed here. Most of them consisted of logs a foot thick driven into the sea floor and connected with barbed wire. Each obstacle had to be blown up, and all of them were.

One team, UDT-11, cleared 1,300 yards of beach, taking out 1,400 obstacles. Each charge consisted of a two-and-a-half-pound block of tetrytol explosive wrapped in a piece of primacord fusing tied in a special knot, with a 30-inch trailer that would be used for tying the charge into the master primacord trunk line. Each block was also wrapped in soft wire, with the wire also used to secure the charge to the obstacle. Four charges were placed in a fabric pack attached to a flotation bladder. Each swimmer could manage five such packs, which meant fifty pounds of explosives.

UDT operations began on March 29 with reconnaissance operations, and then on March 30 and 31 the demolition operations. On April 1, the marines and army troops invaded Okinawa and the long fierce battle began. UDT swimmers guided many of the troops of the first waves in through the channels they had opened. Then the UDT men went to their other duty, to man the machine guns of the APDs against the Kamikaze planes that were coming in by the hundreds.

By April 1, the *Natoma Bay* had expended all its bombs and headed for the Kerama Retto islands to rearm. The ships were attacked by suicide planes, and the battleship *West Virginia*, nearby, was hit by one. The air attacks were heavy and while in Kerama Retto six ships were hit by kamikazes, including one destroyer escort assigned to the carrier.

April 6 was a really bad day, with an attack by a hundred suicide planes, although seventy-five of them were shot down the other twenty-five plowed into ten ships, sinking three destroyers. The fate of the destroyer *Leutze* was indication of the fury of the Japanese air attack. The *Leutze* had already been damaged off Iwo Jima. Now she was a part of the screen for Admiral Deyo's fire-support ships. On the evening of April 6, she was moving toward Ie Shima with the screen when her lookouts sighted an airplane eight miles away, and a few minutes later the guns opened fire on it as it seemed to be heading their way.

One—it turned out to be twelve torpedo bombers and fighters. The *Leutze* was firing 5-inch antiaircraft shells and 40mm ammunition as fast as she could, and so were the other ships of the force. The destroyer *Newcomb* was the first to get hit, when a kamikaze crashed into her after stack, followed in quick succession by another that splashed into the water near the ship, a third that hit deep in the bowels of the destroyer, and a fourth that crashed into the forward stack. The *Leutze* came to the side of the *Newcomb*, assuming that she was about to sink, but when it was seen that she was still going the men of the *Leutze* passed firehoses and helped fight the fires on the other destroyer. Then a plane came in, aiming at the *Newcomb*, and hit on the fantail of the *Leutze*. It was a serious injury, and soon the stern was settling in the water. Lieutenant Leon Grabowsky, the skipper of the *Leutze*, asked and received permission to jettison the torpedoes and depth charges; that helped lighten the ship and prevent further damage. She was taken under tow by the minesweeper *Defense* and brought into Kerama Retto. All this time the men of the *Leutze* were fighting to save their ship. The executive officer, Lieutenant A. G. Capps, was under the kamikaze when it crashed and was pulled from beneath its tail to direct firefighting and control of the forward guns of the ship. The surgeon, Lieutenant J. J. McNeil, carried men to safety and then treated them. Lieutenant D. W. Owens put out a fire in the magazines. Firemen Francis J. Nemeth was securing steam lines that were almost red-hot and would not stop. He was burned to death by the fires. Machinist's Mate Richard Tacey was killed while trying to save some of the engine room crew who were trapped by flames.

That's the way the fighting went all the way at Okinawa, where the U.S. Navy had more casualties than in all the other actions of the war, and so many ships were damaged that Admiral Nimitz invoked censorship on casualty figures so the enemy would not discover how hard they were hitting the navy.

On May 4, the *Natoma Bay* was heading back for Okinawa again and more troop support. On May 11, the American fighters shot down eighty-five Japanese suicide planes and the ship antiaircraft guns shot down thirty-six more. This routine continued through May and June. The *Natoma Bay* took a suicide plane on June 7, and one officer was killed and a number of men were injured, but the carrier continued to operate, even with a hole ten feet wide and twenty-five feet long in the flight deck. They continued operations until June 23, when the ship left again for Guam, and on July 21 left for Pearl Harbor. Everyone was hoping that they would go on to the West Coast, but there was no such luck, and on August 1 they were headed back for Roi in the Marshalls. But there the ship had orders to proceed to San Diego, and she was en route there when the Japanese surrendered on August 14, U.S. dating.

FORTY-EIGHT

Disengagement

The Germans were finally brought to their knees in the spring of 1945, and then all American eyes turned to the Pacific. The high command anticipated a dreadful and costly struggle to conquer the islands of Japan, an anticipation fully warranted by the pattern of Japanese defense and the intentions of the Japanese militarists to take the whole country down with them in their fall.

Because of that, President Harry Truman reluctantly ordered the use of the atomic bomb, and the first was dropped on Hiroshima on August 6, Japan dating. The news electrified the world. From Vermont, Mother LeBaron wrote:

"You can better believe that the news we've been getting the last few days—atomic bomb, the President's message last night and then all today the talk of a Japanese surrender, has us pretty well standing on our heads, and counting the possibilities of all of you being home for Christmas. . . ."

Then, on August 15, fortunately for the Japanese and the Allies, Emperor Hirohito intervened against the generals, braving the palace revolution he had feared for so long and managing to avoid it by facing the generals down. The shooting war came to an end.

The immediate reaction on the home front was jubilation:

Inez called me just at seven, fearing we might not have the radio on. We heard the church bells, auto horns, sirens, and everything else break loose downtown. We went down [a] little later just to look around. The kids had gone completely mad. Trucks were picked up. The wherewithal for bonfires and traffic rules appeared to me to be suspended. I couldn't believe my eyes when I saw one huge "makings" being prepared on the street directly in front of the fire house. . . . Another one, even bigger, was built around the silent policeman at the junction of the road we come in on and the White River Road, right in the center of town. Everyone and his brother was on the street.

The aim of most American servicemen was to get home as quickly as possible. The LeBaron brothers were typical:

"We had all been eager volunteers and were now just as eager to return to civilian life," said Allan LeBaron, who was at that moment of surrender stationed at the naval supply center on Guam. "Our brother-in-law, Norman Strassburg, a chief boatswain's mate aboard a Coast Guard ship, had 42.5 points." He was discharged on September 28. Ted, who was in Quonset Point, Rhode Island, was discharged in the middle of November 1945. Jack LeBaron left Manila and got home to San Francisco, and he got out.

But the other LeBaron boys had to await their turns, along with millions of others.

In Manila Sailor Casey began to fidget in the fall of 1945 as the older members of the 119th Seabees began to go home. His turn came in November and he boarded a transport and set sail for Guam; there was to be transferred to one of the carriers that were being enlisted to get a lot of men home in a hurry. Sailor Casey had braved the rigors of travel in an LST that rolled like a bucket. He had survived the war, but after he got on board the transport *West Point* he was not sure he was going to survive to get back to the United States.

It was the first day out. The weather was calm, peace had again settled on the world, and they were going home. What could be nicer? Casey was sitting with his back against a gun tub contemplating the ocean. Suddenly he became uncomfortably aware that the ship was rolling. Very soon this became the central matter of his consciousness, and a terrible pain coursed through his head, matched by a violent surge of nausea in his belly. He spent the rest of the day sprawled on a hatch cover, and when it rained, he did not move. Later in the downpour, he moved to an opening in the bulkhead where the fire hose was stored. But further than that he could not go. All night long he was sick, and into the next day. By the time they got to Guam he was recovered. The trip to Seattle was a breeze. The first thing to do when they got to Seattle was to get ashore and get a milkshake.

It was the week before Christmas when they arrived and the navy moved fast to get the men out and on their way home for the holiday. The train trip east was a nightmare, with some of the men standing almost all the way from one coast to the other. But nobody complained.

Sailor Casey's last months in the service were spent in the Fargo Barracks in South Boston. In the confusion of moving out of a malaria area nobody had informed Sailor Casey that the atabrine pills he had been taking for months, and which had turned his skin a bright yellow, were a palliative for malaria and not a cure. So when he left the tropical scene he went off atabrine and about two weeks later he came down with a fine case of recurrent malaria. But except for this (and the seizures became less frequent and less painful), those last days in the service were pleasant enough, with little to do but spend the time in the ship's service canteen on the top floor of the Fargo building, drinking Boston Light beer at twenty-five cents a quart. And then he was out and going home.

Allan LeBaron left Guam in February 1946 and was discharged in April. Bill LeBaron, who had served the most actively of all, in the *Wichita*, had earned thirteen battle stars. The *Wichita* came home to the Philadelphia Navy Yard and was decommissioned. But Bill had signed for a six-year regular navy enlistment, and the navy held him to it, although he did not again have sea duty before his discharge. Instead he ended up in the occupation of Japan. He went to Nagasaki, and saw for himself the damage inflicted by the second atomic bomb:

> *I wouldn't expect anyone to believe me if I told them what the place looked like. I thought the reports were highly exaggerated as to the power of that bomb, but after I saw what it did over here I'd believe anything about it. It just flattened everything in that end of the valley and I really mean flattened it right down to the ground. There were just piles of glass*

at the site of a building. The rest of it was all gone. Steel towers three or four miles from where the bomb exploded were either dropped or bent away from the explosion.

Bill LeBaron was involved in the repatriation of American prisoners of war from Japan: "From six to twelve last night I was over handling stretcher cases from the train until they were on board ship. Some of those guys are pretty well starved. I could put my hand around the biggest part of their legs and still touch the thumb and point finger. You hardly know there is anyone on the stretcher unless you look around and see them."

After a short period of resentment at his lot, Bill LeBaron settled down to serve out the remainder of his regular navy hitch with good grace in the forces of occupation in Japan. Sailor Lynch, too, had signed up for a six-year term, and no matter how many times he escaped and went AWOL, they kept bringing him back until he had served his time. Then he came home from the Pacific. In the process of being discharged Sailor Lynch was sent to a psychiatrist, perhaps to try to figure out why he had spent so much of his naval career in unauthorized time on the beach. The psychiatrist heard his story of the frightening hours on the *Lexington* before she went down in the Coral Sea and gave Sailor Lynch a piece of advice. "You go on home to Texas, and find yourself a nice girl and get married and settle down," he said.

Sailor Lynch did not believe he was going to do just that. When he got back to Burnet, Texas, he saw a pretty girl and decided he would take her to bed. He did, too, within a couple of weeks, with one slight hitch in his plan. That was the wedding ring she was wearing on the third finger of her left hand. So Sailor Lynch ended up taking the psychiatrist's advice and as of the fiftieth anniversary of his enlistment in the navy he was still going strong, deep in the heart of Texas.

And what of the ships that the brave sailors had taken across the seven seas and back?

Most of them were scheduled for the mothball fleet, and one by one they were decommissioned and put into storage or sold for scrap. Sailor Askin spent the last few months of his naval career putting ships into mothballs.

The *Natoma Bay* was almost typical. She spent the first few months after war's end as part of the Magic Carpet that brought the boys home from foreign climes. On May 20, 1946, she was decommissioned at Norfolk in a ceremony attended by eight "plank owners" of the original ship's crew. She was destined then for a fate that to some might seem ironic. She was built during the war to fight the Japanese, and she was now scheduled to go to Japan to feed the furnaces of the Japanese steel industry that was being reinvigorated with American help. How times had changed! Japan was no longer the enemy but was now being seen in a new light, as the ally of America in the struggle against world communism. So along with the *Manila Bay*, the *White Plains*, the *Guadalcanal*, and the *Mission Bay*, the *Natoma Bay* was to aid Japan, towed at the end of a line by the oceangoing tug *Elbe* on a ninety-day voyage to Japan. She cost eight million dollars and brought $140,000 at the auction that sent her to Japan. But the *Natoma Bay* was not destined for the ignominy of scrapping, and two hundred miles off the coast of Japan she gave up her ghost, turned on her side, capsized, and sank to the bottom of the sea.

Acknowledgments and Bibliography

The sources for this book were primarily the accounts of the experiences of many individual sailors who served in World War II. They were transmitted to me in interviews, letters, diaries, tapes, unpublished manuscripts, and privately published books. If the bibliography for this book seems incomplete, it is because most of these tales have never appeared in print.

I am indebted to hundreds of sailors and others for suggestions, names, and accounts of war experiences, not all of which could fit into the book. I am particularly in debt to the following: *VFW Magazine*, The Reserve Officers Association of the United States, Olga Gruhzit-Hoyt, Diana P. Hoyt, Hiroko Hattori Hoyt, Henry Pyzdrowski, Rear Admiral W. R. McClendon, USN (ret.), Alfred G. Don, John Sassano, Maury Meister, Rear Admiral Sheldon Kinney, USN (ret.), Tom Hilliard, J. R. Conlin, the LeBaron Family (Alan, Jack, Ted, Bill, and Pearl), Mike O'Dea, Harry Luessen, Clifford L. Legerton, Dean Allard, Mrs. Kathy Lloyd, Mark H. Jordan, Harry Ayres, Van Watts, Carol Kelly, William D. Askin, John Picuri, Daniel E. Keough, Will Molineux, Larry DeVries, C. W. Lynch, Frank Cummings, Theodore Treadwell, Ronald Veltman, James J. Hall, Godfrey J. Orbeck, Rear Admiral E. A. Barham, USN (ret.), Mrs. Roy Davenport, William T. Casey, Sr., William E. Weedon, Dave Mangrum, Larry Flanagan, Robert E. Collins, Gene Eisenhower, J. J. S. Murphy, Wallace Brown, Al Higginbotham, Ken del Mastro Merdin Criddle, Hal L. Roberts, Arthur St. Jacques, Charles Se¹

UNPUBLISHED MANUSCRIPTS

Combat Narratives, Office of Naval Intelligence: Pearl Harbor, Aleutians, Midway, Guadalcanal, Salerno.

Logbook produced by members of the Natoma Bay Association.

The 228 Days of the United States Destroyer Laffey, Eugene Alexander Barham, USN (ret.).

The Milk Tester, the War, and the Price of Eggs in Vermont, Alan LeBaron.

When the War Is Over We Will All Enlist Again, Allan LeBaron.

Chicago, The Best Liberty Town in the U.S., Allan LeBaron.

Jack LeBaron's memoir.

One Man's War: My Life with the Fighting Seabees, William Casey.

Collected Letters of the LeBaron family, World War II.

Diary, William D. Askin, 1945.

Collected materials, Eighth Beach Battalion, U.S. Naval Amphibious Force, unpublished.

Guadalcanal Diary, Mike O'Dea. Sixth U.S. Naval Construction Battalion, 1942.

Narrative, Harry R. Ayers, Jr.

PUBLISHED BOOKS

Appleman, Roy. *Okinawa, the Last Battle*. Washington, D.C.: Department of the Army, 1948.

Barbey, Daniel A. *MacArthur's Amphibious Navy*. Annapolis, Md.: Naval Institute Press, 1969.

Bateson, Charles. *The War with Japan*. Sydney: Yre Smith, 1968.

Blair, Clay, Jr., *Silent Victory*. Philadelphia: Lippincott, 1975.

Busch, Harald. *U Boats at War*. New York: Ballantine, 1955.

Churchill, Winston. *The Second World War*, 5 vols. Boston: Houghton Mifflin, 1949.

Corrison, D. J. *The United States Navy*. New York: Praeger, 1968.

Costello, John. *The Pacific War*. New York: Rawson Wade, 1981.

Craig, William. *The Fall of Japan*. New York: Dial, 1967.

Davenport, Roy M. *Clean Sweep*. New York: Vantage, 1986.

Dockery, Kevin. *Seals in Action*. New York: Avon, 1991.

Dönitz, Karl. *Memoirs*. New York: Bantam, 1960.

Gabriel, Richard A. *Military Incompetence*. New York: Farrar, Straus & Giroux, 1985.

Glines, Carroll. *Doolittle's Tokyo Raiders*. Princeton, N.J.: Van Nostrand, 1964.

Halsey, W. F. *Admiral Halsey's Story*. New York: McGraw-Hill, 1967.

Hess, William N. *Pacific Sweep*. New York: Zebra, 1974.

et al. *Dai Hei Yo Senso Hishi (The Secret History of the*: Nihon Koku Bokyu Sha, 1987.

's War. New York: McGraw-Hill, 1986.

of Leyte Gulf. New York: David McKay, 1969.

l. New York: Stein & Day, 1981.

279

_____. *The Glory of the Solomons*. New York: Stein & Day, 1982.

_____. *Nimitz and His Admirals*. New York: Weybright and Talley, 1968.

_____. *Pacific Destiny*. New York: Norton, 1980.

_____. *Hirohito*. New York: Praeger, 1992.

_____. *Tojo*. Lanham, Md.: Madison Books, 1993.

_____. *The Lonely Ships*. New York: McKay, 1975.

Kaiser Corp. *The Kaiser Story*. Oakland, Calif.: Kaiser Corporation, 1960.

Leahy, W. D. *I Was There*. New York: McGraw-Hill, 1950.

Lehman, Jean-Pierre. *The Image of Japan*. London: Allen & Unwin, 1978.

Morris, Richard B. *Encyclopedia of American History*. New York: Harper, 1953.

Morrison, Samuel Eliot. *History of U.S. Naval Operations in World War II*, 13 vols. Boston: Atlantic Monthly Press, 1950–1964.

O'Kane, Richard. *Clear the Bridge*. Chicago: Rand McNally, 1977.

Overy, A. J. *The Air War*. New York: Stein & Day, 1980.

Sprout, Harold and Margaret. *The Rise of American Naval Power*. Princeton, N.J.: Princeton University Press, 1946.

Padden, Ian. *U.S. Navy Seals*. New York: Bantam, 1985.

MAGAZINE ARTICLES

Van Watts, "The Last Yank," *The California Veteran*, February 1989.

The Wreck of the 709, Cape Breton *Highlander*, April 5, 1967.

Notes

Chapter 1

The sources for this chapter are primarily Samuel Eliot Morison's *History of U.S. Naval Operations in World War II,* as well as *Japan's War* and various other books I have written about the Pacific War.

Chapter 2

The Jack LeBaron narrative was vital to this chapter, as was the story of Charles Sehe on the battleship *Nevada,* which I received in letter form. The official navy interview with Lieutenant Outerbridge was the source for the story of the activity of the destroyer *Ward* that day. Van Watts' story is from his own narrative. Jack LeBaron's story is from his own narrative, and the story of Tom Evins is from Admiral Barham's unpublished manuscript on the destroyer *Laffey.*

Chapter 3

The material about the *San Francisco* is from Lieutenant Bonnell's narrative in the CINCPAC records.

The material about the failed relief of Wake is from my study of the CINCPAC war records in the Naval History Center of the Washington Navy Yard. The LeBaron story is from the narrative of Ted LeBaron. The material about the *Holly* is from Jack LeBaron's narrative. The story of the *Sturtevant* is from an article by Rear Admiral Sheldon Kinney, USN (ret.). The story of Harry Luessen is from letters and material supplied by him.

Chapter 4

The story of the American forces in the Far East comes from the records of the Asiatic fleet, conversations with the late Admiral Thomas C. Hart, and from my *The Lonely Ships.* The primary source for the story of the American ships in the Java campaign is from the combat narrative in the records of the Naval History Center in Washington.

The Watts story is his own recollection; the LeBaron stories are from their own narratives.

Chapter 5

The story of the Battle of the Coral Sea is from the CINCPAC records and war diaries and the combat narrative, and from conversations with Sailor Lynch and with the late Admiral Aubrey Fitch.

Chapter 6

The story of the Sailor Van Watts and Admiral Byrd is from an article in the Walpole, Mass., *Gazette*, written by Watts and published on October 18, 1991.

Chapter 7

The story of Sailor Ronald Veltman aboard the *Hornet* is from a tape supplied to me by Mr. Veltman. The material about Sailor Lynch and Sailor Watts is from their narratives. The story of the Battle of Midway is from the ONI combat narrative, which tells as much about what the navy did not know before, during, and after the battle as about what was known.

Chapter 8

The stories of the men of the *Laffey* come from Admiral Barham's book. At the time the admiral was a junior officer, and he rose to high rank. But he never forgot the chilling experiences of the early days of this war, and ultimately he gathered the materials from many other survivors of the ship and wrote the narrative.

Chapter 9

The story of the *Laffey*'s first battle experience is from the CINCPAC records and from the Barham book. The story of the sinking of the *Hornet* is from Sailor Veltman's tape.

Chapter 10

The story of the Seabees in Guadalcanal is from the O'Dea diary and from material furnished by Captain Mark Jordan, USN (Ret.), who was a senior officer of the CBs in the South Pacific.

Chapter 11

The primary source is the O'Dea diary.

Chapter 12

The sources are the O'Dea diary, the ONI combat narrative dealing with the Guadalcanal battle, and the story of the *Laffey* by Admiral Barham.

Chapter 13

Chief O'Dea's diary was the primary source for the chapter.

Chapter 14

The Barham book was the primary source of the material in this chapter.

Chapter 15

The ONI combat narrative on the invasion of French North Africa was primary to this chapter. The story of Lt. Starkweather's mission is from the Padden book listed in the bibliography. The note about Bill LeBaron is from his narrative.

Chapter 16

Information about the securing of Guadalcanal comes from the O'Dea diary and the Fitch interview.

Chapter 17

The story of the wreck of the *709* is from material supplied by Harry Luessen.

Chapter 18

The story of the movement of the *Holly* to the Pacific is from the Jack LeBaron narrative.

Chapter 19

Sailor Lynch's adventures were told to me in an interview.

Chapter 20

The story of the *Bogue* is from the war diary of VC-9, the naval air unit that served for a time on the *Bogue*.

Chapter 21

Alan LeBaron's narrative was the source for this material on his adventures in Chicago.

Chapter 22

The story of Lieutenant Davenport comes from his book *Clean Sweep*.

Chapter 23

The Battle for the Aleutians comes from the ONI combat narrative and from Bill LeBaron's narrative.

Chapter 24

This chapter depended on material supplied by Sailor Flanagan.

Chapter 25

The story of the minesweepers at Salerno is from the ONI combat narrative on the Salerno landings.

Chapter 26

The story of Lieutenant Commander Davenport's adventure in the *Haddock* is from his own book.

Chapter 27

The story of the *Natoma Bay* is from a two-volume log prepared by survivors of the ship in the postwar years. John Sassano, one of the veterans, kindly lent me a copy of the unpublished work. The comment of the men who sailed the escort carriers that they were "Mr. Kaiser's coffins" was typical navy humor but the underlying seed of truth was borne out during the war when several escort carriers were sunk. The *Liscombe Bay* went down so fast at the battle of the Gilbert Islands that it took down an admiral and his staff. The *Gambier Bay* was sunk by Japanese naval gunfire at the battle off Samar, and several other small carriers were sunk. But they served a very important purpose, and the safety factor had to be sacrificed for speed in building in those critical years of 1942 and 1943.

Chapter 28

The story of the *Natoma Bay* at Saipan is from the ship's book.

Chapter 29

The material about MacArthur's Seabees came to me from Sailor William T. Casey.

Chapter 30

Sailor David Wheeler Mangum's story comes from materials he supplied.

Chapter 31

The stories of the Navy beach battalions, so long unsung, come from Clifford Legerton, who kept diaries and collected materials for half a century.

Chapter 32

The story of the Normandy invasion is from William Weedon's narrative, from Cliff Legerton's materials, from the UDT files at the Navy Special Warfare center in San Diego, and from Sailor Flanagan's narrative.

Chapter 33

The story of the Eighth Beach Battalion is largely from Clifford Legerton's diary.

Chapter 34

The diving story of Sailor John Liuzzi is from material he supplied.

Chapter 35

The story of the *Natoma Bay* at Leyte Gulf is from the ship's book.

Chapter 36

The continuing story of Lieutenant Commander Davenport is from his book.

Chapter 37

Sailor Lynch's continuing adventures were described in materials he provided.

Chapter 38

The story of the Sixth Seabee Battalion is from materials supplied by Captain Jordan.

Chapter 39

The story of the typhoon at sea is from a narrative supplied by Norman Ostrom.

Chapter 40

The continuing story of the *Natoma Bay* is from the ship's book.

Chapter 41

The story of LST *246* is from a narrative and diary provided by Sailor William D. Askin.

Chapter 42

The story of the seabees in Manila is from the narrative of William T. Casey, Sr.

Chapter 43

The letters of Mrs. W. R. LeBaron were collected by her son Allan and preserved for many years. She served as a sort of post office during the war for her four sons, her navy husband, and her navy son-in-law and managed to keep them informed about what each one was doing all during the war.

Chapter 44

Skipper Davenport's adventures continue in this chapter, from his privately published book.

Chapter 45

The story of the *Natoma Bay*, continued, is from the ship's books.

Chapter 46

The story of the UDTs in action comes from materials at the Naval Special Warfare center at Santa Barbara, California, and from the two books listed in the bibliography.

Chapter 47

The story of the *Natoma Bay* at Okinawa is from the ship's book. The story of the UDT teams is from the record at Santa Barbara and the two books on the UDT and Navy Seals. The story of Sailor Sehe and the *Nevada* is his narrative.

Chapter 48

The material about the LeBarons is from Mother LeBaron's letters. Sailor Casey's story is continued in his narrative. The story of the end of the *Natoma Bay* is from the ship's book.

Index